W9-BWC-562

REDEFINING NORMAL

HOW TWO FOSTER KIDS BEAT THE ODDS AND
DISCOVERED *HEALING, HAPPINESS,* AND *LOVE*

Justin & Alexis Black

KALAMAZOO PUBLIC LIBRARY

Those wishing to contact Justin or Alexis Black for speaking engagements
or additional resources may do so at the following:

Justin & Alexis Black
3885 S. 9th St. #83
Oshtemo, MI 49077
www.re-definingnormal.com
press@re-definingnormal.com

Copyright © 2020 by Justin Black; Alexis Black

Redefining Normal

All rights reserved. No part of this publication may be reproduced, distributed or transmitted in any form or by any means, including photocopying, recording, or other electronic or mechanical methods, without the prior written permission of the publisher, except in the case of brief quotations embodied in critical reviews and certain other noncommercial uses permitted by copyright law.

Although the author and publisher have made every effort to ensure that the information in this book was correct at press time, the author and publisher do not assume and hereby disclaim any liability to any party for any loss, damage, or disruption caused by errors or omissions, whether such errors or omissions result from negligence, accident, or any other cause.

Adherence to all applicable laws and regulations, including international, federal, state and local governing professional licensing, business practices, advertising, and all other aspects of doing business in the US, Canada or any other jurisdiction is the sole responsibility of the reader and consumer.

Neither the author nor the publisher assumes any responsibility or liability whatsoever on behalf of the consumer or reader of this material. Any perceived slight of any individual or organization is purely unintentional.

The resources in this book are provided for informational purposes only and should not be used to replace the specialized training and professional judgment of a health care or mental health care professional.

Neither the author nor the publisher can be held responsible for the use of the information provided within this book. Please always consult a trained professional before making any decision regarding treatment of yourself or others.

For more information, email info@re-definingnormal.com.
Printed in the United States of America by Global Perspectives Publishing www.globalperspectivespublishing.com

GLOBAL PERSPECTIVES
— PUBLISHING —

Library of Congress Control Number: 2020914176

Paperback: ISBN 978-1-7345731-3-8
eBook: ISBN 978-1-7345731-2-1
Hardcover: ISBN 978-1-7345731-4-5

For orders, please visit www.re-definingnormal.com

Cover photo by Patricia Norman of Patty Leonor LLC
www.pattyleonor.com

How Healthy Is Your Relationship?

Find out with our FREE GIFT!
Email us at freegift@re-definingnormal.com
Title the email "FREE GIFT"

Follow us on social media: | www.re-definingnormal.com
@redefiningnormal

DEDICATION

For those who find themselves in similar circumstances, this book is for you. We hope it will give you clarity, inspiration, and a sense of control.

"You see you wouldn't ask why the rose that grew from the concrete had damaged petals. On the contrary, we would all celebrate its tenacity. We would all love its will to reach the sun. Well, we are the roses—this is the concrete—and these are my damaged petals."

—Tupac Shakur

"Every kid is one caring adult away
from being a success story."

—Josh Shipp

CONTENTS

"I knew that she was preparing to share harsh details about her past. I wanted to brace myself while simultaneously showing my support. As she began to share, I grabbed her hand to let her know that she was not alone. I felt for her situation and was honored that she was willing to share her story with me. The vulnerability it took to share her experience was inspiring. She was so brilliant, so smart, and amazing—yet she had been through some of the worst things imaginable. I had no idea how she persevered through it all. You truly wouldn't know half of what she's been through by looking at her. That night was the defining moment of our relationship moving forward."

—Justin

"Our parents set the foundation and standard of love. We learn how to love and receive love from them. But if parents don't know what healthy love is themselves, it is inevitable for children to unconsciously inherit unsustainable habits and patterns from their parents. This cycle allows people that are unfamiliar with a healthy definition of love to define what love is for other generations to come. Family plays the most intimate role in shaping our values, morals, and habits; consequently, it can harm us the most. Many adults spend their entire lives healing from their childhoods, yearning for the love, acceptance, and praise that wasn't provided by their parents."

—Alexis

FOREWORD BY MARCY PUSEY

A FEW YEARS AGO, I found myself in one of the most desperate situations of all my parenting. I realized that I had been looking for my own worth and validation as a mother from the *healing* of my children. But not just any of my children, specifically from my foster-to-adopted children. I mean, I had God's unconditional love channeling through my soul into their "rescue" story. Surely my nobility would be evident to all when these rescued children became happy, whole, and healed *because* of what a great mom I was, right?

The reality was, healing didn't come so easily and neither did my validation.

Even with all of my degrees in social services and therapy, and all of my experience working in group homes, wrap-around programs, foster agencies, and private practice...I still fell short. Why weren't my tools and degrees, or even God's love, *working?!*

From deep within that pit, I began to write. I wrote about the challenges of parenting these kids: the challenges within the broken social system, families of origin, society, the trauma-behavior of the kids, and the challenge of my own desperately broken self. As I wrote, I reclaimed hope for every challenge we faced. Hope had been stolen, but I would take it back on behalf of all the hurting families. There's always hope.

So, I wrote and wrote and wrote, books for adults and books for kids. Families came out of the woodwork to share how my books were changing their homes, removing shame and resetting expectations, reframing and retooling the power of love in a more realistic way. And in the process, I reclaimed my *own* validation as a mama. How unfair to have put that responsibility on my children, when it had already been mine all along. I was redefining normal, and it was liberating.

I was thrilled with the way my writing and speaking was shaking up the conversation around social services and our foster / adoption system, but there was a gaping hole. We needed the voices of foster youth. I can speak for my colleagues in social services, and I can speak for moms and dads raising these kids, but I can *never* be the voice of the kids themselves. I grieved the absence of this crucial voice in the conversation.

Then, one day, these two beautiful faces lit up my Zoom screen. I was their assigned Author Success Coach to help them through the process of publishing their book. They were one call in a stream of calls that I'd facilitate that day, helping hundreds of writers see their dream of publishing and impacting the world come to fruition. I had no idea what *that* call would entail.

They began to share their story and I *could not believe* they'd fallen into my lap. All of these years praying for someone to rise up and be the voice in the conversation I could never be—and here they were. They were dynamic, committed, and incredibly self-aware. They were confident and brilliant and knocking out statistics like pro wrestlers. I'm sure my mouth hung open in a silly look of pure delight and shock as they shared their story of overcoming *incredible* life obstacles, which you'll read in the following pages. These weren't kids with lives easier *enough* to heal and find wholeness. They weren't *less* abused, neglected, forgotten, dismissed, rejected, or wounded. In fact, as you'll read in parts one through three of this book, they've lived their own versions of hell multiple times.

And yet, they overcame.

They overcame in messy ways, in beautiful ways, in complicated ways, in miraculous ways...they overcame. And they are overcoming.

And they are taking their overcoming story and putting it into the world because we need to reclaim hope for our foster and adopted children. So few of their own have come alongside them to show them the way, as Justin and Alexis do in this book.

Around 400,000 kids live in the US foster system at any given time, with over 20,000 of them aging out every year. The statistics shout of mental illness, homelessness, lack of education, disease, failed relationships, criminal activity, and high fatality. Breaking free of the statistics is possible, but most kids don't know it. They simply fall in line with the songs of society, following the death march that's been laid out for them.

No more. Justin and Alexis prove, with their own lives, that these youth can bust out of the line and begin living the lives they deserve: lives of love, belonging, acceptance, wholeness, healing, recovery, and happiness. It's not easy, but it's possible.

Justin and Alexis have stepped into a chasm of silence and their voices echo with strength, importance, and a call to all foster youth to believe they can be more than the statistics claim. Their incredible story showers their *belief* and *hope* over every life, every soul, that feels forgotten, unloved, unclaimed, abandoned, and left behind.

Thank you, God, for sending these two into the world, empowering them with a message of pain-turned-power. Their wounds are not wasted, but instead provide a salve for every hurting soul.

I can *never* be the voice of our current and former foster and adopted youth, but I can champion those who *are* with everything I am. Thank you, Justin and Alexis, for your bravery and passion. Together, we are redefining normal, creating spaces and permission for freedom to discover healing, happiness, and love.

Marcy Pusey, CRC, CTP-C
Best-Selling Author of multiple books, including *Reclaiming Hope: Overcoming the Challenges of Parenting Foster and Adopted Children, Parenting Children of Trauma: The Foster-Adoption Guide to Understanding Attachment Disorder,* and *Speranza's Sweater: A Child's Journey Through Foster Care and Adoption*

FOREWORD BY ROB SCHEER

EXPERIENCED THE HORRORS of the foster care system myself at a young age, I always knew that I wanted to be a dad. That was the most important goal I had. I wanted to be the kind of parent that I never had, but I never wanted anyone to know my story of growing up in the foster care system.

I used to believe that love hurts because that was my norm throughout my childhood between continuous abandonment and abuse. As Justin and Alexis have experienced, redefining normal is a lifelong journey that takes courage, hard work, and resilience - the same skills I learned growing up in the child welfare system.

It wasn't until I met my amazing and unconditionally supportive husband Reece that this dream became a reality. It was only through him challenging me to think about all the kids in our own backyard that I was letting down by not sharing my story and by not adopting locally that I took the next step.

He was right. We went to DC Child and Family Services and said we want to adopt a baby, and they told us it would take two years. Two years?! I could not believe it. The social worker suggested a faster route would be to foster to adopt. After some thoughtful consideration, Reece said, "If we can change the life of a child, even for a short time, we must do that." And so our journey began.

It was the surprise of a lifetime when we got the call asking if we would take not one baby, but a sister and brother, ages 4 years old and 18 months! It was not what we had initially envisioned and planned for, but Reece and I knew we would never split up two siblings coming into foster care. We accepted the offer to welcome Amaya and Makai into our home without hesitation. I knew what I had lost by entering the system separated from my brothers and sisters, and we would not allow that to happen to any children we were caring for.

That was when my husband and I founded Comfort Cases a National 501c3 Non Profit to give Hope and Dignity to our Foster Youth. I know firsthand the immense pain, fear and feeling unwanted as I too have had to move home to home with everything I own thrown into trash bags along the way. I have been on a mission to inspire communities to bring dignity and hope to youth across the country just as Alexis and Justin have with Redefining Normal and their other businesses. So far, we've been able to support over 21,000 of the 438,000 youth in the foster care system in the United States.

From my story, published in A Forever Family: Fostering Change One Child at a Time and now from Justin and Alexis' you will see the power and difference that one person can make in a young person's life. They have overcome some of the unimaginable that far too many youths have to overcome as well. It is because of their courage to be vulnerable and transparent that it will invite others to heal as well.

This book is filled with startling statistics that we know all too well to illustrate just how Justin, Alexis, myself, and thousands of other foster youth had the odds stacked against us -- but still, we will rise and must do it together.

Redefining Normal is a must-read and it leaves you with wanting to not only pass it on for others to read it but be part of the change in the child welfare system. I would give this book 5 stars and would recommend it to everyone even if you have never been touched by foster care.

Rob Scheer
Founder, Comfort Cases
Best-Selling Author of *A Forever Family: Fostering Change One Child at a Time*

INTRODUCTION

I N JANUARY 2020, Justin and I were on our way to South Africa. I was going to work and volunteer and Justin was going for his fifth study abroad program. On our way, we stopped in several cities, including Luxor and Cairo, Egypt, where we took in such sights as the pyramids of Giza and enjoyed kofta and koshari. We were exhilarated to be on an adventure together. Everyone knows what happened two months later. Along with so many others, we were emergency evacuated, flying home to Northern Michigan, where we spent two weeks quarantined in an RV just outside my parents' bi-level mid-century style house surrounded by 20 acres of land.

Whirling from the derailment and mourning the loss of the rest of our trip, we set upon an idea. We began writing the book you are holding now. Perhaps it was the confinement that helped us to decide it was time to explore our demons by recounting our story. Having survived so much, and having found each other, we knew the story would ultimately be one of triumph. We also knew that writing about the darkest moments of our childhoods would not be easy. But there we were, furiously writing at the table in the RV's tiny kitchen.

We are writing about our journey for two reasons: we want to share our story in the hope of helping others, and we wanted to grow closer to one another before becoming husband and wife. Most people we know have either been in or are currently in unhealthy relationships, especially those who are, like us, former foster youths. Hailing from Detroit and Flint, Michigan we have seen too many adults spend their entire lives trying to heal from their difficult childhood experiences. Foster youth are particularly at risk of repeating unhealthy cycles of behavior. We were and continue to be on a mission to unlearn all of the unhealthy patterns we witnessed early in life, and to make sure that we don't pass these things down to our children.

We are not perfect, nor are we experts. The purpose of this book isn't to tell people how their relationship should work or even to serve as a model relationship for others. It is only to share our experiences and show people that there are healthy ways of both loving and receiving love, and that we all have the power to build a life of our choosing. We see it as our duty to help others, because so many people have poured love and support into our lives and helped us get to where we are today. We hope that by sharing what we have learned we can save others from going through similar heartache. We are committed to being transparent and vulnerable on our journey to healthy love.

Our story is broken down into four sections with different themes. The first three sections consist of our personal narratives as well as stories on various topics. We had to go on two individual journeys of self-discovery and healing so that we could come together in agreement—the final section of this book.

Although we dive deep into our experiences with the child welfare system, this book is for anyone yearning to understand the components of both healthy and unhealthy relationships while in the process, learning to love themselves.

Here are some statistics you may find startling:

- On any given day, there are nearly 437,000 children in foster care in the United States, with 700 kids entering the system each day. Neglect—a common symptom of poverty—is the number one reason youth end up in foster care.
- There are over 125,000 children waiting to be adopted—most wait three or four years on average.
- It has been estimated that 60% of all child sex trafficking victims have histories in the child welfare system.

- On average, for every young person who ages out of foster care, taxpayers and communities pay $300,000 in social costs over that person's lifetime, with 26,000 young people aging out every year multiplied by $300,000 per person equals $7.8 billion in total cost.

*These statistics are pre-COVID-19, meaning that they've been since exacerbated.

AUTHOR'S NOTE

WE'VE CONSULTED E-MAILS, messages, posts, consulted with several of the people who appear in the book, notes, and memories to construct this memoir. To protect the identity of some of the individuals in this book, we've changed the names and re-created dialogue, while remaining faithful to what really happened. We occasionally omitted people and events, but only when the omission had no impact on either the veracity or the substance of the story. We aren't able to include everything that's happened to us or what we've overcome in this short book. This was meant to give you merely a glimpse of our lives, and how we've beaten the odds set against us.

We do want to provide a trigger warning with regard to domestic violence, trauma, sexual assault, and more.

PROLOGUE

Alexis

I was 13 when I became an orphan and a ward of the state. My mother had died years earlier and my father had just been sentenced to 15 years in prison. At 20, when I was a junior in college, there was much I had yet to understand about the way trauma had shaped my understanding of life and love.

Justin

Due to my parents' drug addiction and neglect, I entered foster care at 9 years old. I lived in four homes over the next 12 years. With no parental support, I arrived at Western Michigan University at 19, my sense of self extremely fragile. Chaos, poverty, and violence had profoundly influenced my understanding of the world and my place in it.

PART 1:
WORDS ON AN
INDEX CARD

What the Statistics Say:
65% of children in foster care experience seven or more school changes
from elementary to high school. Foster youth lose between four and
six months of educational progress with each school change.

Only 56% of foster youth graduate high school while less
than 3% of foster youth graduate from college.

What Does God Say:
"I am fearfully and wonderfully made"
(Psalm 139:14).

ALEXIS

A

FTER FIVE MONTHS of studying and self-discovery among the lush green mountains and beautiful acacia trees of Cape Town, South Africa, I flew home to face something I desperately wanted to avoid. While I was abroad, my boyfriend at the time, Shawn, had been living in my apartment rent-free. We had been dating—if you could call it that— for eight years, and in that time, I'd been on a roller coaster of emotional violence and manipulation. It had peaked in a new way while I was gone.

Shawn was supposed to care for my cats—Leo, Lily and Leia —whom I'd acquired at the recommendation of my therapist. I doted on them as any pet owner does, but due to very dark and specific memories, which I will address later in the book, their safety was of paramount concern to me. Shawn knew this, and used them to inflict torment. He told me that he was neglecting to feed them or clean out their litter boxes; he even denied them clean drinking water. I had to make a series of desperate calls to friends, begging that they come to my house and intervene on the cats' behalf. Far away and helpless thousands of miles away, Shawn had found the perfect way to torture me and leave me in a state of chronic anxiety.

Shawn victimizing my defenseless therapy pets shifted something inside me. After years of abuse I was finally ready to leave him, freed of any sense of obligation to a man who clearly felt no obligation to me.

I came home to an apartment reeking of cat urine. Household items were strewn all over the floor. I confronted Shawn and told him that I couldn't pretend this was an acceptable way to be treated. I had lived like that for too long. I was leaving him.

"So, you don't want to marry me anymore?" He stood at the top of the stairs, yelling down at me. "You don't want to have kids with me anymore?"

It was a sign of the deep dysfunction of our relationship that he could have asked those questions. It would have been funny if it hadn't been so painful.

Meanwhile, I did not know how to ask for help. It certainly hadn't occurred to me to ask my foster parents at the time, Kim and Brian, whom I'd known for seven years and who had given me unconditional love. I never would have thought moving home with them was an option. I have always been too proud—and fearful—to ask for support of any kind from anyone. I was used to figuring everything out on my own. Growing up, I hadn't had much supervision—my biological father was always at work and my mother passed away when I was only six. I was 13 when I entered foster care and have felt self-reliant ever since.

Mercifully, my foster parents offered to help without having to be asked. Kim and Brian came over to help me pack my belongings and move them back to their house. It was just the lifeline I needed. But in order to accept their support, my cats weren't allowed to come with me because they were allergic to them. I had to find another temporary home for my cats until I could have them again. It felt like I was constantly putting them in pet foster care and I was the unstable, irresponsible parent that couldn't support them. The last thing I ever wanted to be was a reflection of my own biological parents.

After moving home, Kim and Brian asked me to promise that I wouldn't date again for at least a year. They wanted me to figure out who Alexis—without a boyfriend—really was. I had dated Shawn from the age of 13 to the age of 21 and my identity had been entirely subsumed by him.

I was running out of the scholarship money that paid for my rent and living expenses, so I chose to apply for the Seita Scholars Program, a scholarship program for foster youth receiving higher education. In order to accept the scholarship, I had to live on campus in Kalamazoo, Michigan at Western Michigan University (WMU) and participate in the Summer Early Transition (SET) week—staying on campus for a week with your cohort to build bonds and begin college together. I had already attended WMU for two years after transferring from The University of Michigan-Flint, and felt this was unnecessary, but hey, there was free food for the week!

It was then that I had to decide: keep all three cats or accept this scholarship. This decision ripped me apart, but thankfully, I had a wonderful friend that adopted Leo and Lily so that I could continue my education.

I moved into Henry Hall on WMU's campus to start SET week. Kim texted me:

Kim: "Henry Hall! That is where Brian and I lived and met freshman year. :)"

Me: "Awww omg!!! Well, I'm with all freshmen so no luck finding my soulmate. Lol"

Kim: "You never know!"

Me: "Kind of doubt it! Lol They are all babies lol I feel so old."

Walking into Bernhard Center, a place for students to eat, interact and connect on campus, I felt confident and cute since I was an upperclassman, and these were "freshmen babies." I walked into a busy room with much conversation. In an attempt to somewhat isolate myself, I found a table where few students sat, which was nearly impossible. The only empty seat I could find was with three other boys.

One guy named Justin tried to flirt with me by complimenting my tattoos. He asked me how my summer had been and I told him that I had just returned from South Africa and that I'd gotten all five of my tattoos there over the course of two days. He was shocked and very impressed by my bravery to do so. It was fun to flirt back, although I thought he was too young for me. He hadn't even officially started college yet! He'd had his senior prom only a few months before.

I sat with Justin and several other kids at lunch. I looked up and saw a student at another table take off his hat and pray. I paused and thought how beautiful it was—I had never seen someone my age do that.

Shortly after, a group of guys on the football team sat down a few tables over. I commented on how "fine" one of the guys was. One of the people at my table stood up in an attempt to play matchmaker and called the guy over, saying I wanted to talk to him. I was mortified. He came over and said, "What's up?" with some annoyance present in his voice. I didn't know what to say and the guy at my table chimed in, "Give her your number so y'all can talk." I instinctively handed over my phone without saying anything and he replied, "Text me" while handing back my phone. My stomach was full of knots and I started to sweat. I looked around the table and noticed Justin walking out of the lunchroom.

The football player texted me shortly after saying "What's up? What you tryna do?"

I knew what that meant. Honestly, I didn't expect anything more from the football player because I've allowed myself to be talked to like that for years and used for my body. I tried to brush off these feelings, but I still had the idea that if I wanted attention or affection, I'd have to give up a piece of myself in order to do so.

I went to my dorm room to lie down and check my texts. Since I was newly single, I had several guys in my messages seeing if I was ready to talk, but I knew what most of them were after. As I lay in bed texting a guy from high school, Justin texted me to see what I was doing. He was on his way back to Detroit and when I asked why, he simply said, "I have to take care of something." My first thought was drugs or a court appearance, because I tended to attract the bad boys. I was pleasantly surprised when he told me later that he had an awards ceremony to attend. I also couldn't help but note his modesty.

By this point, Justin and I had been talking for only three or so days when he asked if he could come to my room because I had a fan and he didn't. Part of me knew why he was asking to come over—to have sex—but I really just wanted company and someone to talk to. I told him that he could come over and watch a movie, and that he was welcome to sleep on the floor. As a sign of respect, he first sat in a desk chair. As the night went on, we slowly began to lower our guards and enjoy each other's company. Eventually, he joined me on the bed and we talked for a few hours about school, past experiences, and our goals. I even told him he was welcome to sleep beside me in bed. Justin made a few advances, but he was instantly respectful when I asked him to stop. I cried silently; something I learned to do as a child, but this time I felt safe. I couldn't remember the last time I had felt that way with a man. Feeling protected and secure, I fell asleep in Justin's arms.

The next day, I called my best friend. "I think he's too young. I can't do this!" I was flooded with excitement and fear.

That day, Justin and I were talking before the program started, and it felt like we were the only two people in the whole world. Justin asked me if I was a Christian and if I believed in God. I felt immediately defensive. After dating an atheist for eight years who constantly dismissed my faith, it felt strange for a man to ask me if I believed in God. I wasn't used to men having expectations of me, especially with regard to religion. Suddenly, Justin said "If you don't find someone else by the time I graduate, *I'll* marry you." I knew he was joking, but I'd never met a man so forward. I laughed it off, knowing he was selling me a dream. *A family and a white picket fence.* But he was too young, and I wasn't looking for a partner.

At the start of the program, two men came into the room to speak to us about resilience. They asked each of us to write down our traumatic experiences on an index card. This was hard enough, but then they read each card out loud, anonymously. I cried as I listened to the pain of the other students. I cried in empathy, and I cried because I realized I was not alone. Other people had been through similarly damaging experiences.

That night, Justin asked me if I'd like to go for a walk. Every time he looked at me, I got butterflies. We sat on the grass outside the library on campus. "Tell me more about yourself," he said. I took a deep breath. For so long, I had been told that I had "too much baggage" for anyone to love me.

Ashamed, I looked down as I spoke, afraid to see his reaction as I revealed my past. *Do I only tell him part of it to test his reaction? Could he love me with all of my baggage, or would my past be too much of a burden for him?*

JUSTIN

WE ARE ALL on the journey to find happiness, but how many of us have pursued it the wrong way, or not known how to define it at all? *Purpose* was the foundational piece that I was missing and somewhat lost track of.

It was 2016. Going into college, I knew two things: I refused to get kicked out of college and move back to Detroit, and I wanted to sleep with as many girls as possible. My foster mom, Mrs. Cora told me that if I were kicked out of college, I could not come back to her house. I was determined to make this work one way or another. Despite this, my mind was on college girls and as a result I decided to abandon my Christian faith when I got there. I wanted to finally be a part of something, a part of a group. I hated high school and never really made any true friends in any of my four years and I hoped that college would be different. Most importantly, I wanted to fit in—no matter what—even if it meant sacrificing some of my basic beliefs to do so. I had this idea that the best way to make lifelong friends was to do what the other college kids did.

On the first day of the Seita Scholars' SET week, we had our orientation in the Bernhard Center. I was nervous and I picked a table that seemed safe, where two other Seita Scholars sat watching a soccer match. Even though I wasn't particularly into soccer, I liked sports in general, so I hoped we could make conversation. A few minutes later, another Seita Scholar came and sat down right beside me.

This student, in particular, carried herself differently from the other scholars. "*There's no way she's a freshman,*" I thought. I did my best at small talk, complimenting her tattoos. She replied that she'd just returned from South Africa, which was where she'd gotten them. I was impressed by her, but intimidated. She was out of my league and she seemed to be strongly implying that she was not interested in spending her time with a kid like me.

I continued my mission to meet as many girls as possible. For most of the week, I had a crush on one of the student leaders from SET week. I found it exciting to talk to an older woman in a leadership role. I so wanted to become the "lady's man" I felt I needed to be. By the end of the day, I had four phone numbers, but I didn't have the number of the one girl I found most interesting: the tattooed junior. She was intimidating and she seemed completely out of reach.

The next day, I saw her again at orientation and I tried to make small talk. I asked if she had Snapchat, and she said no. She asked if I had Facebook and I said no. This revealed our age difference. Finally, I did ask for her name, and her number as well. Her name was Alexis and she was single. I told her she seemed mature, more mature than some of the student staff at the SET week. She didn't seem like the typical college student who partied and messed around with every guy. I couldn't see her doing drugs or alcohol. Alexis was different. Someone who probably had expectations I could never live up to. As our conversation progressed, she told me that she had just ended a long-term relationship. Her distanced manner made a little more sense.

This time, our conversation went a little deeper. She intrigued me and I'd grown invested in spending time with her. I flirted with other girls all week, but the conversations quickly ran dry. I didn't flirt with Alexis. She carried herself as if she'd seen every trick in the book. Our conversations weren't forced either. They were soothing and often comforting. I was at war with my growing attachment to Alexis. It was my persistent desire to be "one of the guys."

That night, I talked to some of them about which girls had caught their eye during SET week. I expected them to mention the conversations they had started. Maybe a few girls' numbers they had gotten. Instead, they told me that they'd already had sex with a few—and we were only three days in! They asked me who I had slept with and I admitted that I had only flirted. I felt the strain of being an outsider once more, and felt the need to hurry up and make my move. I knew this was wrong. The Seita Scholars program was for youth who've experienced foster care. This means that most of the women there have been abandoned by parents and other loved ones, making many of these women extremely vulnerable to guys looking for sex. Statistically speaking, many of these women had probably experienced sexual trauma in one way or another. Still, my yearn to live a college lifestyle forced me to ignore these facts.

With my reckless search for sexual activity, I began flirting with the student staff leader. Everyone saw me, including Alexis. I had been foolish to think I could openly flirt with multiple women with no repercussions, casually returning back to my conversation with Alexis in the Bernhard Center before we started out our activities for the day.

As we sat in the cafeteria of the Bernhard Center, one of the star football players walked past our table with the rest of the team. Alexis said, "Oh my gosh, he's gorgeous!" My heart fell to my stomach. She continued to compliment his looks and I felt extremely jealous. For a second, I couldn't breathe. I wasn't exactly sure why I felt this way. We weren't in a relationship. Why was I so jealous? I felt like talking to Alexis was helping me survive SET week. Though I was flirting with other girls, it was comforting to talk with her. Around her, I didn't have to try to be a lady's man. I could be *me*. But after she exchanged numbers with the football player, I knew any relationship beginning to develop between us was officially over. It was exactly what I deserved.

Later that day, I needed to go to an award event in Southfield, Michigan, roughly two hours from WMU. I was a part of a college-prep group for foster youth and they wanted to hold an award ceremony for those who were transitioning into college. At the event, many of my mentors congratulated me on my success thus far. They were very excited to see me make it to college. This made me feel supported, but the pressure was also on: I realized that night just what a big opportunity higher education presented. I wanted to try new things in college but I had to dedicate myself to graduating. I was the first in my immediate family to go to college and only the second of five siblings to graduate from high school. I was not only representing my family, but so many others in my Detroit community.

I returned to Kalamazoo around 9 or 10 pm. High-minded ambition flew out the window and my thoughts returned to girls. I wondered who was free and began texting all the numbers I had collected. No one responded. I even texted the student staff leader I liked to see if she'd like to watch a movie with me. She did respond, but she turned me down. Just as I was ready to call it a night, Alexis texted back and said I was welcome to watch a movie with her that night. I felt sudden trepidation—what about her football player? I also suspected she wouldn't want to have sex, and I had promised myself I would achieve this goal soon. I went anyway. I was lonely and a little down, and the idea of seeing her made me happy. My excuse was also that I didn't have a fan and was drenched in sweat every night as the July heat set my room ablaze.

As soon as I entered the room, I felt the calming breeze of her fan and relaxed into its pleasant whir. I did not want to ask if I could sit on her bed, fearing that even the question was a breach of boundary, so I sat in her desk chair instead. We talked about our day and I told her about the awards ceremony. Anxious to know more about her new friend, I skipped straight to her exchange with the football player.

"So wassup with you and ol' dude?" I said.

"The football player?"

"Yeah."

"Yeah, I can tell what his intentions were. He thought I was 'one of those girls,' if you know what I mean."

I thought to myself, *Man, I wonder what she would think if she knew I was "one of those dudes" too? Just looking for sex…*

Alexis could really read people. She understood who people were and what they wanted within the first few minutes of conversation.

"All these guys think that they're ladies' men." She looked right at me. "Even you," she said.

I reeled inside.

"But I know you're not really like that," she added quickly.

"You put on a front to impress people, but you're really a baby," she said, laughing at our age difference.

I wasn't exactly looking for a partner at the time, but I felt Alexis taking hold of me that night. I enjoyed talking with her, and she surprised me and made me feel liberated from external expectations. We talked and laughed all night—much to the annoyance of her new roommate. I talked about the troubles I had in the group home where I lived before coming to college. She talked about how amazing her foster parents were and that I should meet them sometime. I never had conversations like this with women. Most conversations were mainly overtures for sex, either on my part or the girl's, and there was usually another layer, too—maybe the girl wanted to make her boyfriend jealous, or they wanted to get attention from another man by being with me. It was usually a game of chess and had nothing to do with real communication. I never learned that being real could make a conversation so pleasurable, and have never been taught the value of authenticity. Being with Alexis was an entirely new territory.

My lady's man persona, such as it was, evaporated into the night. We both shared many aspects of ourselves. We felt the smoothness of genuine friendship. It was one of the headiest evenings I've ever had. Both of us really needed that kind of support and friendship. Eventually, we sat on her bed as we watched the movie on her laptop. About 20 minutes into the movie, she laid her head on my shoulder. Forty minutes into the movie, we wrapped our arms around one another. Part of me still hoped for sex, but now I didn't want to disrupt what we'd started. Still, I made a few hesitant attempts, and she quickly shut me down.

I was slightly embarrassed and felt like I had abused her trust. I'm not sure where our relationship would be or if we would be married today if she had let me have sex with her that night. Sex would have clouded our judgment and built a foundation based on my need to become "one of the boys."

We cuddled until we fell asleep. That night was perfect. At about 4 a.m., she asked me to leave before the other students became suspicious. I left her room smiling ear to ear.

The week had been smooth sailing, but now it was time to deal with reality. A professional poetry group was prepared to present for SET week. We were a group of foster youth entering a world with which we were unfamiliar as first-generation college students with a lot of trauma in our pasts. There were about 30 of us in our cohort. Statistically speaking, only 3% of foster youth graduate from college. As a Black foster care youth, my chances were even lower.

On an index card, we were instructed to write down the things we had been through that people wouldn't know about by looking at us. The cards were anonymous, and we had the choice to share as much or as little as we wanted. I hadn't dealt with my trauma and I was shy about sharing many of my experiences. One by one, I saw the other scholars handing in their cards covered with words. I felt ashamed that I was too embarrassed and afraid to be vulnerable with my peers. Even shielded by anonymity, I couldn't talk about my past. The poetry group began to read the cards and the room went silent. It seemed as if half of our cohort had dealt with sexual trauma and abuse. I later thought to myself that some of the cards discussing sexual trauma could easily have been men.

After we finished, Alexis and I began to talk once more. With the poetry group challenging us to embrace our experiences and be comfortable with ourselves, we were inspired to go deeper with each other. And so, I asked her if she believed in God. Most people ask, "Do you go to church?" However, given my experience with church folk, I knew that attending church doesn't necessarily equate to true faith in God.

"Wow! Nobody has ever asked me that." It was my turn to surprise Alexis.

Thoughts of worry and regret drilled my brain:

> *How could I have attempted to take advantage of these young womens' weaknesses? Surely, I had disappointed God during this entire process. How could I have called myself a Christian? How shameful could I be?*

We began to talk about our relationships with God. She said that she had been going to church ever since she was little, but it wasn't until she met her foster parents and saw an example of a healthy and loving family that it finally clicked. We both had had bad experiences with religious people who followed propaganda without understanding the principles of Christianity. I think we were both surprised by how intimate our conversation had gotten. It was chemistry that came from a deeper place.

To blow off some steam, we played in a volleyball game with the other scholars. She smiled at me the entire game and something in me knew that she felt what I was feeling. The index card activity lingered with our entire cohort for the rest of the evening. Alexis and I went for a walk around campus, sharing stories from our time in foster care. At last, we sat down in the grass.

I knew that she was preparing to share details from her past. I needed to brace myself while continuing to support her. As she began to share, I took her hand to let her know that she was not alone. The vulnerability it took to share her experience was inspiring. She was so brilliant, so smart, and so unique, even though she had been through some of the worst things imaginable. I realized which index card was hers. I had no idea how she had persevered. This was the first step toward our pursuit of happiness: a journey of reliving our past to prevail over the obstacles that are still present in our lives. You truly wouldn't know half of what she'd been through by looking at her.

PART 2:
IDENTITY

What the Statistics Say:
Based on factors such as the environment, neighborhood, education
and parental influence, a child's success can be determined by a
0.6-mile radius around the home in which they grow up in.

Every 73 seconds, someone is sexually assaulted in the United
States with 80 to 90% committed by someone the victim knows.

What Does God Say:
"I knew you before I formed you in your mother's womb.
Before you were born, I set you apart and appointed
you as my prophet to the nations"
(Jeremiah 1:5 NLT).

WHAT DID THEY TELL ME ABOUT MY IDENTITY?

(Trigger warning)

Only 3.4% of all rapes ultimately lead to a conviction of the offender with at least two-thirds of rapists in the U.S. getting away with it.

As many as 200,000 rape kits sit unopened in police storage across the country and over 1,100 in Michigan alone.

ALEXIS

MY FATHER DISOWNED me until I was 2 years old, when my mom chased him down and demanded he take responsibility for his child. When she passed away four years later, I moved in with him full-time. He worked periodically throughout the day, leaving me at home with no supervision. Walking past lower-income apartment complexes on my way home from school in second grade, it was tradition for me to watch *The Maury Show* every afternoon, a show known widely for DNA paternity tests, lie-detector tests, cheaters, and out-of-control teens. I don't know exactly how it started, but I ended up watching *Girls Gone Wild*, R-rated movies, and a bunch of other explicit shows after midnight.

We moved around frequently; my dad was repeatedly fired and repeatedly finding new jobs. Each neighborhood was the same as the last, populated by perverted older men, liquor stores on every corner, and parents who kept to themselves unless their children were involved in trouble.

At seven years old, I began to notice I was being sexualized by both men and women, and I quickly internalized this message. I decided I wanted to be a Playboy model when I was in the sixth grade and my biological father bought me a Playboy jacket. I even started telling people that was what I was going to do. In my "Heiress Diary" by Paris Hilton from the sixth or seventh grade, I wrote: "*I LOVE BOYS, I'm outgoing, very mature, sexy and I love my body.*" The words "Boy crazy" were repeated several times throughout.

I can't remember a time when I didn't have a boyfriend, even in the first grade! I was always playing damsel in distress on the playground, hoping for someone to save me. Or I was asking to play house, and I was always playing the mom and wife. Even at six and seven years old, there was dry humping—I was always the one being humped, even inside a toy playhouse in the basement of a funeral home with a boy twice my age. Clearly, I wasn't the only child exposed to sexual behavior at a very young age.

In middle school, men in their 30s and 40s would ask me inappropriate questions and ask if I had a phone so that they could text me. At that age, I was even asked what my body count was (meaning how many people I had slept with). I was surrounded by other 13- to 16-year-olds that had "fuck buddies." In my apartment complex in Flint. A common tactic among the boys I knew was to spread the idea that sex would make your butt bigger. Tragically, young and vulnerable girls, wanting very much to please and be sexually "perfect," would take the bait.

I lived with my mother until the age of six, and in that time, I was already being sexually abused and molested by family members, babysitters, friends, and neighbors, both male and female. I have countless stories of how men abused their authority and strength to exploit me; and female friends and babysitters who just wanted to "try things" with me. One boy—my mother's best friend's son—chased me around the house wearing a Scream mask and wielding a knife. He found me hiding—and sobbing—in the closet. Then he lay me on top of his groin while he took a nap. I was too scared to move.

Then there was the son of a friend of my dad's, who pretended to be looking for a lost remote on the couch in order to fondle my legs and butt. On another night, he dry humped me with six kids sleeping on the ground next to us.

I was often left alone with the son of my father's girlfriend, who was 16 when I was 7. He called me "Sexy Lexy" and also dry humped me when his mother was out. I saw him a few days later and I couldn't bear to look at him as he walked past our car. I felt deep and painful shame.

When I'd visit Greg, a family friend, at his house, he would require that I "do stuff" to him if I wanted to play video games or watch TV. If I'd protest, he'd say "Well, I guess you don't want it that badly." I was eight or so at the time. If I stayed the night—and there is no easy way to write this—I could expect to be raped. He'd use Ziploc bags as condoms. I was learning early and frequently: if I wanted something, I had to give up a piece of myself in return. Even though this happened so often at home, it never felt normal. Something even deeper than shame tells you that these kinds of incidents are wrong, pathological, even criminal. At the same time, another part of your brain becomes desensitized in order to survive.

One time, I was playing hide and seek with my brother, Zach, and his best friend. I was hiding behind the couch when the friend "found me." He started kissing me and touching me all over my body. I was only five or six years old. Years later, when I was 11, the same boy came over to my apartment when my dad was at work. My godmother, whom I called "Aunt Bev," came over to check on me, and because I'd forgotten to lock the front door, she found us lying together in bed. She was livid—screaming for us to get out and that I was on punishment because she can't trust me alone. I was incredibly grateful when she discovered us. I would not have wanted to do anything more than exchange kisses and I had no idea if he would be willing to leave it at that as he was trying to pull down my pants while I was pushing his hand away

Not long after, I had a boyfriend who lived in our apartment complex. It's hard to believe, but my dad allowed me to sleep over at his place. I would sleep on the couch and my boyfriend would sleep on the floor next to me.

We would stay up all night kissing and talking about having sex. It was nice to feel wanted—for any reason—by someone my age. It felt rebellious too; I knew my father would explode if he knew I was allowing another male to touch me in that way.

When I was in the sixth grade, there was a boy that my best friend and I had a crush on named Jaylen. He lived in the building directly across from me. I went over to his place one time to see if he wanted to play basketball or hang out. After letting me in, he locked the door. I looked him in the eyes and could tell that something was different. He wasn't smiling and happy like he usually was. Cautiousness and fear ran through my body. I knew something was off. When I came towards the door, he blocked it and threw me down on the ground, holding me while he unbuckled his pants. I wrestled with him until I was able to get him off of me, lunging towards the door as he grabbed my ankle before I could unlock the door and escape. I never told my best friend what happened. I just told her that she should stay away from him.

This pattern of abuse continued even into college. When I studied abroad in the Dominican Republic, my class and I stayed at an all-inclusive resort. I had never really had alcohol before and suddenly, I was being offered unlimited drinks. I got on a boat with classmates and a grown man from the resort began handing me drinks. When I was almost too drunk to stand, he pulled me behind the boat, tried to pull down my swimsuit bottoms, and force my hand into his shorts. I was fading in and out. The next thing I remember I was fighting him off, and when I saw a male classmate, I yelled, "Don't let me have any more drinks!" I blacked out, threw up on the boat, and woke up in my room. My first thought wasn't *"How did I get to my room? Did anyone do anything to me?"* No…it was *"Oh my God, what if Shawn finds out?"* The abuse was secondary to the terror of losing my boyfriend.

In my early twenties I was victimized again. One late Saturday morning after Justin and I started dating, I went to get a massage at a local spa. During the massage, I started to fall asleep as I usually did but then I was awakened by a hand grazing my vagina under the sheet. My body clenched and I lay there frozen, waiting for the massage to end. I didn't know if I made it up in my head or if I dreamt it so I didn't even tell Justin about it until I saw a news article with the masseuse's face at the top. I knew what it was about before I had even read the title.

Young, vulnerable women are often abused on a regular basis. As we enter adulthood, we carry these dark and frightening experiences that have altered us dramatically, shrinking our self-worth and ability to form meaningful and healthy relationships with others. We are scarcely aware of how profoundly changed we are, not just by the experiences themselves, but by the continuing burden of carrying the memory of them. As children and teens, we internalize the crimes that have been committed against us and process it as shame, as though *we* have done something wrong, rather than having been wronged as tiny children. Almost inevitably, that child's shame expresses itself in toxic behavior when she becomes an adult. People who meet abused children as adults, acting out the worst of what they have learned, assume we are inherently toxic people, knowing nothing of what we have endured and how that shapes our behavior. Meanwhile, there is another self, deep within: the real person, buried beneath that shame and heartache.

I want to talk about how I ended up in foster care.

My brother and I had different fathers. When I was about four, my biological father built a house on a golf course close to Niagara Falls, where my mom, my biological father, and brother Zach lived while my dad worked at General Motors (GM). I didn't find out until years later that my dad was fired for selling cocaine in the parking lot at work. We lost the house he'd built and filed for bankruptcy. Afterward, my mom took Zach and me back to Michigan to move in with my Uncle Jeff, who happened to live across the street from Zach's father.

On May 30, 2000, I was at day-care in Flint when Zach's dad came to pick us up. I remember thinking this was strange since he didn't usually pick us up. Our mom did.

The next day, I went to class as normal at Cody Elementary School.

"Excuse me, Mrs. Rhodes?" a familiar voice asked, I disregarded it; I was engrossed in my painting. Usually, my mom volunteered as a teacher's helper in my kindergarten class, but today she hadn't shown up.

"Is Alexis Sulzman in this class?" (Sulzman was my brother's father's last name, and while I lived with my mother, it was mine.) Another voice—one I would know anywhere—my father's. I looked up, startled, and even from a distance, I could tell something was wrong. I realized the other voice belonged to my father's sister, Aunt Kristy, who still had her police uniform on.

Now they were whispering with my teacher. I couldn't catch the words, but I saw distress pass over my teacher's face, and a knot formed in my stomach. Her hand flew up to her mouth. Then she took her hand down and I saw her mouth the words, "I'm so sorry," to my aunt and father.

What happened in the next few days was a blur. *Where was my mom? Where was I?* This room looked vacant, with only my dad, Zach and me in it, and a big wooden box at the front. The box was dark brown with silver railings on the side. The rectangle case looked like someone had cut it in half, exposing the inside, which was a beautiful cream or light brown color. There was also a large pillow in there, with someone resting on top of it.

"Is she sleeping?" I asked my dad. He winced, but never replied. He was standing next to me, staring down at her with a lifeless, distant look on his face. His chin trembled and his eyes were glossed over. I still couldn't comprehend what was happening. She lay there with her hands crossed, one on top of the other, across her chest.

She died on May 31st, 2000. Looking at court records later, I discovered that my parents had been fighting over custody of me. I never unearthed the details. Maybe my father just wanted to make life hard for my mother, or maybe he didn't want to be forced to pay child support. The case was closed in March 2000, just two months before she died.

Ten years later, during my sophomore year of high school, I ran on the track team and was preparing for a 4x200 relay. Usually, my best friend India was the first leg and I was the anchor, but this time I was the first leg. My Uncle Jeff and my brother came to the meet, which they usually did once a year since it's about an hour's drive from Flint. Right before the meet, I was in the locker room getting ready when I was told over the phone by my aunt that my mom had committed suicide. I texted my brother, who was sitting in the stands. He replied, "Yes, I knew." I felt betrayed. We had a promise that if we ever learned the truth about mom that we would be the first to tell each other. For years, we were told that she fell at work and broke her neck. This didn't sit well with me because when I'd ask family members what happened, they would tell me to ask my dad or that "You know already." My mom vanished and they assumed that I would accept this explanation and somehow deal with it.

I stayed in the locker room, missing my relay and other races. I didn't care anymore. My coach, Ms. Pollini came in to check on me and after telling her what happened, she asked if I'd like to sit out the rest of the meet. I was shocked. She never lets anyone miss practice or meets. I was barely able to speak through my tears, but I managed to tell her I wanted to be alone.

In court documents I later found, my father blamed my mother's suicide on him being fired. "My life has been destroyed over someone accusing me of two transactions of cocaine…I have been dismissed [from GM] and now my ex-girlfriend and the mother of my daughter has committed suicide over this matter." Again in another document, "Please look into my case for me. My daughter and I—her mother committed suicide—would really appreciate it."

I had been told that she had slipped and fallen, breaking her neck. Actually, she hanged herself at work, at a restaurant called Ponderosa in Flint, where she worked as a waitress. Her life savings (exactly $15,600 in hundred-dollar bills) was stuffed into her green apron and photo buttons with Zach and my face attached to it.

Zach and I never received the money that was meant for us. *Did she kill herself because she knew what my dad was capable of? Was she trying to protect me? Or was she taking the easy way out, abandoning me in the process?*

Years later, while I was working at Target, I overheard coworkers discussing their craziest work experiences. One woman, Tameka, said that she had to keep working after discovering someone who had hung herself in the bathroom.

I froze. Then I raced around the corner.

"Did that happen at Ponderosa in Flint?"

She looked startled. "Yes, why?"

"Was her name Linda?"

"Yes."

"That was my mom."

I ran into the bathroom and sat on the floor. I had finally met someone who knew her.

Tameka helped me contact other people who had worked with her. I wanted to try to fill in the gaps of who she was and what had happened.

I was told that my mother was incredibly fearful whenever a particular man came into Ponderosa and sat in the back booth. She would run into the kitchen and tell a coworker that she didn't feel safe—that a man was watching her in the back. I am certain my biological father was somehow involved.

Before my mother died, I had spent only weekends with my father. Afterwards, I had to move in with him full-time. I began a quest for a mother figure, calling nearly every woman in my life "mama." I could see this with my brother as well—he would only date single mothers with children.

We moved around a lot, and I remember at least one time when my father and I were homeless, couch-hopping through his friends' houses. But what I remember most clearly is that this was when the abuse began in earnest.

I always smelled Canada House whiskey on my father's breath. He had at least one glass every night. First, he poured in some ice, then a little coke, and then the liquor, stirring it with his finger before sucking off the liquid —a sound I will never forget. He could easily drink a fifth a day. One night he got so drunk that he fell on his way to bed and cracked his head open on the doorframe.

What started out as "just" touching got worse over time. He would first touch my leg as his way of signaling: it's time. He cleared his throat as he entered my room, and then I'd smell the alcohol on his breath, wafting through the darkness. Next, I heard his belt unfasten and his pants unbutton. I'd freeze, lying ramrod straight in the middle of the bed, face down, arms crossed underneath my chest, legs crossed at the ankles, hoping that this would deter him. He touched my leg. *Here we go again. When will it end? God please make it stop.* I start thinking about what I have to do the next day, playing basketball, being with friends, anything to help my mind escape what's being done to me.

My biological father sexually, mentally, and physically abused me for eight years.

When he was done raping me, he would go back into his room. If he heard me crying, he would scream through the wall, "Stop crying before I give you something to cry about."

I got in trouble in first grade because of passing notes about having sex. When asked by the principal where I got these ideas from, I blamed it on my older brother for talking about sex around me.

In sixth grade, while we lived in Maplebrook apartments in Flint, I found porn in my father's room. I think my dad wanted me to find it. He would play it sometimes while he did stuff to me asking me if I wanted to try things in the film. He showed me how to pleasure myself in the shower and would even stand there and watch sometimes.

Living on the bottom floor of our apartment building, it was easy to see into our apartment if the blinds were raised. At night, I would keep my window cracked with the blinds raised a few inches. One night, as I was laying in bed I turned over and saw a boy watching through my window. *How long had he been sitting there? Did he see me get undressed?* I screamed, which prompted my dad to run in my room and prompted the boy to run away. I noticed the same boy looking through the window a few weeks later after my dad was done. *Oh no, did he see what just happened?* I was afraid of being caught. I had already internalized my father's crime as my own and felt deeply ashamed of the time I was forced to spend with him.

Years later, I remember a boy named Deon, who was several years older than I was, reacted to my history in a strange way. "Wow," he said, "Your dad has heart for looking you in the eyes while he did that to you." The expression meant courage—Deon was expressing admiration for my father's shamelessness. It was shocking and grotesque, but now it serves as a reminder that much of my community was steeped in pathology. There were many other such kids—and adults—who did not respond to my plight with the expected horror or outrage. While not every child was being abused by their father, it is now clear to me that there was a pathological value system within the circles in which we traveled—something that corroded the safety and happiness of the kids growing up inside them.

I contemplated killing my father several times. From the kitchen, as I unloaded the dishwasher, I could see the back of his head while he drank and watched television. Holding a knife, I found myself imagining what it would be like to be free. What if I could end the sexual abuse, the screaming, the being called a bitch again and again? I tried to imagine the knife sliding into him, would it even work? Would he grab the knife back and kill *me*? I tried to imagine the sirens and the ambulance and the police cars rolling down our street, the lights in the windows but couldn't get myself to do it. The consequences of going to prison outweighed being free.

We would never really talk, just scream at each other at the top of our lungs. Cops were never called; neighbors would only bang on our ceiling with brooms or their feet to try to get us to be quiet.

He started to get more courage. Each summer, we would go to North Carolina with family and rent a beach house. My dad and I would always share a room and he raped me with family in the next room. He would always tell me to act happy and put a smile on my face when people were around.

I was deathly afraid of my dad. In sixth grade, I received a B- in a class and on the last day of school I wouldn't leave until I'd negotiated my way up to a B. I stayed for an hour to complete the required extra credit assignment, because I knew what was waiting for me at home if I didn't.

In seventh grade, I wore a thong to the skating rink on a Friday night. When I got out of the car, I bent over to grab my bag and he saw the thong. He made me get out of the car, bend over so he could see it, get back in the car, and then slapped me right across the face. I was grounded for four days.

I thought abuse was normal. I didn't realize that it wasn't until I told two of my best friends in the seventh grade. I started texting them "It happened again" every time he attacked me. They recorded this in their phone calendars, unbeknownst to me. This helped my case, once I did finally tell the authorities.

Every night, I would listen to "Imagine Me" by Kirk Franklin. I would play it after my dad was done with me, while wrapping my arms around my dog Jake's neck, crying into his marble black and white fur. It gave me hope. It made me feel safe. I heard this song one time when I went to church with a friend and held onto the lyrics...

Imagine me
Loving what I see when the mirror looks at me 'cause I
I imagine me
In a place of no insecurities
And I'm finally happy 'cause
I imagine me
Letting go of all of the ones who hurt me
'Cause they never did deserve me
Can you imagine me?
Saying no to thoughts that try to control me
Remembering all you told me
Lord, can you imagine me?
Over what my mama said
And healed from what my daddy did
And I wanna live and not read that page again
Imagine me, being free, trusting you totally, finally I can
Imagine me
I admit it was hard to see
You being in love with someone like me
But finally I can
Imagine me
Being strong

And not letting people break me down
You won't get that joy this time around
Can you imagine me
In a world (in a world) where nobody has to live afraid?
Because of your love, fear's gone away
Can you imagine me?
Letting go of my past
And glad I have another chance
Imagine Me by Kirk Franklin

My biological dad would always threaten, "If something ever happens to me, you'll go live with Mark and Karen (My aunt and uncle)." I'd reply, "Over my dead body."

I never liked going to their house. It was always fake smiles, no real connections, and my dad was always saying awful things about them. The abuse got so bad in sixth grade that I told a counselor at school. When CPS came to my house, I denied that I'd been abused.

That night, I got one of the worst beatings of my life. He kicked me with his steel toe boots, which he wore because he worked in construction. He kicked the wall, leaving a hole. He left and I had to clean it up through my tears and pain. I went to my neighbor, who was my friend's mother and also my babysitter at the time, and told her that he had kicked me and that I had to go and clean it up. All she said was: "You'd better go do that before he gets home."

Starting in the sixth grade, I was allowed to go to the mall for hours on end. My father would drop my friends and me off when the mall opened and pick us up when it closed, or I would have to be home by 9:30 p.m. if I found a ride home. He didn't care how I made it home, just that I did. Of course, we would get into trouble at the mall, riding carts around, getting kicked out and banned from coming back. Friends would have sex in the bathrooms, and we would get guys' numbers and make out on the side of the building. I couldn't understand why I was always the last pick when guys came to talk to us.

One Saturday, we were being dropped off and I had all my friends in the car. I'm sure I said something smart and my father smacked me so hard my ears started ringing. He called me a bitch, and took me home. Sometimes he would sit in his lazy boy chair in front of the TV, and force me to stand on his left side so that I was just close enough to slap and degrade me, screaming that I was a bitch *just like my mother.* I quivered in fear as the spit from his words landed on my face. My child brain tried to make sense of this. Could it be his resentment of my mother that drove him to abuse me?

As my situation continued to deteriorate, my friend Jasmine told her mother what was happening to me. Her mom called to invite me for dinner, and because I hung out there all the time, often spending the night, I thought nothing of it. When I got there, Jasmine wasn't home. It was just her mom and me. She asked me if there was anything I wanted to tell her, and she promised that she wouldn't be mad. I thought maybe she had caught me doing something that I shouldn't have been. Then she revealed that Jasmine had told her everything. I knew that she knew. She told me that I had one week to tell someone before she did.

Almost a week later, on June 1st, 2007, I went to the Soulja Boy concert with a few friends. I had to argue with my dad because he didn't want me to go somewhere with an all-Black crowd. On top of his other toxicities, my father was racist and filled with hatred. My friend's mother managed to persuade him to let me go.

The next day, I was dropped off at the Courtland Mall, as usual. I had gotten into a bad fight with one of my close friends, Mya, and no one in my social group would talk to me. To top it off, I saw the first boy I had ever had sex with—my first "love" at the mall with another girl. I went into Staples next door to be alone—crying in the bathroom, and terrified to go home because I didn't have a ride anymore and the mall was closing soon. My friend Aaliyah came and got me and took me home. We sped home but still got there a few minutes late. He was drunk again. I knew, because when I came in the door he immediately started smacking and punching me, throwing me into the wall. I fell down and when I made it back up, he threw me back on the wall and I heard a pop. I had dislocated my shoulder. There was a rack of golf balls on the wall and he grabbed them and started throwing them at me as hard as he could, hitting me or bouncing off the door behind me. I was flailing, trying to cover my face, my leg raised trying to block the blows.

Begging him to take me to the hospital that night, he forced me to go about my normal routine of cleaning the bathroom and taking the dog for a walk with little to no movement in my arm. I called all of my friends and told them what had happened. I didn't care anymore. I couldn't hide it anymore. Thankfully, they weren't mad at me and just wanted to help.

The next day, I woke up to go to church with Aaliyah as I did sometimes. It was excruciating to take a shower. I couldn't cry silently through the pain anymore. He heard me getting ready, barged into my room and said,

"Where the fuck do you think you're going?"

"I'm going to Church!"

"No, the hell you aren't. You aren't going anywhere."

I ran out of the house with nothing but the clothes on my back and refused to stop until Aaliyah's mom arrived, picking me up for church. Near the end of church service, I went into the bathroom and tried to calm myself down. I had no idea what to do next. I just knew that I couldn't go home.

I came out of the bathroom and my friend told me that my arm was blue. I tried to hide it, but it was difficult to do so in a T-shirt when one arm was clearly different from the other. Everyone seemed to be in a hurry to get on with their day, but I was panicking. I couldn't go home. We got into Aaliyah's mom's car. There were at least seven people in the car, Aaliyah's siblings, her parents, and her brother's best friend. I was frantically texting Aaliyah (who was sitting in the furthest back seat) that I could not go home and didn't know what to do. She said that she was going to tell her mother, who happened to be a police officer. I begged Aaliyah to instead persuade her mother to let me come home with them, but Aaliyah said it wasn't an option because they had plans that day. Aaliyah, terrified at the thought of me going home, shouted to her mother in the front of the car.

"Mom, Alexis can't go home!"

"Why?" her mother asked. I froze in the back seat, not believing this was actually happening.

"Her dad has been coming into her room at night and touching her."

Everyone looked back at me as I sat in the back seat, frozen with fear about what would happen next but also relieved that the secret was out. No one said a word.

Her mom immediately pulled the car over. She turned back to me.

"Is that true?" she asked quietly. I was incredibly scared to admit it. Another friend whispered that if it were, I could come to live with her. This gave me courage, and I managed to whisper the word "yes."

Aaliyah's mother took me back to their house and called the police. An ambulance arrived to take me to the hospital, and they collected everyone's cell phones for possible evidence. I had nothing but the clothes I'd worn to church.

At the hospital, I stripped down, put on a gown, and hoisted my legs into the holsters. The nurse swabbed my vagina for a rape kit. Jasmine and her mother stood nearby to support me. Because it had been a few days since the last incident, they didn't find any evidence. I told them that if they went to my house and tested the sheets, they would find something.

The doctor came in and said, "Your aunt is on her way to pick you up." My heart dropped. I could hear my dad saying *If anything ever happens to me, you'll have to go live with Mark and Karen. It's a family agreement.* I wouldn't have said anything if I knew that I would have to live with her. My dad had always used that as a way to get me to stay quiet. I felt utterly betrayed—my friend had promised I could live with her. I was too young to understand that legally, I couldn't just move wherever I wanted to.

Now, I would have to move away from everything I knew and loved to live with people that I hated spending holidays with and attend my ninth different school (high school being my tenth). Jake had been left in his cage for days because my dad had been arrested and we didn't have anyone to go check on him. He was hungry and aggressive and had to be put down. The only thing that comforted me through my father's abuse was gone.

Jasmine, who I was supposed to live with—the only justification that I had for telling—moved out of state shortly after. Something in me broke after this and I severed myself from any conscious drive to find a mother figure.

For the next few months, my biological dad would call my aunt and uncle's house, trying to talk to me, until we had a no-contact rule in place. Every time the land line rang, my heart would drop to my stomach with unbearable anxiety.

Between this time and his trial, I had to give a statement at least five times to several officers and to a social worker. Then, on October 21st, 2008, I testified against my father in a court of law. I had just begun the ninth grade. This was one of the most difficult things I've ever had to do—to recall, in front of both family members and strangers, every detail of my dad beating and raping me.

I had written a letter to the judge before the trial, asking that he get only eight years, the exact duration of his abuse. At the trial's conclusion, his parental rights were terminated. I was officially an orphan. As my father was led away, I also gave up on finding a mother figure or anyone to protect me. I knew I had to figure everything out for myself.

On November 24, 2008, I went back to Flint to attend his sentencing. I thought testifying was difficult, but this might have been even harder. He apologized for what he did and said that he had found God. He said he hoped that I would forgive him. I ran out of the courtroom crying. I did not believe him. He had lied to so many people, denied the abuse for so long, hurt me in so many ways. Suddenly he had found God? He was still trying to stall his prison term by changing lawyers and trying to appeal. He was not sorry, and I could not forgive him.

He received six counts of first-degree child abuse, the most severe of child abuse charges, and was sentenced to a minimum of 15 to 25 years in prison.

I never took time off school during any of this. My Aunt Karen and my boyfriend at the time Shawn were supportive and empathetic with how much strain this was having on me. School was a distraction and served as my coping mechanism. **My education was the one thing that no one could take away from me.** I would check out the maximum number of books from the school library and read them all at once. I would create extra homework for myself on top of my daily assignments and track practice when I lived with my aunt so that I didn't have to participate or socialize. *I can't get in trouble for not talking or participating if I'm doing homework, right?* I would sit at the table immediately when I got home from track practice until it was bedtime, every night.

After my dad went to prison, he would write letters to the family. I found these letters in 2018, while cleaning out Aunt Bev's house after she passed. He had written that I had made up everything because I had wanted to move out and live with my best friend. Now I was too deep in, he wrote, and couldn't take back my story. *He added: I don't know what else to think. I've been wracking my brain like crazy trying to figure this out. I truly thought that our problems would pass and that this was all just a phase in her life that would pass. I still can't believe she hated me that much to do this to me. I truly believe she's too scared to back out now."*

Of course. I made it all up, right?

I often say that I am lucky because my family unequivocally believed me. I've been told that there had been signs over the years—he would tell relatives that I had "nice tits" or a "plump ass," and that I acted differently when he was around.

After a few months, I went to visit Aaliyah. Her mother asked me, "Are you upset about going to live with your aunt because you can't be "fast?" Referring to being promiscuous at a young age.

I was at a loss for words. Was anyone who had been sexually abused at the age of 13 simply "fast." Was this an appropriate question for a young girl who had been violated and victimized by her own father for nearly a decade? Aaliyah's mother was a police officer. If she had no idea how to understand an assault survivor's perspective—how confusing my world already was for just how *young* I *still* was—who would?

WHAT DID THEY TELL ME ABOUT MY IDENTITY?

*The Black community comprises approximately 40%
of the homeless population, 50% of the prison population,
and 45% of children in the foster care system.*

Almost 70% of Black families are single-parent households.

JUSTIN

MY IDENTITY WAS to mirror whoever got the most attention around me. My parents were busy doing their own thing and the drug dealers in our neighborhood regularly looked out for us. In my neighborhood on Dexter Ave in Detroit, the drug dealers got all the money, girls, and attention. At about seven or eight years old, I actually wanted to be one. I dressed how they dressed and talked like they talked. As an eight-year-old with super nappy hair that I never brushed, I looked silly wearing a durag, but it had become a reflection of who I was becoming.

Drug dealers are often seen as monstrous villains by people outside of the hood. But most kids growing up *in* the hood idolize the local drug dealers, seeing them as the closest thing to success. In neighborhoods like mine, these guys were like celebrities. We glorified their Rolex watches, new Jordans, and exotic cars. My siblings and I would always do favors for them. If they were chilling on the block and wanted food, they would give us a $50 bill to run to the Coney Island restaurant up the street for a $5 Cheeseburger deluxe. After we brought back the food, they told us to keep the change. This gave them an ego boost and made us worship them even more.

We had a basketball rim in front of our house that they always used. It was a janky old rim donated by a church. Most dealers paid us to use it even though they were intimidating and didn't really need to ask. I think they wanted to either show respect or flaunt some of their money. They would bet hundreds of dollars on jump shots. After losing their money, they would double up, spending roughly $500-600 gambling. All of the kids gathered around our house to see who would win. It became a spectacle with the whole block as an audience. I was the kid grabbing rebounds and passing it back to them, just trying to grab some attention.

Having the basketball rim in front of our house made our home well-known throughout the neighborhood. Part of the reason why we idolized these guys was because they looked out for us. They saw how we were living, so some of the dealers gave us their old clothes and sometimes a little money if we did them a favor. We were dirty kids on the block who were easily the poorest in our neighborhood. The dealers we were cool with didn't sell to my mom. That may seem odd, but they made our situation less stressful.

Some of the dealers were cool and felt bad for our family, but others were not. The dealers that sold to my mom were always threatening and intimidating. I remember some dealers knocking on the door, looking for my mother. Frightened by the danger that they could inflict, she whispered in a trembling tone of voice, "If 'such and such' knock on the door, tell them I'm not here." I knew she owed them money and the violence of the community crept to our front door.

My mom's issues started to affect me personally when she took money from me as a child. Even back then, I had an entrepreneurial mindset—selling snacks I bought from the store at a higher price and reinvesting the money I saved. I barely spent any of the money on myself, saving every penny I earned in a clear cookie jar on the living room table. I left it there knowing I could trust everyone in the house. Every dollar I got from the dealers was also saved in the cookie jar—almost $30.

In a sudden panic, my mom told me she needed the money to pay my grandma. I knew it was a lie, but I obeyed her wishes and handed over the money. After attempting to relaunch my savings, my brother Andre stole most of it for weed. With numerous addictions in one household, having money in the house became a project of failure.

My mother's drug addiction would lead us to a point where one of the neighborhood dealers threatened to shoot up our home. We immediately went to a friend's house a few blocks down the road until things cooled down. As a kid, I wasn't as worried about the situation. I had grown familiar with their threats and I figured nothing would happen. All I remember is that we stayed next to a basketball court and that the people we lived with had cereal. While enjoying the sweet taste of off brand Frosted Flakes almost three times a day, I remained unbothered.

My transition into the foster care system was a wild one. My mom and dad were separated at the time and my mom had a new boyfriend who enabled her addiction and other bad habits. Around early October of 2005, my mom welcomed a former co-worker to stay with us as she escaped an abusive relationship. My mom had a heart for those experiencing physical abuse because she had dealt with similar issues with my dad. Though addicted to drugs, my mother was comforting to the weak and needy. If a friend of ours became homeless, without hesitation she'd offer a couch or our room as a shelter. My mom tried to make sure that no one around her had to suffer. Unfortunately, addiction blinded her of the true suffering we endured throughout life.

Her former co-worker only stayed with us for a week, but she noticed the quality of life we were living. We were behind on rent for months and regularly without hot water and heat. The refrigerator was always empty until the first of the month when we received our food stamps. Hundreds of roaches would scatter in the bedrooms once you turned the light on. We lived with roaches, bed bugs, and any other thing you could think of. When my mom's drug addiction got worse with her new boyfriend, her former co-worker truly saw us at our worst.

One or two days after she left, Child Protective Services (CPS) came knocking on our door. We assumed she called because we never heard from CPS until she came around. The entire neighborhood knew the conditions we lived in. The majority of the parents in our neighborhood earned their living by drug money or some dead-end job. The kids in my neighborhood always joked about my mom being a crackhead. Not only were our circumstances normalized but comical to the children in our community. Even though all of the signs were there, I never believed my mom did drugs. When she went to rehab for a short time and CPS paid regular visits, my heart never allowed me to accept that she was addicted to drugs until she actually said the words, years later.

To maintain his role as the provider, my dad would visit every other week to shower us with McDonald's, KFC, and other fast food meals that distracted us from his recurring abusive behavior. This made us excited every time he came around. Even though his abuse was the very reason he was forced to leave, he oddly became the hero.

As CPS became more aware of our situation, we eventually went back to our old neighborhood in Southwest Detroit as an escape. In the late 90s and early 2000s, my parents lived on 25th Street while my aunts and uncles lived on 23rd. Back in the 1950s and 60s, when my dad's side of the family lived there, the neighborhood was beautiful. My grandparents moved from the South and raised my dad and all five of his siblings on 23rd Street. My grandfather dropped out of school at the age of 12 to begin working and helping his family financially. When my grandfather met my grandmother, they had a traditional working-class family—my grandfather was the bread-winner and my grandmother took care of the children. After Detroit started experiencing economic difficulty, the crime rate rose, and the majority of the city started to deteriorate.

Today, our old block looks like a bomb hit the entire neighborhood. There are maybe two or three houses per block. The rest of the block is filled with abandoned houses plagued with drug abuse. After my grandparents died in the late 1990s, the neighborhood, along with their old house, was abandoned. On the run from CPS, my mom and two older brothers, Khalil and Andre, eventually squatted in one of those abandoned houses only a few blocks down from my grandparents' old house. My pregnant sister's boyfriend came along to live with us. There were six of us living together in one abandoned house. We had no water, no heat, and were without any source of income. My mom was regularly gone, so my sister Tiffany and her boyfriend assumed the role of our parental figures at 18 and 20 years old.

Though she was sometimes a mother figure, I believed Tiffany yearned for attention from men being that she never knew her biological father. Following the path my mother set before her, she dropped out of school in the eighth grade and became pregnant with her first child at 18. Though my father accepted her as his own, I feel that there was always a void that needed to be filled.

At the time, my brother Andre was a hothead whose impulsive behavior often landed him in trouble. Similar to my father, he was often fueled by pride and resentment, behaving as if the world owed him something. His reckless behavior would lead him to becoming a father at 14 years old. His girlfriend began to spend the night with us in the abandoned house during her pregnancy.

My oldest brother Dylan lived on his own and was unaware of our living situation. Dylan became a distant loner that often kept to himself. Abandoned by my mother earlier on, I feel that he found comfort in Marvel and DC comics while spoiling himself in any and everything that he missed out on as a child.

Shortly after we started this new journey, my dad returned. This gave me instant hope. After CPS got involved, my mom's boyfriend quickly fled the scene. This opened the door for my dad to return, and my siblings and I were excited. My dad was always one of the well-respected dudes in our neighborhood. He related easily to everyone and he was cool with all the drug dealers. I couldn't find many people that didn't like him. My dad and I used to watch old Kung-Fu movies on our dusty VCR and mimic what we saw, horse playing after the movie ended. All my siblings knew him for carrying a Colt 45 in a brown bag in his hand. It was odd seeing him without it, especially on a Saturday night. When he was intoxicated, he'd tell my siblings and me funny stories about his childhood as we sat him on the porch and watched him drink the night away. My parents often said, "Do as I say and not as I do."

It gave us hope that my dad knew the ins and outs of fixing houses, as did his promise to restore the abandoned house we lived in. As a child, I believed every word he and my mom said to me. The idea of having a new house—one that my dad would build—sounded amazing. This dream sustained me in those years of living in that dark, abandoned house.

This wasn't the first time we were homeless. We were frequently kicked out of houses. Though our house on Dexter is where we stayed the longest, it was common to be without heat or water. Christmas with no heat was especially devastating; presents were the farthest thing from our mind.

My dad's promise to fix the house on 25th made things different this time around. We came back to our old neighborhood and I wanted to believe it was a fresh start. Slowly but surely, we made the house our own, hung pictures of our grandparents and put furniture in the living room. I became attached to it. My parents had gotten back together, and I felt that all was well. I dreamt of my dad fixing up our house and creating a resurgence within the neighborhood.

My dream was to reestablish what my grandparents had built. I believed this house could be the house we always wanted and needed. This could be the house where my nieces and nephews would grow up and my kids would one day visit. I thought of this house being known as grandma and grandpa's house for my children and great-grandchildren. This idea sparked a dream of rebuilding our neighborhood and bringing glory back to the city of Detroit. I wasn't exactly sure what I wanted to do in life, but at the age of eight, I knew it was our responsibility to rebuild the city and our neighborhood.

Unfortunately, the bad influences of the community only worsened my mom's drug use. Strangers throughout the neighborhood who were also addicts regularly showed up at our house. My dad continued his drug dealing and this was the first time I had seen him in action. I grew up around dealers so discovering that my dad was one as well didn't mean much to me. Our house officially became known as a trap house, a house on the block known for drug use and drug dealing. Addicts would sit on the couch next to me as they waited for my dad to arrive. They would often try to make small talk with me, but I ignored them most of the time because I knew they were addicts.

From the outside looking in, these may seem like extreme situations, but I had a lot of fun during those times. I was eight years old and I didn't go to school, which I thought was cool. We used an extension cord from a neighbor's house to plug in a TV and play video games. My parents were either gone or hiding away in their room, so I had no one telling me what to do. I believed my dad would eventually make this into a real home. But most of all, I was ignorant of what was going on around me. I didn't know anything outside of the life we lived and extreme circumstances became daily activities. Seeing addicts in our house became normal and didn't bother me after a while. Strangely, life seemed good.

As the Michigan winter began, I started shoveling snow to make a little money. Living in an abandoned house during the fall wasn't bad, but when winter came along, things weren't pretty. Detroit's winter winds are brutal. Living in a home with no heat became unbearable. Without running water, we had to scoop snow off of the ground, carry it inside in buckets and wait for it to melt to use as makeshift showers. No one in the house had a bed so we regularly piled up clothes to sleep on to avoid feeling the wood and sharp nails sticking out of the floor. We lived on baloney, peanut butter and jelly sandwiches, and anything we could make easily. To this day, the smell of gasoline recalls those gasoline heaters we used to warm our dinner in abandoned housing.

By the end of January, everyone in the house was sick. Both Khalil and Andre had miserable stomach viruses that passed onto me. Shortly after, I became sick as well, vomiting and having diarrhea simultaneously. Our living conditions were taking a toll on our health. With my sister Tiffany only a few months from having her baby and my brother Andre having his first child any day, as an eight-year-old I began to realize how bad our situation was. Meanwhile, my mom told us to make her funeral arrangements, instructing us on the music she wanted played and other details.

As spring arrived, Child Protective Services somehow found out where we were staying. My dad had been making excuses for months of why he couldn't fix the house and resorted to hiding from CPS. I began to lose faith in my parents. They told us that we would have the house fixed by the time CPS came to visit again. They never had any plans to fix the house at all, and my dreams of making it a home were long gone. I thought fixing the house would be the first piece of making us into one happy family. When CPS finally visited, our parents told us to hide. I ducked behind the living room couch in case they peaked through the windows. We all remained silent as we heard the social worker knock on the door.

We did our best, but my parents had no choice but to let us go. One month later, we entered foster care at the start of spring. As the youngest two boys of five siblings, my brother Khalil and I, at age 11 and nine, entered the foster care system together and journeyed through the system for years. Because he was two years older, he became my role model. When he decided to play football at 12, I did the same. Once he pursued music at 13, I quickly followed. Journeying through the foster care system, Khalil played the role of a father figure and I mimicked his every move. We had an unbreakable bond up until we were separated at 17.

My sister Tiffany, 18, was preparing to start a family of her own. She gave birth to her first child that April. My 14-year-old brother Andre temporarily lived with my uncle for a few months. He always had a conflict in every home in which he was placed, making no living situation a viable long-term solution for him. Eventually he went AWOL. All four of us separated on our individual journeys; it was up to us to figure out life on our own, with the foundation set by our parents.

I still clung to the faith I'd had in my parents. At the same time, I felt that they had let me down completely. Here is where my issues with trust began. If I couldn't trust my parents, I reasoned, who would I be able to trust?

DESPERATE FOR LOVE

One in three adolescents in the U.S. is a victim of physical, sexual, emotional or verbal abuse from a romantic partner.

ALEXIS

BEING SEXUALIZED AT a young age influenced my thinking and behavior. In middle and high school, I would allow boys to touch my butt and give me tight hugs pretty much every day. I accepted and even liked it when boys called me "Snowbunny," unaware it was a stripper name. Most days I would change my clothes once I got to school. I was obsessed with what I wore. One typical outfit: a short plaid pink, black, and white skirt, with very high wedges to match. With a thong underneath, I wore a pushup bra with a V-neck shirt to finish the ensemble. I wore makeup every day and always put a ribbon in my hair. I thought I was even cuter with my brown and gold Baby Phat coat; it was my signature look. Once, my high heels gave out on me while running to class.

Exposed to pornography at a very young age, I developed a distorted image of what made women desirable, and I made it my mission to emulate that image. The intercourse and other sex acts I had experienced unwillingly with my father were by their very nature violent and dehumanizing. As is common with sexually abused children, I became very good at disassociating—taking my brain outside the room to escape the horror, shutting off to avoid feeling the pain of it all. But the hugs and kisses I experienced at school offered me actual pleasure and somehow left me feeling loved and worthy. I was hungry for affection, for validation, for a comforting embrace. What boys offered was a sense of gentleness that felt like balm after my father's drunken violence. But this also set me up for other types of abuse, such as the emotional torment of Shawn.

I was obsessed with boys. I kept track in my planner of which boys were interested in me. I even tried to steal my friends' boyfriends because I wanted the love and affection I saw them receiving. I wanted someone to hold and kiss me like they did. When I succeeded, it ruined two of my strongest friendships. Deep down, I didn't want sex anyway. I wanted intimacy, security, and love.

Almost every Friday night, my best friends and I would go to the skating rink around the corner. We would spend the night talking to guys, dancing, and flirting. I used to love the overnight lock-ins because then you could talk to guys all night and even fall asleep cuddling next to them anywhere you could find a spot on the ground. One Friday night after we were dropped off at the skating rink, we ended up going to the bowling alley next door. I was 13 and my boyfriend at the time, Troy, was 16 or 17. He and his friend went out back to smoke weed, and we followed. The police came and we ran around the building, hiding in the bushes. I looked down and smacked my lips. *How the hell did I already mess up the brand-new Nike Air Forces I just got that day?* I wasn't as concerned about being caught. There are things you can handle and understand as a pre-teen, and things you cannot really grasp.

At 12, I was getting nude photos from guys almost twice my age. They would get upset that I refused to show them the kind of photos they wanted in return.

On my 13th birthday, I invited friends over to my apartment. It was the middle of January in Michigan, fresh white snow layering the ground outside. Since we lived on the first floor, I could see it accumulating on the windowsill. Shortly after the party started, my dad left and just told us not to make too much noise. Troy asked me if I wanted to go in my room. We lay in bed together as I waited for him to make the first move. I really didn't know what to do. Although I'd experienced the mechanics of intercourse every time my father raped me, I didn't know what sex was like with someone you liked or felt that you loved. I was scared. Troy started to take off my pants as he got on top of me and kissed me while he entered my body.

All of a sudden, headlights shone through the blinds and I heard my friend banging on the bedroom door, screaming, "Your dad's back!" We scrambled to get our clothes back on. For some reason, I couldn't get my other leg inside my pants. I ran out of the room and then Troy ran out behind me. My dad was standing there. I didn't know if he saw us coming out or not. He said "Alright, the party's over, everyone let's go." He took everyone home and didn't say anything about it.

Troy broke up with me shortly after. He stopped talking to me altogether and told his cousins not to answer the house phone when I called—which I did, probably five times a day. I was desperate to hear his voice. *How could he leave me after what we just did? He told me he loved me and wanted to be with me.*

Before my birthday, I spent several days at his house. I told my dad that I was hanging out with Troy's female cousin when in reality, I was just there to see Troy. I would sit on his lap with my legs wrapped around him, kissing while he would touch my body.

I thought this was normal—sneaking around, fooling around with boys, smoking— so many other people I knew were doing it too. There was no one protecting me and telling me that it wasn't normal at all. There was no one there to tell me that the hole in my heart couldn't be filled with chasing boys or in gaining their very temporary attention.

In 2008, in the summer between eighth and ninth grades, I was in a bowling alley in Flint with a couple of friends when a light-skinned guy came in smiling, walking with my friend. He said his name was Shawn and he shook my hand. I found myself grinning from ear to ear.

He sat down on the wall, his beautiful brown eyes fixed on me, as I prepared to bowl. He gave me chills. To have someone look at me the way that Shawn did made me feel as if I were the only girl in the world. He asked me for my number, his smile ever present. I was mesmerized.

He lived in Flint, and I lived in Rochester Hills with my aunt and uncle about 45 minutes away. We spent every waking hour on the phone or texting each other. We were head over heels in love. I was only 14 and he was 16. All I wanted to do was talk to him and see him. I had a sense of hope whenever I talked on the phone with him, as though I would have both love and a future. Every few weekends he would take the bus to the Great Lakes Crossing Mall and my aunt would drop me off so I could see him. He made me feel like a queen: happy, good, loved, adored.

He was my rock through the trial and sentencing of my dad, he helped me deal with my aunt and uncle and the stresses of high school, and he even came with me to visit my mom's grave on Mother's Day. After about six months of dating, he began talking about sex—a lot. He would ask me to touch myself on the phone while he listened. We did this together frequently. One weekend, we made a plan for me to sneak into his grandmother's house while I told my aunt that I was visiting my brother in Flint. We had sex. I was scared because I loved him, and I was worried that he wouldn't find my naked body attractive. But he was gentle and kind and told me that I was beautiful and that he loved me.

After a few months, Shawn's tenderness evaporated. He became possessive, jealous, and cruel. Our nightly routine was to sleep on the phone together. I've always been afraid of the dark and our conversations before bed helped ease the anxiety of going to sleep alone. This started as something soothing and romantic but became demeaning. He wanted to stay on the phone just to make sure I wasn't talking to or sleeping with anyone else.

In high school, Shawn would often end our relationship and cut ties with me before school, later admitting that this was a tactic to upset me and deter me from talking to other guys throughout the day.

I couldn't begin to count the hundreds of hours spent crying and begging Shawn to stay in a relationship after telling him how much I needed him and that we were meant to be together. There were multiple late nights weeping in the laundry room calling Shawn for hours. Desperate for him to return my calls, I left countless texts and voicemails.

His neglect and abandonment were a form of punishment, he treated me like a child. He ignored my calls for weeks, blocked me on social media, and only communicated with me via email when it was convenient for him. *When* I could prove that I was trustworthy, he'd tell people we were together. After vacations, I would see pictures posted on social media of just him even though we took photos together, saying that he was with family although it was a trip I planned for us.

I always felt like a second option, shameful to be with, and easily disposable to the man who was with me during my most challenging moments of life. I held on to every text and email just in case it was the last. I held on to them for dear life, printing them off in case my phone was taken by Aunt Karen, to read as a reminder that I was loved and cared for—even if I was only worthy of it momentarily. He used to have eyes for only me, now he had eyes for every girl that passed.

In the mornings, I would wake up as if in a nightmare, so distressed that I became nauseated. This feeling was paralyzing. It took thirty minutes of self-soothing in order to get out of bed in the morning. There was so much tension in my body that it made it hard to breathe and move, as if all of my muscles were constantly clenched tightly together.

The summer between my sophomore and junior year, we were off and on even more. He broke up with me two days after our two-year anniversary and ignored my calls for over a week.

While visiting my cousin for an out-of-state softball game, Shawn finally answered the phone. I was ecstatic to at long last hear his voice. But a woman picked up the phone.

"Hello? Where is Shawn?"

With laughter in the background, she responded "He's busy right now."

I went to Facebook, where I found photos of Shawn with another woman. I froze as tears ran down my face.

My world came crashing down around me. My whole existence was wrapped up in him and he was gone.

I visualized leaping out into the street to finally end my pain and suffering. No more would I have to endure the agony that life offered. I accepted my life for what it was and accepted my fate.

I locked myself in the bathroom until Aunt Karen convinced me to open the door. As she consoled me, I told her I wanted to end my life. She suggested taking me to a hospital in Flint, to ensure that they'd accept my health insurance. I secretly hoped that Shawn would come to save me. With this in mind, I said yes, forcing a smile as I left the bathroom. When I got to the hospital, the doctor asked if I wanted to be an inpatient or an outpatient. I assumed that meant that I would be able to stay at the hospital overnight, in my own room, and finally enjoy peace and quiet for a bit. But I was put inside an ambulance and taken to a psychiatric hospital, where I was put on suicide watch and multiple medications. I was set up with a psychiatrist and received points for taking showers, eating, and making my bed. The gloom of the place overwhelmed me, and I pleaded to be let out. I was allowed 30 minutes of phone time a day, which I used to call Shawn. Finally, he answered and told me that he didn't want anything to do with me.

After leaving the hospital, I spent the rest of the summer isolated from the world, sleeping, doing puzzles and paint by number kits, which helped me escape my thoughts. I continued to use medication but remained depressed. I lost 20 pounds only weighing 130 pounds to begin with. Sometimes, I would sit in the living room hoping that Shawn would suddenly show up in his car to see me or take me away.

It seemed like I was always disappointing everyone around me. At least alone, I thought, I could only disappoint myself.

After a month or so, Shawn emailed to invite me to his graduation. I thought this meant we were back together, especially because I would be a part of his family celebration.

A few weeks later, my Aunt Karen saw the email. Disappointed that I'd started associating with Shawn again, she called Aunt Bev and told her she was packing all my things and putting my belongings in the driveway. Thankfully, Aunt Bev's neighbor was willing to drive an hour to help me gather my belongings.

It was the summer between my junior and senior years and I was terrified that I would have to go to a new school and start a new life once again—away from everything I knew and loved. On the flip side, I convinced myself that my Aunt Karen's disapproval of Shawn was the reason we hadn't gotten along. Once she was out of the picture, I told myself, Shawn and I could finally be happy together.

A few days later, I moved 35 minutes away from my high school to live with Kim and Brian, my new foster parents, only to reenact old habits. On the second night of living in my new home, I sneaked out to see Shawn. Though they genuinely cared for me and trusted my judgment, my loyalty lay with Shawn. He was a master manipulator, and wanting love as much as I did, I was a willing puppet. *Don't you miss me, Alexis? Don't you want to see me?* Sometimes we'd have sex at 2 am in the back of his car or in the movie theater on weekends. I felt addicted to sex, though I realize now I was trying to satisfy my craving for affection.

I had at least three pregnancy scares in high school. I'm not 100% certain, but I think I had a miscarriage once. With my sex life a secret, I was afraid and ashamed to tell anyone. Searching the internet for solutions, I decided to punch myself in the stomach. I also considered taking pills or throwing myself down the stairs.

A few weeks before my high school graduation, Shawn and I had conversations about getting our names tattooed on each other. Rushing me to do it before I graduated, this was his way of branding me and discouraging me from talking to other men in college. I got his name, the date of our anniversary, and a lily on my lower back. He got my first name on his back right shoulder. I finally belonged to him now and he had claimed me as his girl.

During my last semester in high school, I attended a weekend conference where I was scheduled to receive a prestigious $20,000 scholarship. Being one of 102 people chosen out of over 70,000 applicants to be granted the award, I was elated to fly to Washington D.C. to accept it. I saw my name in the newspaper! Photos of me were posted all over the entire school and on their website. I felt accomplished and successful. Shawn, on the other hand, saw my accomplishments as a threat to his masculinity and my devotion to him.

The conference consisted of speaking with a Supreme Court Justice and a variety of celebrities. But those two days were filled with loneliness and resentment, with Shawn threatening to end our relationship every day. I spent the last night of the conference crying alone in my hotel room. I sobbed openly at the airport the next day, hoping for even one stranger to ask me if I was okay. But everyone avoided eye contact. I was sixteen years old, and I felt utterly alone.

When I landed in Michigan, Shawn greeted me with open arms and kisses. He swung me around as though we were in a movie, and he handed me a card telling me how much he loved me—as well as a bouquet of flowers. It was as if nothing had happened. *Didn't he just break up with me? Maybe everything's okay now.* I told myself I had made too much of our fight. In the back seat on the way to dinner with my foster grandparents, I tried to hold his hand. He shoved it away, mouthing the words, *"don't fucking touch me."* The floor dropped out from under me. I realized that it was all a facade for my foster grandparents. Shawn was amazing at disguising his insecurities. During dinner, he smiled and made jokes. After we left them, we walked to our car, preparing to drive back to Flint. Shawn yelled, "Get in the fucking car!" The arguing began.

We screamed for the entire drive home. He demanded that I pull over the car in the middle of the highway. I did as he asked and he began to walk on the side of the road, just to prove his point that I had better listen to him next time. I raced after him, trying to apologize for anything he thought I had done wrong.

This became a regular occurrence. It became normal for us to sit in the car for hours as he degraded me, calling me naive, irresponsible, selfish, and immature. The only reason he kept leaving and coming back, he said, was that he had hoped that it would get better—but *I* fucked it up every time. I was reminded that I was worthless without him. I always felt in debt to him. Constantly proving that I deserved his love. Clapping his hands with every word, he'd say "PLAY-YOUR-ROLE," while deepening his voice.

Shawn's demands filled my head: *"Give me 30 days of no complaining. Start with 24 hours and work up to it. In order for us to get back together, we need to be healthy first. Why can't you be one of those girls who could get and keep their man? Talking to you makes me want to shoot myself in the face."* One night, he emailed me a video about five things to do to keep your man.

After graduating from high school, I moved back to Flint to rent us an apartment together, naively excited for the new journey ahead of us. Little did I know that this apartment would become hell.

Desperate to make Shawn feel as welcome and at home as possible, I furnished the place with a new bedroom set, living room set, and a TV. I also painted the walls. I wanted something that felt permanent; something that provided the sanctuary I so deeply desired. When we purchased each piece of furniture, Shawn would say, "So what happens to this if we break up?" Sometimes he would say, "What happens to this *when* we break up?" I'd protest, "Why do you say *when*? Can you say '*If*' next time?" We had our routine down pat; I knew all my cues.

If I wouldn't stop trying to cuddle or touch him, he would tell me to move back to my side of the bed, or sleep on the couch or at the foot of the bed as if I were a dog. Every morning, I would wake up afraid; his moods would change by the day. I would lie in the dark, frozen, trying to assess his frame of mind, vigilantly watching his behavior for signs of how our day would go.

There were times that I would be on the phone discussing a scholarship opportunity or a potential job and Shawn would be in the background berating me, "Bitch, shut the fuck up." "Bitch" became my second name.

Shawn often locked me out overnight. If I tried to return to our house, he would shove the door hard in my face. Arriving at the doorstep of family or friends, I would downplay the altercation as minor. *Was I ashamed? Did I know what was happening was wrong? Or did I believe what he said, internalize it, and hope that others wouldn't discover how unlovable and difficult I was?* I was playing out a cycle of longing for love, fleeing abuse, covering for my abuser, and returning to the scene of someone else's crime, again and again. I had learned this cycle, of course, and my role in it, from the man I had called "Dad."

Shawn bought me a promise ring as a tactic to give me hope of a future together. Since I was a little kid, I had wanted a man to give me a ring. Not long after, furious when I interrupted his PlayStation game, he blew up, and in a moment of rage, flushed my prized ring down the toilet. I stood by, helpless.

Shawn would tear up all our photos and throw them in a box, then place the box on top of a dumpster. Then he would text me to report what he had done. I would sneak out and tape them back together, hopeful that we'd make up.

I thought that if I used my scholarship money to buy us a home and help Shawn get a job, he would settle in and trust me, but he refused to look for work. I created a resume for him and applied for jobs on his behalf without any guarantee that he would accept or show up if he received an offer. I even bought him a car. Whatever it took for me to be loved, I did it. "You're my girl. I shouldn't have to ask you to help me, you should just do it," Shawn would say.

I thought love meant buying him food and providing him with shelter. It was almost if I had become the parent he never had. Shawn had grown up in a single-parent household where his mother was his only source of love. It wasn't until later that he found out how she made her living. One of his closest friends informed him that she was a prostitute after paying for her services. With his mom being the closest person to him in his life, this crushed him to his core. I received the brunt of his lingering anger.

My relationship with Shawn was a roller coaster, to say the least, but there were enough highs to keep me holding on. Sex became an addiction for both of us. It became routine to argue and have sex immediately afterward, almost as if it were planned. The roller-coaster distracted us from our struggles, the constant volatility actually shielded us from even scarier truths.

My body started to react negatively to birth control and sex lost its steam after a while. This caused one of our biggest arguments. Shawn humiliated me in front of his grandmother's house. He yelled in front of everyone that our sex life had become miserable and he wanted someone who could please him. I was so ashamed that I threw up. Standing over me as he continued his rant, Shawn told me I was useless. I stood there helpless; the situation eerily similar to when my dad would humiliate me.

Our relationship became a cycle of breaking up and getting back together.

At night I would read blogs on how I could be a better partner. *What am I doing wrong? Why am I always the problem?* I blamed myself for everything. *How can I make the man that I love feel that way?! God, please help me. I'm sorry I'm too difficult to be loved.*

Shawn came to me slurring his words and reeking of marijuana. I knew trouble would follow…:

"I talked with a few friends about you and your dad and we all think that you could have left if you wanted to, meaning that you wanted it to happen." He said, looking to destroy me even more.

"I need you to admit it.

Look me in my eyes and tell me to my face that you could've left if you wanted to.

This was all your fault.

I won't be with you until you tell me that this was your fault, you could've done more and left if you wanted to.

I will never be with you if you forgive him for what he did to you."

He questioned me further about my past the night before Thanksgiving. Shawn called me and asked if my dad ever made me perform specific sexual activities. I decided to be truthful, knowing that I couldn't change the past. I reluctantly said yes. He hung up and wouldn't answer any of my calls. Still showing up to my brother's house to carpool for Thanksgiving dinner, everyone went inside, but Shawn told me we needed to have a talk. Shawn screamed at the top of his lungs, calling me disgusting and dirty, as if I'd consented to being abused by my father. He told me that I needed to wash my mouth out with bleach. With no one in my family saving me from his attacks, I felt unprotected and disgusted with myself. If no one stood up for me then it must mean that I deserved it, right? I internalized his remarks and accepted that his perspective was justified. *I allowed my father to sexually assault me. I am disgusting, filthy, and someone who doesn't deserve to be loved.* The identity Shawn shaped for me allowed for his abuse to continue for four more years.

After that Thanksgiving, public humiliation had become the usual. That December, Shawn visited me at University of Michigan-Flint, where I was attending my freshman year of college. We stood in line in the cafeteria, and I impulsively offered my extra dining dollars to the students behind me, in a casual gesture of kindness. Shawn burst into a jealous rage. I knew I had screwed up, and here came his predictable torrent of anger. But it turned out to be a blessing. Something began to shift inside me that day. Some of my determination to hold onto Shawn at any cost dissolved. He had profoundly humiliated me in front of all my peers, and when the semester ended, I felt I could never go back to UM-Flint comfortably. Although more drama had yet to play out, this marked the beginning of the end. And when, entirely because of this humiliation, I transferred to Western Michigan University (WMU) that fall, I couldn't know that the move would re-shape the rest of my life.

Shawn did follow me to Kalamazoo that fall, but by October, we had broken up. I dated another man briefly, an old friend from high school, who treated me so gently and lovingly that I felt like a queen. I would drive across state to his house and collapse into long, lush naps, feeling that I had made it to someplace safe, at last. His name was Tony, and I enjoyed feeling good with him, dressing up for him, being made to feel pretty and special. Unfortunately, while I slept, he was taking my car out for rides to get drugs. When I discovered this, I broke things off, feeling more foolish and helpless than ever following similar addictions to Shawn. Would I ever catch a break? Would I ever be lucky in love? Or was I fated to eternally choose the wrong men, the men that would hurt me and take advantage of me?

Meanwhile, Shawn had been sleeping in his car outside of my apartment. He sent me apologetic texts claiming that he couldn't bear to live without me. Our psychodrama had to play out its final act, and I felt it enclosing me once more like a net.

Shawn even went over to Kim and Brian's house, yelling that they were ruining my life by telling me that I shouldn't be with him. That they didn't know what was best for me, and he did. He'd been with me since I was 13. He yelled angrily at them. Afterward, Brian asked me if Shawn owned a gun and asked the neighbor to watch their house.

I wanted to finally be done and cut all ties. The only thing still connecting us was the tattoo of his name on my back. I booked an appointment with the first tattoo artist I could find. I was a little skeptical when I pulled up to someone's house and went down to their basement, but I didn't care. This was getting covered up no matter what. I cried while I was getting it done because getting his name covered felt like the weight of our relationship had finally ended. I was released from bondage and finally free. After the coverup, I got a tattoo on my shoulder saying, *"There is Always Hope,"* to remind me every morning of the message.

I got his name covered up, but was I truly ready to deal with my past? The journey of healing was far too frightening to face, leaving the door open for Shawn to reenter my life.

DESPERATE FOR LOVE

---

*More than 40% of Black women will experience
domestic violence in their lifetime.*

*Black women are 2.5 times more likely to be
murdered by men than white women.*

JUSTIN

WHEN PARENTS ARE absent, there often seems to be a hole in a child's heart; they are left unsure about themselves, and always questioning their own decisions. This leaves many children vulnerable and desperate for love, yearning for affection from any source available. Without understanding what love meant, I confused attention with love.

Because I never received much attention from my parents, I became one of those children—desperate and vulnerable as a child. It always seemed like other things were pulling their attention, and sometimes rightfully so. When poverty, drug addiction, and domestic violence is generational, most kids don't get the attention and nurturing they need. Before entering the foster care system, my mom was consumed by her lifestyle until I got into trouble in school. She'd usually put me on some form of punishment while my dad was more of the disciplinarian. He would whoop our ass in a heartbeat. Just like most Black kids in the hood, I had my fair share of ass whoopings and stories to go along with it.

I remember the time when I received my worst whooping. I was about six years old and my siblings and I were having a water fight in front of our grandpa's house on the Northwestern side of Detroit. We were living with my grandfather on my mom's side at the time. During this period in life, we moved around often, my grandpa was always willing to let us stay with him until he died about two years later.

It was a sunny day in June of 2003 and all the kids were outside playing. My dad was just coming home from work and didn't want to be bothered. My mom warned me that my dad wasn't in a playful mood and that I shouldn't bother him. I told her that I was going to involve him in the water fight regardless. She laughed and warned me that once the whooping began that she couldn't help. I neglected her advice and continued with the water fight. My dad walked down to our house with his Colt 45 in hand and sat on the porch annoyed; something had happened at work. Finally home and ready to relax, I ran up behind him and poured a full cup of water over his head, completely drenching his shirt.

I scurried away laughing, hoping this would somehow brighten his day. As I peeked behind me, I saw him chasing me, grunting through his teeth. He snatched the back of my shirt and things went downhill from there. Ripping down my pants and underwear, he grabbed me by my leg and held me upside down. With the other arm, he grabbed his famous belt, covered with metal dollar signs, off of his waist and the whooping began.

All the kids in the neighborhood witnessed my beating before continuing their activities. It wasn't uncommon. In fact, many of my friends and I comedically swapped stories of times when we received our worst whooping. It's safe to say that when it was time for a whooping, I got all of my parents' attention and then some.

My parents, always fighting, left my siblings and me in search of someone to love us. With their attention torn away, all five of us grew up desperate for love. They would get into terrible arguments over money—amounts as small as five dollars. It was always "I paid you this money" or "I bought you this food." Their priorities were far from us and we needed to learn to adjust to life without their affection. Their relationship consisted of emotional, mental, and physical abuse that would last for decades.

I was roughly six years old when I saw my parents' first physical altercation. I was sitting on the living room floor, inches from the television, watching Saturday morning cartoons, as I often did. My mom would usually tap me on the head and tell me to back up before I went blind, but she was preoccupied with an argument between her and my dad. I heard them arguing in their bedroom and progressed to the living room. Arguments were nothing unusual, so I continued enjoying my cartoons since it was none of my business. But this time, I had no choice but to direct my focus toward their altercation.

My dad called her degrading names such as "filthy," a "dirty bitch," and more. I kept my eyes on the television screen, but their voices had grown louder than the volume on the television, forcing me to hear every word. It wasn't until he began threatening my mom that I turned my head towards them. The last thing I remember was my dad degrading her repeatedly and threatening to spit in her face. She said, *"If you gon spit on me then do it!"* He gargled up as much spit as he could and spat directly in her face, slamming the door behind him as my mom and I sat in the living room, stunned.

My dad was forced to leave the house regularly when he and my mom would fight. I began to play outside more often to avoid getting caught in the middle of their disputes. After returning from my outside activities, I would see the damage done inside the house as my parents fought once again. My dad left for an extended period of time once my siblings forced him to leave.

The situation happened a year later after moving away from my grandpa in 2004. I was seven years old and playing basketball outside with friends. I was one of those kids who wore a headband with the NBA jersey—Steve Nash, to be specific—Even though I couldn't actually play basketball. We all knew that the kids who wore the basketball jersey with the headband couldn't really play. With the basketball rim being right in front of our house, all my friends could hear the dispute. I heard my parents arguing so

I attempted to distract my friends by diverting their attention toward the basketball game.

"Hey! Who's on my team? We got first ball." I said, hoping that the situation would subside.

But after the actual fight started, we all stood there filled with worry. My mom screamed for him to get off of her. I froze and didn't know what to do.

The tricky part about domestic violence between your parents is that you feel obligated to be loyal to both your mother and your father. Even with my dad regularly beating my mom, I still loved him and never got involved. Looking back as an adult, I feel that I could've done more to protect my mother. At the same time, I was only a child when all this occurred and didn't know what to do.

My siblings weren't as gentle and forgiving. My brothers Khalil and Andre ran inside to attack my dad, my sister and her boyfriend followed. Shortly after they went inside, I heard my dad screaming at the top of his lungs. I knew things had taken an ugly turn, even worse than before. Seconds later, I saw my dad running outside covered in blood. I later found out that my sister had stabbed him to get him off my mom.

The entire time, my friends and I stood there frozen, not knowing what to do. After my dad ran away covered in blood, my friends looked at me speechless, as if I had answers to what had just occurred. Their parents called them home as the spectacle ended. The parents weren't as surprised or alarmed as their children. At first, we were known as the house with the basketball rim where the dealers played ball. Then our family became known for our crazy situations in our neighborhood. Either my parents were fighting and arguing, siblings fighting each other or other kids in the neighborhood, or one of us was getting a whooping outside for everyone to see.

Every week there was another incident. We literally had fights where our entire family would fight another family that we had a problem with. Oddly enough, that was one of the ways we bonded as a family. To this day, my family talks about the classic fights we had—almost as if they were joyful memories.

I could tell you a million crazy stories about life on Dexter. As an eight-year-old, I would only get attention if I stirred up trouble for myself. This made it normal for me to fight, abuse, and do crazy things to other people. It was almost as if we were trying to see who could take the trauma, abuse, and violence to the next level. Every other week our family had another enemy. **It wasn't that I liked what we did but it was the only way to be a part of the family and get the attention that I craved.** I needed to join in on the chaos. Eventually, this became normal and I started to like fighting other kids. **It was so easy to use violence to solve our problems that it seemed like the only option.** After having conflicts with almost every family on the block, I lost all my friends and would eventually be alone. This made me become even more desperate for my family's love and attention and even more desperate for their approval.

My teachers at school felt the impact of my home troubles. As a third-grader, I started to be interested in girls. The problem was, I went weeks without showering, wore the same clothes, and regularly wore shoes without socks. On top of this, I had no idea how to talk to girls so I did what I saw the guys in the neighborhood do to their girlfriends—grab girls' butts to get attention. My friends and I would see how many butts we could grab in a day. It became a normalized game we would play—almost as normal as tag or hide and seek. They would challenge me to touch the cutest girl's butt and I did without hesitation. My friends in school would always challenge me to do and say the wildest things. I knew how crazy it was and I willingly accepted. Whatever it took to keep them around and to have me at the center of attention, I'd do it.

Just like any other child, they regularly abused their power over me, having me steal snacks from the store or give them answers for a test. I didn't care what they asked me to do, all I knew was that I had friends. This still didn't stop them from clowning me for my appearance. To go along with the bad smell, I never brushed my hair. The adults on the block used to call me *beedabeed*, a nickname to reference how dry and nappy my hair was. Eventually, the nickname made it to my school and my friends started calling me the same thing. Once the kids in school started to make more jokes and embarrass me in front of the entire class, I began to fight anyone and everyone at school. The main kid leading the flurry of jokes was the same kid who had convinced me to steal for him and let him cheat off of my papers. He was the first of many of my school fights. One day he made a joke about my hair.

"Boy, it looks like you homeless. Yo mama ain't never brush yo hair?"

I froze as the kids in the class laughed at his jokes. It didn't stop there.

"Look at this bum ass nigga, dude don't even have socks on."

Others started to chime in.

"Yea, and that's probably the fifth time he wore that shirt too, dirty ass!"

Steam was coming out of my ears as my blood began to boil. I was the laughingstock of the class and completely hated myself. I waited until later in the day when we were in the middle of class to retaliate.

I wanted to embarrass him just like he had embarrassed me. The class was quiet, and everyone was working on an assignment. I remained calm the entire time as I walked across the room pretending to sharpen my pencil. Before he could even look up, I punched him right in the face and he fell out of his seat. I began to stomp his face into the ground with all my might. The anger that had built up from their jokes was all released in that moment. I didn't stop until the teacher came to break it up.

He was the most popular kid in the third-grade class, and everyone admired him. After I beat him up and embarrassed him in front of everyone, I became one of the popular kids in our grade. Kids I never knew started to talk to me and be nice to me—including the girls I always wanted to talk to. It felt good to be the center of attention. It felt good to be feared and to be the bully. It was like I was finally receiving the love and respect I had wanted. This love filled the void of what was missing at home.

I'm not sure if the teachers noticed my dirty clothes and other signs of neglect, but they sure noticed my behavior. I wanted to be the class bully because that's who all the girls liked. I think even the girls in school saw that I was putting on an act. One time, our class was in line for the restroom and a kid cut in front of me. I punched the kid and violently stomped him while he was on the ground. As an eight-year-old, this became who I was, a pillar of my identity.

When Andre found out why I was suspended from school, he laughed and cheered me on. I was celebrated for beating kids up. I wondered, *"Was this how I needed to get their attention?"* That wasn't too bad. I began to abuse all the kids in the neighborhood. I choked kids with extension cords, sucker-punched the bigger kids, and slapped the kids who I didn't like. I became extremely violent and it mirrored the behavior of my siblings.

One afternoon, we used our cat as a chew toy for our new dog, just to test his limits and see how far it would go. The dog snatched the cat by its neck and swung it back and forth until its neck snapped. We tossed the body of the lifeless cat across the street into our neighbors' yard and went about our day. I felt slightly uneasy but joined in on the laughter with my siblings to avoid being the outsider. My mom returned home furious that her cat was killed, but she soon moved on as well.

My violence became a form of entertainment: my older brothers would have me fight their friends' younger siblings. They bet to see whose little brother would win the fight. Embarrassingly enough, I got beat up by a kid a lot younger than me. He had a huge head and didn't feel a thing. After that fight, they started to lose faith in me. I lost their attention, but it actually felt like I was losing their love. Whatever it took, I needed to get it back. My behavior only got worse and I would eventually beat the crap out of the kid to get payback, along with a sense of empowerment. Until I was about ten or eleven years old, I fought my problems with physical force, head-on. It wasn't until I entered the foster care system that my violent behavior began to slow down. I was about a year into the foster care system and separated from most of my family.

When I moved in with my oldest brother Dylan, I felt bad putting him through the suspensions and phone calls home from school. He was only about 26 years old at the time and wasn't at all ready for the stress of raising my brother Khalil and me. I didn't want to risk being kicked out of his home. But without violence, how would I earn anyone's attention?

While living with my parents, we were the family on the block known for violence. I'm actually just realizing this as I write, but I always wanted to do something to get my parents' attention, good or bad. I wanted my parents so badly that it translated into me being desperate for attention in school. I was trying to figure out who I was through my pain. In school, I was either quiet and isolated, a class clown, or a bully.

WORTHINESS

---

*The average abusive relationship lasts 7 years with the survivor
attempting to leave 7 times before leaving for good.*

*1 in 3 women and 1 in 10 men will experience
domestic violence in their lifetime.*

ALEXIS

W E ACCEPT WHAT we think we deserve. Victims commonly return to their abusive partner as they've grown used to their methods of abuse. I had been abused since I was a child and had no idea what it meant to be in a healthy relationship. The process of discovering happiness seemed exhausting.

Hoping for pity while taking advantage of his title as my first love, Shawn reached out to me when his apartment building burned down, looking for somewhere to stay. Kim warned me that it was a trap. Cautious of his intentions, I went to breakfast with him in Kalamazoo to get a clear understanding of what he wanted. He dropped a bombshell, telling me that he got another girl pregnant. My heart skipped a beat, waiting for it to be a joke and hoping he would laugh it off. I burst out of the restaurant. Shawn ran after me laughing. "Relax, it was a joke. I needed to see if you still cared and had feelings for me. I knew the Alexis I loved was still down there somewhere."

In 2015, I was preparing for my first study abroad program to the Dominican Republic. Shawn suggested that I put all of my belongings in his place promising that he would take care of my cats until I returned. Our agreement was short lived, and I immediately regretted the decision. "Get your shit and these cats out before I put them outside," Shawn said once his jealousy grew once again. In a panic, I called Brian and begged him to shelter the cats.

I'd often hear, "If you'd act right and make me feel loved, then maybe I would stay." This only pushed me to try harder to earn his love.

I'd get up at 3 a.m. to make him breakfast and lunch before he went into work, hoping I could get a kiss before he left for the day. Since he never answered my texts and phone calls, I wasn't sure if he would be coming home after work or hanging out with friends. I would leave sticky notes around the house letting him know how sorry I was in case I did anything wrong. I tried to be more "fun" so that I wasn't always the girlfriend left behind. This meant that I needed to smoke weed, drink alcohol, and partake in things that contradicted my lifestyle.

Because I never hung out with him around his friends, I never knew about his uncontrollable binge drinking. Once I confronted him, he spat back saying, "And you wonder why I don't invite you around my friends!"

Livid and reckless in his drunkenness, we got into a huge argument as he stormed in the bathroom and locked the door. I was on my knees banging on the bathroom door begging for him to *please* answer. It felt like he had locked me out for hours. He opened the door, looking down at me sitting in a pool of tears and said, "Get up and shut the fuck up!" as he walked out of the apartment.

He tried to make me choose between him and my friends. Shawn found reasons to hate my foster family and keep me all to himself when he felt like I wasn't giving him enough attention, even when attention wasn't what he wanted.

When I left for the Dominican Republic, Shawn's insecurities once again reached a destructive phase. As I packed my luggage, he went through my suitcase to approve each piece of clothing. He had long policed my work and school clothes; this was nothing new.

On the trip, I had to be acutely aware of where men were in photos, so that I was never "caught" too close to another man. If he texted me and I didn't reply immediately, he started questioning what I was doing and where I was. Often, I would text him to "check in" with photos of where I was and what buildings I was entering, to prove I hadn't done anything wrong. This kind of territoriality and possessiveness is very common in domestic abuse, and although the woman may realize its pathological, she can find herself trapped in the "comfort" of these predictable patterns. I was clearly not yet free of Shawn, despite my stabs at independence.

"Why weren't you there for me?"

"Why did you let me down?"

These were the underlying questions behind every one of Shawn's accusations. From buying him a vehicle to paying his bills, I knew he wanted me to fill the role of his mother, a woman who had let him down again and again. **I was both a punching bag and a substitute, fated to consistently disappoint him precisely because I was a stand-in for a parent he had resented.**

I went on another study abroad program to South Africa in 2016. At the time, Shawn was staying in my apartment and presumably caring for my cats. Caring for them and being loved by them were crucial parts of my recovery. I wasn't even gone for two days before he broke up with me yet again, following with comments such as "I'm so alone. I don't have anyone to hold me or hug me. I need someone." He made sure I knew that he was involved with other girls and that this was punishment for my independence.

As further punishment, he stopped sending me pictures and videos of my cats before cutting me off entirely for weeks on end. Thousands of miles from home, from Kim and Brian, from my beloved pets, I had never felt so helpless and alone. I felt intense self-hatred, left alone to stew in insecurity for hours on end. I'd send Shawn messages of apology and promises to "do better," playing directly into his hands and the endless, exhausting cycle of our dysfunction.

For hours before going to bed and when I would wake up, I would sit and read our texts and emails over and over again—like a lifeline for answers or comfort.

As a hail Mary, I decided to invite him to visit me during spring break in Botswana and Zimbabwe. Naturally, I paid for his flight. Looking back, it is hard to imagine how I could have arranged for such an emotionally abusive set-up. How could I not have known, deep in my bones, that the trip would be a disaster? I am sure that on some level, I did.

Shawn made it to the house and then made a display of refusing to hug me. "Let's go inside." he said. "Why didn't you do your hair and makeup for me?" He took out his phone and showed me a picture of myself the weekend prior with friends where my hair was smoothly pressed down by my shoulders and makeup embraced my bright blue eyes. He said, "Am I not special enough for you to look that good for me?" Then he snatched the bottom of my shorts and said,

"Why are you wearing such short shorts, do you want any guy looking at you?"

I replied, "I wore these for you, babe. I did do my hair and makeup for you!"

"Why didn't you straighten it the way I like it, then?" he responded.

He was just getting warmed up.

Shawn would snoop on my iPad and go through my pictures, messages, and social media accounts. He saw a photo of my housemate with his arm around my shoulder in a group photo and began to create an entire narrative that I was sleeping with him and hiding it from him. I left class early to come home and comfort him.

"I know you slept with him, just admit it. It would make your life so much easier if you did." I stood there prepared to admit to accusations just to please his emotional responses.

Several people in my house spoke with me about Shawn: the energy in the house was different. I was obviously unhappy and distracted. When we went to the beach with our housemates, Shawn took the opportunity to pick on me for forgetting to shave my legs that day, saying it was "so disgusting" while laughing out loud. Embarrassed, I remained silent. My housemate Haley stood up for me.

"Why does it matter to you if she shaves her legs or not? She's a grown woman and can decide for herself if she wants to or not."

Before she said that, I was looking down at my feet, taking in his words. For the first time, I looked at him with my back straightened and I finally took a deep breath with a surge of confidence.

It was difficult to balance his presence with my studies. I chose to take five courses as opposed to most other international students who took three.

For a long time, I didn't think people would believe me if I told them how cruel he was behind closed doors. Shawn could be so charming and charismatic in public. But when we were camping in Zimbabwe, two of my friends came to me to tell me that Shawn was an "asshole" and that he called them "bitches" for not making him eggs for breakfast. I was stunned. Something else in me broke loose. I had thought he'd reserved that hateful word for me. Knowing that he might call anyone that for any reason freed me a bit—maybe I wasn't such a terrible woman after all. Maybe he was the problem.

The campground was incredibly quiet that morning and he started screaming that I was worth less than the dirt under his feet. He didn't care who could hear him anymore since he would never see them again. He always came back to how broken I was and how much baggage I had and how difficult it would be for anyone else to love or accept me. Despite all this, I allowed him to sleep with me that night. I cried the entire time.

Sex was used as a way to punish me. It made me feel dirty, useless, insufficient, ugly, and unattractive, taking away my dignity as a woman, as a partner. I truly believed that I deserved to feel hurt and pain. I was damaged goods.

As long as my identity and worth were based on another human being, as they had been for those years I was with Shawn, I knew that it would continue that way.

I finally managed to break things off for good. My friend came to help me cancel Shawn from my phone plan, pretending to be me on a call with a T-Mobile representative. I didn't have the strength to say the words myself. Not long after, I had a dream...

I was traveling with classmates when I smelled fresh ocean water and coconut juice as if I were residing in a tropical environment. I was led to a memorial where I would be separated from the others. I traveled to the second floor of a mysterious building which no one was allowed to visit. As soon as I arrived, the police came, and I quickly hurried out of the building to get away. Confused on where to find the exit, I found myself trapped at a dead-end. The cop snatched me off the ground as I begged him to let me go. He demanded that I take my pants down or I would die in prison. Obeying his orders, I slowly pulled down my pants, weeping for someone to help. The police officer began to rape me as I begged him to stop. He said he wouldn't until I fully submitted to his commands. While he was dragging my lifeless body to the lobby, another officer approached us to ask what had happened. He responded in a stern and assuring voice, "Everything is fine...she paid her debt."

This dream symbolizes the vulnerable and fragile who are "in debt" to society. We operate our entire lives under a microscope, seeking to satisfy those who have imposed their will upon us. The policeman represented all the men in my life who mirrored serpents with their methods of deception. **I was indebted to this world and my body became my offering.**

Eventually, my accomplishments became a way of repaying this debt that I had imagined for myself. Life at this stage was about distracting myself from reality, excelling at school as a coping mechanism. I was always reminded by my campus coach in the Seita Scholars Program to reflect on my need for external validation, why I never allowed myself to relax and spend time alone. When you're constantly moving, you don't have to face the difficult realities of life. When you don't journal and write things down, they didn't really happen, right? I became good at hiding the pain by crying in bathrooms, lying about how I was feeling, and downplaying how bad my relationship had gotten. It was easier in my mind to hold it in and stay busy. Staying busy was a good excuse to neglect my self-care because I was being productive and doing well, right? When I received some of the highest academic honors undergraduate students can receive, such as two Presidential Scholar awards, the Gilman International Scholarship, and the Newman Civic Fellowship I questioned whether I was really worthy of receiving them. *"Why me?"* I'd ask. The imposter syndrome of feeling like a fraud and undeserving of these achievements didn't help either.

One day, Kim called me. "Alexis, you know I'll love you no matter what you accomplish or don't. You're my daughter and I'm still proud of you."

This was the first time I had ever received such a warm acknowledgement. Some of us are set on a path from childhood—having been deprived of security in those crucial first years—of endless searching for real love and validation. Her phone call will always stay with me. In that moment, I felt loved for who I was, validated, and even mothered. The call also sparked an epiphany: failing, falling short, or completely missing the mark was okay. As long as I enjoyed life and respected myself in the process, peace and happiness were attainable.

WORTHINESS

JUSTIN

HAVING STRONG PARENTAL figures instills self-confidence and a sense of worthiness. Good parents validate their child's sense of importance and recognize them as an individual with their own needs. They also guide by example, and in doing so, instill character in their kids, a firm understanding of right and wrong, and the sense of security they need to make mistakes and learn from them as they shape their consciences. And of course, parents are supposed to provide stability. I was only able to figure these things out later, backward, after taking stock of what I didn't have growing up. I never exactly felt loved by my parents and that's why I believe I've felt worthlessness throughout my life.

I left my brother Dylan's house at 11 years old. When my brother Khalil and I moved in with him, I hadn't realized the degree of responsibility involved with raising two children. With his patience in decline, he might've expected this to be a temporary placement as my mom went through the process of stabilizing her life, but it never happened. Also, his lifestyle of enjoying fast food or luxury dinners while my brother and I ate scraps left over in the fridge became unsustainable. That, combined with the fact that we lived in a bug-infested apartment, made things especially uncomfortable.

When I moved in with my Auntie Cheryl at 11, I found out where my parents lived and was thrilled to see them. It had been over a year and I was desperate for them to be a part of my life, regardless of our checkered past. I often ignored the trouble in our family in the hope of finding normality.

Auntie Cheryl took offense to my desire to see my parents. She felt that they only wanted to be parents when it was convenient for them. She knew they continued to abuse drugs and neglect their responsibilities as parents. Khalil and I just wanted them to be a part of our lives. When I became a teenager, I would scrape up money from my allowance or from cutting grass in the neighborhood just to catch the bus and visit them. From Auntie Cheryl's perspective, she became our enemy and our parents became our saviors.

Our parents would buy us whatever food we wanted with their food stamps, and we did whatever we wanted at our parents' house. I played video games all night, ate tons of junk food, and escaped from the problems I had back at my Auntie Cheryl's house. Auntie Cheryl's house came with too many rules and regulations. Though they were for our own good, Khalil and I hated following rules because it was so uncommonly expected in our family. Whether eating together as a family or routinely doing chores, it took years for us to get used to an ideal family culture.

As a new foster parent, it was difficult for my auntie to adjust to the situation. Her house was the miserable, boring house where we needed to do chores and share our food. In my mom and dad's house, we ate when we wanted and did what we pleased. There was little to no balance and we lived in almost two completely different worlds.

I had become a ward of the state years ago and my parents' parental rights were terminated. Along with losing custody, it had become illegal for my parents to be around children. Regardless, my aunt knew how much we wanted a relationship with them and she didn't want to get in the way of that. Even with my parents' drug use, she felt it was necessary to give them the opportunity to be parents. She eventually started giving my brother and me a ride to their house when we became an annoyance. Little did she know that this would only damage us further, causing resentment within our regular household. We frequently visited my parents. It became a once or twice a month occurrence. As much as I enjoyed visiting my parents, I had questions that needed to be answered. The unlimited junk food and video games were cool but there was still this sense of emptiness inside me. This prompted a burning question I had for my mom, but I couldn't bring myself to ask her, so I asked my dad instead, not knowing how he would respond. Sitting in my parents' bedroom I asked,

"Is ma still doing drugs?" My tone was shy and my voice very quiet.

Sitting next to me on the bed smoking a cigarette, my dad said, "That's a question you gotta ask her."

He went to grab her from the living room. She came in and sat next to me, knowing it would be a difficult conversation. I couldn't look her in the eyes. She said, "You wanted to ask me something, son?" I don't remember if I even asked her the question. I just remember sitting there in silence. Their lifestyle resembled the one they lived on Dexter; I already knew the answer...

When I was about ten years old and lived with my oldest brother Dylan, my mom made an honest attempt to become sober and change her life. We had family meetings to reconnect and build a solid foundation. It happened one day when we were having a family meeting with my brother Khalil, my mom, a social worker, and me. The social worker asked a series of questions, but I could only remember the first and second. She asked, "For what reason did your children enter the foster care system?" My mom replied, "Because I *had* a drug addiction issue." The social worker then asked, "What drug specifically?" My mom said, "I was addicted to crack." My heart dropped and I felt as if all the breath had been snatched from my lungs. I had lived in denial for so long that until I heard her say the words, I never really believed it.

At the time my mom lived in a recovery house, with other women who struggled with addiction. I never saw her so strong and healthy in my life. For the next few months, she came to visit us regularly. She even brought us to meet her housemates. I remember she came to visit us one time and she told us about the Bible verse that carried her through recovery. From that point on, I knew that Bible verse by heart:

"The Lord is my shepherd; I have all that I need. He lets me rest in green meadows; he leads me beside peaceful streams. He renews my strength. He guides me along the right paths, bringing honor to his name. Even when I walk through the darkest valley, I will not be afraid, for you are close beside me. Your rod and your staff protect and comfort me. You prepare a feast for me in the presence of my enemies. You honor me by anointing my head with oil. My cup overflows with blessings. Surely your goodness and unfailing love will pursue me all the days of my life, and I will live in the house of the Lord forever."

Reading it today takes me back to the time when I saw my mom at her best. She gave Khalil and me hope that we could overcome any obstacles or hardship the world offered us.

Eventually, though, my mom would stop attending our weekly family meetings, and the social worker was unable to find her. The recovery house informed us that my mother had left. We discovered that she was living with my father again in the old house on 25th Street. Khalil and I had to move on with our lives.

When we were depressed, lonely, and in need of strength, we recited our scripture, Psalms 23. It carried us through more than nine years together in the system.

Five years later, when I was 15, I sat beside her and asked if she was still addicted to drugs. I heard the words again but this time it crushed me even deeper. She told me that all of her children (me and my other four siblings), were all out of the house and she was only responsible for herself—saying it as if we all graduated and went off to college. In reality, CPS took all of my siblings and me away, we were fighting our way through the foster care system.

My brother Khalil and I were 15 and 17. My brother Andre and sister Tiffany were living barely sustainable lifestyles as they entered toxic relationships and moved from home to home. My oldest brother Dylan was the only one who had some sense of stability and independence, having lived on his own since the age of 16. Dylan called my mom by her first name, never identifying her as his mother. I never heard him call my mom his mother.

I was lost, anxious, and searching for sanity. Having my mom tell me that she could do drugs if she wanted to because we were all out of the house was the blow that sent me into a very deep depression. As an adult, I now have a better understanding of drug addiction and how it works, but as a 15-year-old, I wanted their love and attention so badly that I'd do literally anything for it. As the relationship between my parents and my auntie worsened, it became harder to find a ride to see my parents. If we didn't visit them, then we would not see them. I wondered if they really wanted to come see us at all. *Just please come to my football games. Come visit me at home. Please, mom… show that you love me. That I exist.* They say the opposite of love is not hate, but indifference, and indifference was exactly what I felt from my mother when she easily washed her hands of any responsibility for her children.

Through my nine plus years of experience in the child welfare system of Detroit, I always wondered why my parents never thought to check on me much or see how I was doing. My parents lived about 30 minutes away the entire time. We all lived on the west side of Detroit and I don't remember a single visit from them. I felt worthless and spiraled into suicidal thinking.

It would have been easier to accept the absence of parents in my life if they were deceased. That would have made it okay that they hadn't come to see me. Whether I caught the bus in 15-degree weather or caught a $50 taxi round-trip, I made sure I could see my parents. No matter their neglect, addictions, or selfishness, I always wanted to be around my parents. I realize now that I wanted to be validated by them. I wanted my mom to tell me she loved me and that she was proud of me. Actually, my parents always told me that they were proud of me, but it felt empty and insubstantial.

During one of my last times visiting with my parents as a teenager, I finally received the truth from my dad's heart. People say when you're drunk you usually speak your mind and dad always knew how to cut deep when he was drunk. My parents were having a heated argument that nearly resulted in violence again. He called my mom all types of derogatory names, which had become normal at this point. My mom mentioned that they shouldn't be arguing in front of us. He said he didn't care and called my siblings and me a burden that he didn't want. I stood there helpless, feeling like I had nothing else to live for.

Though I would return to my parents' home for holidays, this feeling of worthlessness haunted me even as a young adult. I remember buying my first car in 2017. During the process, I wanted my dad by my side as I perceived this moment to be something that should be shared between a father and son. While driving out of the parking lot, I had a panic attack. I assumed that I would ruin it and that I wasn't worthy of anything nice. I couldn't breath and every muscle on my body began to shiver. As these panic attacks continued, I asked God *"Why me? Was I just a product of two people coming together for sex? Why am I here and why did I deserve to suffer?"*

PART 3:
DEFINITION OF LOVE

What the Statistics Say:
On average, 24 people per minute are victims
of rape, physical violence or stalking by an
intimate partner in the United States.

What Does God Say:
"Love is patient, love is kind. Love endures with patience and
serenity, love is kind and thoughtful, and is not jealous or envious;
love does not brag and is not proud or arrogant. It is not rude; it is
not self-seeking; it is not provoked [nor overly sensitive and easily
angered]; it does not keep a record of wrong. It does not rejoice at
injustice, but rejoices with the truth [when right and truth prevail]"
(Corinthians 13:4-6 AMP).

SELL-OUT

ALEXIS

OUR PARENTS SET the foundation and standard for love. We learn how to love and receive love from them. But if parents are unaware of what healthy love is themselves, it is inevitable for children to unconsciously inherit destructive habits and patterns from their parents. **This cycle allows people that are unfamiliar with a healthy definition of love to define what love is for generations to come.** Because family plays such an intimate role in shaping our values, morals, and habits, consequently, they can harm us the most. Most adults spend their entire lives healing from their childhood and yearning for love, acceptance, and praise that wasn't provided by their parents.

When my mom died, I went to live with my dad. This is when I was first taught that love hurts. It's violent, unpredictable, violates boundaries, and sets up a pattern of fear and despair. Ideas such as filling voids with money started in my father's household. My family has always been transactional. In order to receive you must give; preferably cash. Every Christmas, I would receive over $500 in gifts and was still never satisfied, especially when I saw my cousin or a friend receive something that I didn't get. Granted, my dad would buy me gifts and give me anything I "wanted" as a tactic to get me to stay quiet or rationalize what he was doing to me for years. Nevertheless, the lesson was still there: you show how much you love someone through material things. As I became more aware of this, I started to notice this with other family members and their style of parenting or their intimate relationships. With my brother, he'd buy his girlfriend a $300 gift and if she only spent $250, he would ask for the difference. To me, this felt transactional and…empty.

When Justin and I spent our first Christmas together, we spent over $200 on each other because that was how both of us expected love and relationships to go. That night, we talked about how that made absolutely no sense for us, that we must show our love through time together and experiences. We didn't need to prove our love and value to each other through money spent or things acquired. We've seen too many people trying to prove how much they love their partner or their kids through gifts. We want to break that pattern. Gifts can be symbols of love, but giving them does not equate to love. Tenderness, mutual respect and admiration, stability: these are among the signs of love given and received.

My brother Zach got a woman pregnant. I immediately called him to ask if it was his. With the culture of misogyny still deeply rooted in my family, he said she had no value outside of the holes in her body and that he didn't have any room for a car seat on the back of his motorcycle.

He posted memes on social media of "Plan C," which meant punching a pregnant woman in the stomach. He was adamant that this was not his child. Just like my dad, he never took responsibility for his actions. When I told him that I believed *her*, he did what all men in my life had done. Once he got his point across through text, social media, and email, he would block me so I couldn't respond. He wrote:

> "*Coming from the snowbunny who loved hood life and now is all*
> *Christian cover-up and changing and wants a suburban lifestyle.*
> *Remember the lifestyle you called boring and lame growing up?*
> *You're a sell-out! You think cause mom died I have a psychological*
> *disorder? Bitch, please. I've been over that since she died, I barely*

even cried. So, get over yourself. Join the real world, you've been
condemned and brainwashed to believe in the horse shit you
now follow."

Though he did all he could to avoid the truth, the child was his after all.

I reflected on how he treated the women in his life. I knew very well how men with fragile masculinity operated. I had seen how chronic anger could plague men. I could see his unresolved trauma playing out. He resented our mother for dying and sought new mother figures in his girlfriends, whom he then abused out of retributive spite. I knew that pattern all too well. He resented my efforts to build a new life for myself, to pull myself out of the mental and spiritual poverty in which we had been raised. This reflected the inherent pessimism of the culture in which we grew up. Rather than being inspired to aspire to bigger things, he aimed to shoot down anyone who tried to leave the nest of dysfunction and pathology. Justin has seen the same tendency within his community. My brother had a full-blown antisocial personality disorder. We'd been raised in an environment in which people believed that giving children love would make them "weak." My brother's broken soul spoke to the results.

I had no choice but to leave him behind. I outgrew the family culture I once considered normal to start a path of healing on my own.

In 2011, my junior year in high school, I lost the one man whom I had always admired and trusted. My Uncle Giles was more of a Godparent who helped raise me since the time I was only five or six years old. Months earlier, I had seen Uncle Giles cough up blood, and when I asked him what was wrong, he said that he would be okay. When I asked him if he would be coming to my high school graduation, he said "I wouldn't miss it for the world." Watching his tall, healthy body wither away in front of me with no explanation or acknowledgment ripped me apart more than words can say.

His wife, Aunt Bev, became the closest person to me. A few years later, in the middle of class, I received a call from Aunt Bev's best friend, who told me if I wanted to say goodbye to Aunt Bev, I would need to come immediately...

I stormed out of class with no regard to my professor's instructions, driving over 100 miles an hour, hoping that when I got there she would miraculously heal by virtue of my presence. When I walked in, she said "Alexis! I'm so glad you made it. Now I get to be with Uncle Giles, so don't be sad for me." Not even two hours later, I watched the doctors take her off of life support.

Their house had always been my home. When people asked me where I'm from or where home is for me, I've always said their house. Now they are both gone. Where is home at now?

SELL-OUT

*"The Lord, the Lord, a God merciful and gracious, slow to anger,
and abounding in steadfast love and faithfulness...forgiving iniquity
and transgression and sin, but who will by no means clear the
guilty, visiting the iniquity of the fathers on the children and the
children's children, to the third and the fourth generation"*
(Exodus 34:6-7).

JUSTIN

NRESOLVED TRAUMA CAN easily be passed down from generation to generation. **Trauma can be passed down as culture and normalized within a family.** The reason why it remains within a family for so long is because it is often unidentified and then mislabeled. Multiple families have labeled their unresolved trauma as love. When you identify trauma as love, you then accept everything that comes with it.

Throughout my life, my dad and his siblings always praised and honored our grandparents, being sure never to criticize their relationship. Based on what I heard from many of my aunts and uncles, they had the perfect family and they were happy together. I think a small part of it might be the fact that they wanted to respect their deceased parents but the idea that they did no wrong was always suspicious to me. From the stories they told of my grandparents, I always wondered if there were more to their story than what was said. *Why did I never hear anything bad about them when so many of my aunts and uncles have displayed such violent behavior throughout their lives?*

My mom once told me a story about the time when she was pregnant with either me or my brother Khalil (I'm not exactly sure which one). My mom was pretty far along into her pregnancy and her and my dad got into an intense argument. When my mom and dad argued, they always did and said things that were viciously cruel. After the argument, my dad told his sisters that the baby may not be his in order to evoke a vengeful response from his family. Auntie Cheryl physically attacked my mom for lying about who the father was. These types of incidents occurred regularly as my mom continued to tell me stories about my dad's siblings.

Living with my Auntie Cheryl, I always heard stories about my grandparents and how she adored their relationship. She said she had never seen someone love a woman like her father loved her mother. Every once in a while, she would mention that my grandma and grandpa used to argue. She provided little to no detail about what would happen or what they would argue about other than describing their arguments as "very intense." She went on to say that my grandpa moved out of their house on 23rd St. to a house down the block because of the intense arguing. I always wanted more detail into their relationship and how they raised their kids.

My dad more than likely learned how to deal with his anger the same way my grandparents did. This means that **domestic violence has run through at least three generations in my family.** I always wondered why such stories of violence were normal among my aunts and uncles. From shootings and stabbings to running each other over with cars, the behaviors were normalized.

Defining "family" can be tricky. My relatives believed that family meant sticking together no matter what. Growing up in my Auntie Cheryl's house, I remember my entire dad's side of the family knowing Bible scriptures like the back of their hands, but I had yet to feel the love of God while around my family. I grew up surrounded by religion. My auntie, her son, my brother

Khalil, and I went to church every Sunday. We even joined the choir for a while. We went to an old traditional Baptist church where service could go from 10 am to almost 2 pm (causing me to miss the beginning of the Detroit Lions game every Sunday). We loved the traditions of Christianity but lacked a spiritual relationship with God. We dressed up for church, screaming and shouting as we caught the Holy Ghost, telling other people when they needed to get right with God. But we did not have the sense of peace and purpose that I would later find in Christianity. Going to church never stopped family gossip, familial violence, and our violence toward others, or the hatred many family members felt toward one another. When my aunts and uncles had problems with each other, things got ugly. If a physical altercation didn't occur, there would be an overwhelming amount of gossip within the family. One member's deep dark secrets would be casually revealed by another in a mean-spirited play of revenge.

Because of this, it took awhile for me to have an understanding of love from a Godly perspective. Our family talked about how sweet and amazing God was, but I never saw much of it in our family. The problem was that we rarely dove deep into the scriptures and inconsistently practiced the principles we learned. My first connection to God started when I was a ten-year-old living with my brother Dylan. He was an atheist but my curiosity for a spiritual connection never was minimized. I began visiting the apostolic church up the street by myself every Sunday. After a while, my brother Khalil started to join me for service, I'm guessing for some form of fulfillment as well. We looked crazy coming to church as we had no understanding of the expected etiquette. I came dressed in my WWE T-shirt and basketball shorts. My brother would dress slightly better in a polo shirt and jeans. Other than our school uniform, we had no nice clothes to wear to church.

Even though we weren't aware of the proper church attire, our desire to have a relationship with God was authentic. When we moved in with my auntie and tried to wear those same clothes to church, she immediately took us to buy a suit and dress clothes for Sunday services. Living with my auntie, church and religion became almost forced. If my brother and I wore "inappropriate" attire to church or dared to question the Bible or any of my family's religious beliefs, there would be hell to pay. This is why I feel like the young people of our generation have turned away from God. So many people have blindly followed religion without asking questions for themselves. With these strict religious traditions, the young population has turned away from God to seek answers outside of the church. For me, there is a philosophical component to a religious life, a strong need to ask big questions and seek meaning in one's life. It is about analytically studying biblical scripture more than meaningless, drawn out entertainment during service that takes the attention away from God. It is also about consistency. If you go to church and sit through the service, you have to listen to the words, interpret them, and apply them to your own actions in life. Church is not merely a spectacle, or just for holidays, or dressing up. **It is about behavior, and choices, community, and meaning.**

Strict religion didn't stop me from asking questions. I kept asking questions, but I looked to God for the answers. I became very curious and began to read the Bible all the time. I even started bringing my Bible to school and silently prayed in class before my tests. My desire to read the Bible and get closer to God started as a pre-teen. But as a teenager, my desperate need for love and approval from my peers overshadowed my love for God. Being the Godly kid who prayed and read the Bible before and after class wasn't cool and wasn't getting me any girls. And trust me, it's lonely being the kid who doesn't talk to any girls.

Each year Khalil and I lived with my auntie, the relationship worsened. It got to a point where we weren't her nephews anymore but just two foster kids living in her house. Khalil and my Auntie Cheryl butted heads regularly as he became older and his interest in girls grew. My brother was going out every night messing with girls, disregarding her rules in the process. Khalil would skip school (and sometimes football practice) to hang out with girls. He would eventually get caught and completely broke his trust with Auntie Cheryl. Our relationship with her became more distant as my brother and I turned against her. The tension was obvious, and she stopped hiding it. She openly disrespected us without remorse, degrading us while on the phone to other family members. Calling us lazy and saying we didn't do shit around the house was normal. We became the talking point of the gossip in our family. Khalil and I would visit our cousins and hear disturbing rumors said about ourselves.

"I heard y'all getting on Cheryl's nerves again."

"Yea, I heard she's about to kick y'all out."

Or if I were to walk past the kitchen while visiting another auntie, someone would say,

"Aye! I heard y'all be eating up all of Cheryl's food, don't come over here eating up all our food."

It was the epitome of humiliation.

It was common for my auntie to come home yelling about a chore that wasn't done and threaten to kick us out on the street. Almost every day when she came home, we expected to be yelled at about *something*. This wasn't a home anymore, nor was it love. At the time, I believe she allowed us to continue living with her for the monthly foster care stipends. She was out of work at the time and the money we brought in as foster care youth provided food and groceries for the house. After it was clear that we had overstayed our welcome and the love and respect were gone, I followed my brother's path of open rebellion by disregarding her rules.

Freshman year of high school, I was a class clown, expressing my home-life frustrations during the school day. Every day, I dealt with the fact that we could be kicked out at any moment. It was hard to focus on school and I was always irritated at home. The constant threats and housing insecurities also affected my behavior in school. **The facade I portrayed at school, combined with the mental and emotional warfare I had waiting for me at home, often resulted in me crying alone in the bathroom.** I prayed that God would relieve my burden and give me hope and happiness. Tears running down my cheeks, I'd plug my earphones in to drown out the noise of the world, listening to the lyrics of one of my favorite songs *The Vent* by Big KRIT.

> I know you've been down so long
> So I'll be stronger for you
> I know you've been down so long
> Cause I've been down too
> Yes I understand
> What you're going through
> Yes I understand
> Cause I'm going through it too

These words gave me comfort, reassuring me that Khalil and I weren't going through these situations alone. I heard my mom speaking these lyrics to me and imagined her rescuing me from the ravages and deprivations of the foster care system. I never approached my parents with the idea of moving back in with them because I knew it wasn't going to happen. They were struggling to survive themselves—they could not take care of anyone else.

Things came crashing down at the end of my sophomore year of high school. I went to Old Redford Academy at the time, a charter school in Detroit. The guys had to wear full suits as uniforms. The girls wore skirts, button-up dress shirts and a blazer. If the boys forgot something as little as their belt at home, the principal would send us home. It's safe to say that our school was pretty strict. Two weeks before final exams, I was suspended from school for play fighting and childishly giving the security guard a fake name as if I would escape the situation.

I was suspended from school and indifferent to the consequences that followed. I hung out with my brother Andre, looking for even more trouble. I told him I wanted to get my ears pierced, a decision I knew would cause even more disturbance at home. My auntie didn't want us to have any tattoos or piercings so that we could eventually find a good job. She always told us that those were adult decisions and we weren't old enough to make those decisions yet. I decided to get a piercing anyway. When I went home, I regretted my decision, but it was too late. I was in the kitchen washing the dishes, headphones covering my ears, when my auntie asked me a question. I slowly pulled them down and looked into her eyes, afraid of what was going to happen next.

During our six years of living with my auntie, she yelled at us a lot, but I had never heard her yell like this. The tone of her voice told me that our time together was over. Her eyes seemed to glow red. An enormous vein pulsed in her forehead. "WHAT? WHAT?" She said. I couldn't remember anything else as she screamed at the top of her lungs. She immediately called our foster care worker—we had two weeks to find a place to live before being kicked out. This wasn't the first time we had a meeting like this, so I expected things to blow over.

As much as I resented my auntie, I was afraid of living with someone else. On the one hand, I needed a change. On the other hand, I risked being separated from my brother to live with a stranger. We revisited the conversation regarding our housing situation a few days later, and her attitude had not changed. She was tired, worn down, and in her eyes, she had done all that she could do. After living with my Auntie Cheryl for six years, it was time for Khalil and me to move to another home.

About five days later, she told us to wake up at 7 am to cut the grass. I didn't want to leave on a bad note, so I prepared to do so. Khalil felt differently. He was angry and bitter, refusing to do any chores since she decided to kick us out. I overslept and woke up at 7:35 am, panicking. I knew my auntie expected us to be rebellious and not cut the grass, but I wanted to prove her wrong. I woke up to her yelling to someone over the phone calling us "lazy niggas" that needed to get the hell out of her house. She stormed into our room as we began to pack our bags. We had no idea where we were going but we knew we needed to leave. Before I could explain that I had woken up late, she started yelling at my brother and me.

"So y'all not cutting the grass! REALLY?!"

"HELL NO!" Khalil said.

She grabbed our clothes out of the closet and began to throw them in trash bags.

"Good, I'll help y'all get the hell out of my house."

The altercation escalated as my brother and auntie began to argue in the kitchen. Soon, she'd pulled a knife on him. We grabbed what we could and ran out the door, just as our brother Andre arrived to pick us up. We were to stay at our mom's house until we could find somewhere else to go.

THE CYCLE

ALEXIS

A FTER MY DAD was arrested in 2007, I moved in with my Aunt Karen and my dad's brother, Uncle Mark. The resemblance between my dad and my uncle brought back memories of abuse. Simple things such as the way they walked and ate were oddly similar. Even the way they yelled at me was nearly identical. After I came out about my dad's abuse, Uncle Mark was reluctant to take me in. Understandably, he was afraid that my trauma would disrupt the emotional stability of his children. His wife, Aunt Karen, advocated on my behalf.

Being my strength in times of distress, my Aunt Karen and I formed a bond that allowed me to be vulnerable as I moved into their home. We would make chocolate chip cookie dough together every time something came up with my biological dad. One night, there was a thunderstorm and the power went out in the whole neighborhood. We made cookie dough by candlelight and ate it together on her bed, as we talked into the morning hours.

She supported me through my dad's trial and remained by my side the entire time as I struggled to testify against him. She sat there and listened to the details of my dad's sexual and physical abuse of me.

The entire time living there wasn't terrible. We definitely had some good "family" times where I felt loved and like part of the family and loved. I am thankful that they took me in when they did, and in their minds, they did the best they could do. However, I mainly have memories of feeling like the black sheep of the family, the problem, the cause of their marital issues.

I felt that she wanted to be my savior, and tokenized me as a display of her amazing work. I would listen under their bedroom door late at night as my aunt talked to family members and friends about how difficult I was to control and how hard it was having me in the house. She would say things like "I don't understand why she doesn't want to be here, I don't know why she doesn't want to be more involved and be with her friends more" and "I'm doing all I can do."

Yet, when I would ask to go to friends' houses, she would say in the car, "I have to haul your ass around..." If upset, Aunt Karen's first instinct would be to go in the basement, grab my luggage that I moved in with, and throw my clothes in it while threatening to kick me out. She often reminded me that if I go to another foster home that would most likely be much worse than hers, pressuring me to accept her abuse. Then I would beg and cry for forgiveness and promise to be better next time. She implemented a rule that when she came home from work, I had to come out of my room to acknowledge her arrival.

I felt that she cared more about looking like the picture-perfect family with a beautiful spotless home in a nice, upper-class neighborhood, kids involved in traveling sports, going to a good school. We would have house parties, dinners and get-togethers, but before they walked in the house, it had to be spotless and I was told to "look happy."

My aunt would always say that if she ever caught Uncle Mark cheating, she would leave him instantly. Well, she caught him cheating and, recalling her threats, I panicked. I was the only one in the house who knew; my cousins were oblivious. I went to school the next day crying, strung out with anxiety. I came home and within the next day or so, we went out to dinner at Buffalo Wild Wings like nothing had happened. I was sitting there in silence because I couldn't understand how you could act like nothing happened. Then, in the months to follow, my uncle wasn't allowed to take his cellphone on trips without my aunt and I was put in the middle of their conversations. For example, my aunt would call me to ask if Mark was home and what he was doing. He would ask me to communicate some message to her since they weren't talking, all while my cousins knew nothing about what had happened.

I remember before one of my homecoming dances, my aunt dropped me and my best friend off at the mall to shop for my dress. I tried on several dresses that I knew I couldn't get but thought would be fun to try on. I took a picture of myself in the dress and tried to send it to my friend as she went off to a different store. I accidentally sent it to my aunt and for some reason, I guess it was sent multiple times. My aunt texted back, "Since you want to dress like a whore, why don't you make a sign and stand on the side of the road and find a ride home because I'm not coming to get you." Needless to say, we were stranded and now my friend's mom needed to come get us. The worst part was that when I got home, my aunt told my cousins (right in front of me), "Alexis isn't a good role model. She's not someone you should look up to." This is something that has always stayed with me. Fortunately, I think this statement has motivated me to be a better person and someone worthy of admiration.

My uncle, who's my blood uncle, never stood up for me or protected me. When I made it to the state championships for the club Business Professionals of America, my aunt gave me only $20 for the whole weekend to use for food. While looking down at the ground in embarrassment, I had to ask my teacher to please pay for my meals because I ran out of money by the second morning after mainly eating snacks from Starbucks.

Then, when I made it to nationals and my teachers came to my 5th hour period to announce it to my whole class, I was beaming with excitement. But when I got home, my aunt said that I couldn't go because she didn't think that I worked hard enough for it since I was only the runner up.

When my friends came over, they would joke that it felt like they were being watched or that there were cameras in the house. Aunt Karen was good at making you feel like she was the rational one and you were not. I watched her scream at my cousin until she cried, just to hug her and say she loved her right after. I have many more stories, such as when she told me I looked fat in my dress right before my track & field awards ceremony.

My aunt was always hurt and offended that I wouldn't allow them to adopt me.

I never really started to heal from the trauma of my dad until college because every time I would go to counseling it was to talk about home situations or how my boyfriend was leaving me.

When you leave an abusive situation and enter foster care, you're supposed to be in a healthy environment to unlearn those habits, learn new ones, and heal. But my trauma was just compounded. I always felt like a burden to my family and my romantic partners. I wrote many times in my journal asking *"Why do I make other people's lives so difficult? Why do I put so much stress on Shawn and others that I love?"* I think that's another reason why I learned to be so resourceful—so that I didn't create more work for anyone around me.

It's not surprising that my confusion and struggle with love was fueled by my family, but it was also entrenched in my environment. I don't remember one friend being in a healthy relationship until I got to college. Everything that I consumed—movies, media and everything else—gave me low expectations of myself as a woman, as a foster care youth, and as a survivor in rape culture dominated by men who think it's okay to "grab a woman by the pussy," so eloquently quoted by U.S. President Donald Trump.

THE CYCLE

JUSTIN

FOSTER YOUTH ARE a vulnerable population. Most teenage youth who have nowhere to go usually enter a detention center, not because they have done anything wrong, but because it is so hard to find people willing to take in teenage foster youth. Many of us are moving from home to home with nothing more than a trash bag full of clothes. After settling into a new home, in the back of our mind we're always expecting it to be temporary. We expect something to go wrong that'll put us back on the streets. It takes faith to enter a home believing that this is the one. That both you and the family you're with are fully dedicated to making a better future for you. Most youth never get to that point with a family, eventually ending up homeless or in a detention center with nowhere else to go.

After leaving my Auntie Cheryl's house, my brother and I moved in with Khalil's best friend's parents. Our time with them was short-lived as I lived with them for only eight months. The Bennett family had pretty much had enough of me. In foster care, it can be the simple things that will make you leave a placement. Whether it is slacking off on chores, bad grades, or simply the fact that raising kids that aren't your own is extremely difficult. Ultimately, the mom in the house wanted me gone but the dad fought for me to stay.

Mr. Bennet took me to the backyard, "Listen, son, my wife wanted you gone but I fought for you to stay. This means no bullshitting around. If I catch you slacking, that's your ass." He said with a firm grip on my shoulder. I appreciated him advocating for me to stay but I was seeing way too many red flags in the situation. I felt like I could easily be thrown in the middle of the conflict in their marriage. Even as a teenager, I understood the importance of agreement in a marriage and I became the problem in the house. I didn't want to be the cause of their arguments and possibly the reason for their divorce. Also, having the dad in the house hover over me constantly would be way too much pressure on my shoulders. I knew I had to go elsewhere but the problem was that I didn't have anywhere else to go. I was stuck and didn't know what to do.

The next day, I met with my social worker to weigh out my options. It was 2014 when I moved into a group home right outside of Detroit. The process of moving into a new home was depressing and I was frightened to move houses for the third time in nine months. I remember being interviewed before moving into the group home. The home was uniquely structured—four young men lived in a house with two house parents. While in the house, the parents (along with multiple mentors and tutors) were focused on helping young men in the foster care system transition into adulthood. The opportunity seemed perfect. The change in scenery was much needed and I was leaving my family's influence in Detroit and becoming my own man. The most difficult part about the entire situation was leaving Khalil. We had been together in the foster system for about eight years. I wasn't ready to leave but I had no other choice.

During the interview, we talked about my plans and intentions while living in the house, along with their expectations. To avoid being homeless or placed in a detention center, I told them whatever they wanted to hear. I was emotionally drained, mentally fatigued, and my tears had run dry. The only part of the conversation I remembered was the list of things I needed to do to avoid getting kicked out. My brother Andre had told me horror stories from his time in a juvenile detention center-like facility. After the interview with the house parents, they asked me if I had any questions or concerns. I felt that it was time to be honest and vulnerable.

"We've pretty much done all the talking. Do you have any questions for us?" Mrs. Cora said.

I paused for a moment, taking a deep breath into my nose and out of my mouth slowly. I said to them,

"This seems like an amazing house with great people. I don't have any concerns, really. I've felt that so many people in my life have given up on me. All I ask is that you please don't give up on me."

I wanted to make this relationship work more than anything. If I was going to get kicked out of another home, I was going to make sure it wasn't my fault this time.

I later found out that there was an opportunity for me to move into the group home after leaving my Auntie Cheryl's house. Unfortunately, Mrs. Cora read over a report from my auntie and my social worker detailing my behavior and decided I wasn't a good fit at the time. Learning this information was upsetting, no one cared about my side of the story. I was mislabeled and prejudged. But, for the sake of my housing, I left the past behind me. I was tired of worrying if I did something that would get me kicked out. *Did I eat too much of their food? Did I forget to wash my dishes? What did I do wrong?* **These types of questions haunt the mind of foster youth living in a new home.**

Despite this early conversation, we walked on eggshells. The Bennett family often said, "You're living in our house, eating our food." This made us feel like powerless outsiders. The "You're in my house so you follow my rules" attitude had been a burden for me throughout my time in care. Luckily, the monthly foster care stipends my auntie used to receive were now given to me directly as I transitioned into Young Adult Voluntary Foster Care (YAVFC). A recent policy passed in Michigan which extended foster care benefits until the age of 21, instead of 18. This gives foster youth a greater chance at autonomy.

When I entered the group home, I felt welcomed and loved. I was still desperate for parental figures and Mrs. Cora and Mr. Melvin seemed to be the perfect fit. They supported me in ways in which I had never felt supported before. If I struggled in Spanish class, Mrs. Cora and other members of our church would connect us with a Spanish tutor.

I wanted to go to college, but my grades weren't even close to good enough. My GPA was a meager 2.3. After my first semester living in the group home, I earned a 2.4 GPA. I was actually pleased, because this was at least a little higher than my cumulative GPA. But Mrs. Cora was not pleased at all. I didn't understand why she believed so deeply in my potential, but she told me she expected more. She even wanted to ground me and take away my phone. Because her role was similar to a resident advisor than a mother, she had no jurisdiction to do so. Still, it made me feel cared for—this was so unlike the indifference I was accustomed to from guardians. She believed in me. She made me feel important. This was such a new sensation for me—this was what it was like to have an attentive parent. Because of this, I decided I would be the first person in my immediate family to attend college.

Mr. Melvin and I would build decks and other projects around the house together as a father and son might. Mrs. Cora would comfort me whenever I came to her to discuss my family troubles. Her hugs were tight and warm, almost as if you were healed by her touch. She promised that they'd always be there for me. My brain told me to wait until I knew they were sincere. I was not ready to open myself completely, nor have total faith in them. But my heart opened despite myself as I nestled in her arms. I needed a mother so badly.

The burden of living under someone else's roof may seem small but large problems lurk within this system. Conditional support is frightening, especially to a child. Within two months of living in the group home, I was diagnosed with scabies, an infestation of tiny mites that gather in the upper layer of the skin, where they live and lay their eggs. Scabies causes intense, constant itching, which worsens at night and causes an angry rash.

I suffered with scabies for two years before I received a diagnosis. I was relieved; finally, I would get a proper cure. I told Mrs. Cora immediately.

She believed that I kept it a secret intentionally. She accused me of having known for a long time and deliberately hiding it from her. Her accusation felt like a betrayal of our trust, not like something a mother would hurl at a child. In fact, I had thought it was eczema. I told her that I had no idea where I might have gotten the disease, but I couldn't rule out the group home where we lived. The only places I had slept had been the group home and in my biological parents' house.

I was relieved to at least have a diagnosis, despite the conflict with Mrs. Cora. My skin had become very dry and cracked. I scratched awkwardly throughout the day and had reached the worst stage of scabies; my skin had begun to deteriorate.

Mrs. Cora was insulted by the suggestion that my scabies could have come from the group home. I shouldn't have been in school after my diagnosis, but I had an important test to prepare for. I was just trying to keep my distance from everyone and act as if everything were normal. Not long after I told her, she called the front office at my high school and asked to speak to me. Mrs. Cora began to interrogate me. I told her again that I wasn't sure where the scabies came from but I couldn't rule out the group home. She became furious and we began to argue. The school receptionist gave me the side-eye; the whole office could hear her berating me through the telephone. Fighting back tears, I realized that she wasn't the loving person she had initially seemed to be. She told me to put all of my clothes in trash bags in the garage when I got home.

Even before this moment, we had many small conflicts about things that made me feel uncomfortable, but I remained silent to ensure my housing. My first week after arriving in the house, it instantly became the youth versus the house parents. When I first arrived, Mrs. Cora and I went food shopping and she bought me whatever food I wanted. It was cool, but I was suspicious. While shopping, she gave me the rundown on the other three boys in the house. Her comments were demeaning, to say the least. She talked about their hygiene, their lack of attention to detail, and their other flaws. She also shared personal information about them that I knew was far too private to be shared so casually, let alone with a stranger. I realized that there was no telling what she'd say about me once she discovered my flaws. I later discovered that she spied on all the kids in her house. Privacy was nonexistent.

As soon as I found out I had scabies, I wanted to do all I could to protect everyone else in the house. I put my mattress on the side of the curb as I prepared for a new one that would arrive wrapped in plastic. I spent more than $50 washing all my clothes at the laundromat, but refused to store them in trash bags in the dirty garage with the trash cans. I told Mrs. Cora that I preferred to bag up my clean clothes and put them in the basement, but when I came home from school, I found my clean clothes thrown on the garage floor, spilling out of the trash bags. They were right by the filthy trash cans, exactly what I'd wanted to avoid. **Those trash bags filled with my clothes were a reminder that I was just another foster youth. This wasn't a home, nor was it a family.** It was just another stop on the way to college. I sat in the garage with tears streaming down my face. How could I let this happen to me? I put a hole in a new dresser in the garage with my fist, then cried myself to sleep.

It was hard to ask for help because Mrs. Cora and Mr. Melvin wanted me to be independent.

"Stop relying on other people and figure things out yourself." They'd always say.

I understood their perspective but there needed to be a healthy balance. Oftentimes, they decided to leave me to figure things out on my own. Neglecting me at times when I really needed assistance made me very confused about the nature of our relationship. Foster youth have already been abandoned enough; we don't need anyone else forcing us to "figure things out".

But I continued to hope and pray that they could be the parents I had always wanted. They always said that we were like their children and I believed them. They even adopted one of the boys in the house and I wanted something similar. They would ask me, "What are we to you? Who do you usually introduce us as?" I wanted to be respectful of my biological parents while accepting them as parents also. I told them I wanted them to be my foster parents. This was a huge step for me, but I wanted parents in my life, people I could rely on. For a time, I convinced myself that's what they were.

Maintaining my emotional stability was a struggle. It was always hard to decipher whether our house parents wanted to become our actual parents, emotionally involved and invested in us, or if they wanted to treat us like any other foster youth in the system. Different events like prom and graduation would become awkward when I would invite Mrs. Cora and Mr. Melvin to come and support me. They'd turn down those invitations, stating that they didn't feel comfortable because those were more of family events. It seemed as if inviting my biological parents was futile—they couldn't come to support me either.

Desperately in need of somewhere to call home when I left for college, I saw the group home as a refuge and ignored the troubles we had in the past. Over my first holiday break during freshman year, Mrs. Cora and Mr. Melvin welcomed me back with open arms. I was excited to visit and stay with them for a week. Even though I had other options, such as visiting my brother Khalil (who had his own place at the time) or staying on campus and receiving help from the Seita Scholars Program, I caught a two-hour train from Kalamazoo just to come back to the group home. I wanted to come home to a family, but I came back to something different. Shortly after arriving, Mrs. Cora informed me that I needed to pay rent for every day that I stayed there for the holiday break. Maybe this was how family worked?

It wasn't until my sophomore year, when I landed an internship in Washington D.C., that I knew I needed to sever the relationship. I needed somewhere to stay for about three days before flying to D.C. Since they lived roughly ten minutes from the airport, I was hoping that Mrs. Cora and Mr. Melvin could give me a ride. The day before my flight, I asked Mrs. Cora how much money she needed for gas. She asked me, "What do you think you should give?" During my time living with her, she taught me how to calculate how much I needed to pay someone for gas money if they gave me a ride. I calculated that she needed about $5 for gas money. I asked, hesitantly, if that seemed like a fair price, adding that if she needed more, I was willing to go to the ATM. She said it was fine.

I made it to the airport, ecstatic that I finally had the love and support I needed. The flight was smooth, and I was anxious but excited to start my internship in D.C. On the morning of my first day of the program, I received screenshots from Mr. Melvin. They were of Uber prices from their house to the airport. The prices ranged from $50-$60. He texted me, "You really paid Mrs. Cora $5.00 for gas? Wow…Why did you think that was enough?" I was completely caught off guard. I tried to explain that Uber rides from the airport fluctuate depending on the day and time. Along with this, Mrs. Cora and I had agreed on a price. He said, "No, you pay people for their convenience and time also." I hadn't thought that was true for parental figures, but now I was more confused than ever, and extremely hurt.

I started the first day of my D.C. internship on a terrible note. I was done being vulnerable with people who didn't show up for me. I felt like I already had parents who had abused their power; I didn't need anymore like them.

TURNING POINT

What the Statistics Say:
In the U.S., there are more than 400,000 children living
in the foster care system without permanent families,
with the average age being eight years old.

40-50% of former foster youth become homeless
within 18 months after leaving care.

Almost 80% of inmates incarcerated in our prisons have spent
time in foster care with Black men being six times more
likely to be incarcerated as white and Hispanic men.

What Does God Say:
"For my father and my mother have forsaken
me, but the Lord will take me in
(Psalm 27:10).

ALEXIS

Pay attention to your patterns. The ways you learn to
survive may not be the way you want to live."
—Dr. Therna

LIVED WITH MY aunt and uncle for about four years and with each incoming worker, I would ask to switch placements. Each worker told me something like "You need to make this one work. You live in a nice home and go to a good school." After asking six or so foster care workers, I gave up trying. I wouldn't tell my aunt that I was doing this because I didn't know if it would make the situation worse or not.

On July 27th, 2011, when I was in Grand Blanc, a Flint suburb, with my Godmother, Aunt Bev, I was wrestling with Shawn (this was one of our good days, thankfully) and he was jokingly keeping me from going to the bathroom. I had my phone in my back pocket. I really needed to pee and instinctively ripped down my pants and plop...my phone fell in the toilet. I freaked out and hurried up and soaked my phone in rice for a while. When it wasn't turning back on, I called Aunt Karen to tell her what happened and what my options were for getting it replaced with insurance.

Within a few hours, she called back Aunt Bev and told her that she caught me talking to Shawn again on the phone records as well as through emails back and forth. At that moment, she made the decision to kick me out, saying that I could not come back —I needed to stay at Aunt Bev's house until I found a home to live in.

My feelings were all over the place at this point. I was terrified that I would be sent out of state or to live with horrible people like my aunt had threatened. I was also relieved that I was out of her house—anything else would be better in my book. At the same time, I felt an overwhelming sense of relief: was I ready for this next chapter in my life, or were these more rebellious feelings since I could finally be with Shawn? I had racing thoughts of transferring schools, finally being with old friends I had in Flint, and being more independent.

My social worker at the time, Tina, called me and said, "Alexis, I have the perfect placement for you in Oakland County so that you can stay at the same high school. Just stay with your Aunt Bev a few more days and trust me. I don't know your religious affiliations, but these parents are Christians and they won't shove it down your throat. They are great people and care about fostering teenage girls. They just got done fostering another teenage girl and asked for a few days before taking in another one."

Although I had a difficult time trusting at that point, Tina advocated on my behalf more than any other worker I'd have before, so I was willing to give this a shot. I was just happy that I could stay at the same high school. A few days later, I had an emergency placement meeting at the foster care agency I was going through. Aunt Bev, Tina, and her supervisor at the agency were all present in the room to try to come up with a solution for the next steps. I remember being remarkably calm as I sat and analyzed Kim. She was soft-spoken with welcoming eyes and a calm demeanor. After introducing ourselves, she pulled out a sheet of paper with "House Rules" written on them.

"You can stay with us if you can abide by these rules:"

- No cussing at us.
- No hitting.
- No stealing.

"I can do that!"

This list seemed extremely easy and honestly like common sense. *I wonder what the last girl was like for you to have to make a house rules sheet like this.*

She asked if I was comfortable coming to her house for the night or for the weekend to try it out and see what I thought. "I'll come for the weekend!" Surprised at how well I was handling the situation, we headed out with a suitcase and got into their Honda CR-V. It's funny the little things that you remember like when I was looking down at Kim's feet as we crossed that street in Downtown Flint thinking, "Wow, she has nice feet!"

I didn't realize at the time that this was the day before Kim's birthday. Now she jokes that I was her birthday present that year.

We drove about 45 minutes to Lake Orion, Michigan, to a beautiful two-story home in a suburban neighborhood with freshly paved roads and sidewalks, green grass, and yellow lilies lining the front of the porch. When we entered the house, I saw toys thrown around, blankets hanging over the couch and dishes in the sink. Just like Kim's outfit of a faded grey shirt, khaki shorts, open toed hiking sandals with chipped toenail polish sticking out the ends, their home seemed less rigid and more laid back than what I was used to. I noticed that they didn't have a TV in their living room. At first, I thought this was odd—the TV was the centerpiece of life with Aunt Karen. We ate around the TV, gathered around it, spent whole evenings in front of it. But family time to Kim and Brian was no electronics in the living room as a place to talk and connect.

This was a stranger's home, yet it immediately made me feel at ease as it was a stark contrast to my Aunt Karen, who always had her short brown pixie haircut highlighted and styled perfectly, pristine makeup, and business attire.

At this time, Kim and Brian only had two kids, Anna and Eli, who were 3 and 1 at the time. Kim was a stay at home mom while Brian worked at a local church. She loved to cook and bake. One day when I came home, I was so excited for dinner as I could smell freshly baked bread from the front door.

Rushing into the kitchen, I asked "What's for dinner?"

She said "Leftovers."

Confused and slightly disappointed, I said "But you're cooking?"

"This is for a friend from church who just had a baby."

I was still working at Little Caesars at the time, about thirty minutes away from where we lived. I was working the cash register when I saw Kim and Anna come in the door. My heart started to pound because I thought something was wrong until both were smiling at me from ear to ear. Anna ran up to the counter to hand me a little baggie of 2 or 3 mini cookies. Kim explained, "Anna made these, and she was insistent on giving you some before you got home from work so I suggested that we bring them to you!"

These moments clicked for me and I often get emotional when recalling them because they showed me even more of her selfless love for other people and how she puts other people first. I can see this still today. Even with five kids, she finds time to host trainings to prepare other people to be foster parents.

One Bible verse that encouraged Kim and Brian to foster was Isaiah 1:17 "Learn to do good; seek justice, reprove the ruthless, defend the orphans, plead for the widow." (Interestingly enough, Isaiah is the name of my foster brother who I was the first to hold and 1-17 is my birthday)!

The second or third night after arriving, my foster dad, Brian invited me out to eat as I drove their car to Buffalo Wild Wings. Brian wanted to get to know me and make me feel more comfortable living with a man in the home. This was especially important being that I never felt protected by any of the men in my life. At dinner, Brian said, "You can drive my car to school." I was shocked that I went from a home that felt like I could never earn trust and there was a rule for everything to one that immediately I was trusted until I'm not. Thankfully, because of the McKinney-Vento Act, a policy put in place to help foster youth stay in their original schools, I was able to get gas cards from my high school to drive to school every day.

I learn who people are by observation. I wanted to observe their behaviors and how they treated each other, and I wanted to wait a few days to see if their behaviors would change, as my aunt's had. When I first moved in, I mainly stayed in my room and came out only to eat dinner and go to the bathroom. I was waiting for the yelling to start and for the climate in the home to change. After a few days, it still hadn't. They also didn't press God or religion on me, ever. I never felt watched nor did I worry about them changing into different people. This was who they were. When I lived with my aunt, she claimed that she was a Christian and I told myself that if this was what Christianity looked like, then I'd never be one.

But, after observing them, I saw that they lived each day in the word of God, went to church, and communicated in a healthy way (i.e. no screaming, hitting, or yelling). After a couple months of living with them, and their frequent offers to join them at church on Sundays, I finally agreed. I hadn't been to church in a couple of years and realized how much I missed it. I knew that I wanted to go back, maybe just not to their church. I was used to going to a Baptist-style church.

It wasn't until I moved to Kalamazoo, after I transferred from UM-Flint, that I started to go to church more regularly. My friend Lauren invited me to go with her. I was captivated by the preacher, who talked about the power of faith and healing during his sermon. His words touched my heart, giving me the blueprint for overcoming the insecurities of my identity. Lauren and I walked to the altar for prayer near the end of service. Both the pastor and his wife laid their hands on my shoulders for prayer. Never had I seen the wife of the pastor stand alongside her husband with such power and authority. I was instantly inspired. I stayed behind to talk with her and she was even more electric during our conversation. Who knew that she would become my mentor and give me the name of my first business? I've been going to that church ever since!

When Justin and I started dating, he started to willingly go to church with me as well since he was also looking for a church to transition to while in college. The lead pastor of our church eventually began to mentor Justin as well. An example of how important mentorship is—Justin and I never imagined becoming authors or business owners until my pastor planted the idea, teaching us about publishing, website development, and more.

Who we surround ourselves with matters. Kim and Brian introduced a new way of living, thinking, giving, and loving unconditionally. It was the little things—like going on walks together. Before, alone time always consisted of groundings, taking away of phones, or yelling. The first time Kim asked me for a walk, I thought I was in trouble or something bad was going to happen. This was a realization for me because parents' time with their kids should be a time of connecting and relationship building, not something they associate with fear or punishment.

On one of the walks with Brian, he said to me, **"You are our flower, because we get to witness you bloom."**

I felt like I had just started to really connect with them when Kim and Brian came home one day and said, "We're moving." My heart dropped to my stomach and I didn't hear anything they were saying other than the word "Kalamazoo." I had never heard of it before, so it could've been in another state for all I knew. I felt abandoned and didn't know where I was going to go. Knowing this, Kim and Brian worked to keep me in the same school and even the same family—I moved in with Kim's parents who got licensed so I could stay with them. Apparently, they had told me before I moved in that there was a possibility that they might move, but I must have buried it, not wanting to imagine it could happen.

Sometimes, I felt like I was on a different planet when I was at Kim and Brian's house. Even their kids had never seen adults argue or yell until the oldest was 10 years old. Justin and I would look at each other in surprise about different things that we noticed—that the children were not allowed to camp out in front of the TV all day, that they listened to Christian songs and actually embodied the words. I've never been around people so mindful of what they put into their minds and bodies, and more importantly, their souls. They would read, share what they were thankful for, and pray together every single night. This consistency has been transformational for both of us. As children, no one paid attention to what Justin or I were exposed to, how we spent our time, whether we had safe plans or what time we were supposed to be home. The idea that parents are responsible for providing structure, safety, and routine was entirely new to us.

It didn't fully hit me how my childhood was so significantly different until I looked at my siblings, ages 10 and 12, and thought about how I couldn't imagine them even thinking about sex and how jealous I am that they were appropriately sheltered by two amazing parents. I didn't realize how important it is for parents to teach their kids how to regulate their emotions and communicate their feelings. Parents are supposed to translate children's expressions of pain and decipher what they need and want. When children have no safe port in the storm of their own feelings, the anger turns inward and results in lashing out, hysterics, and other destructive ways of seeking attention that are often misinterpreted by others, causing the child to repeat unsuccessful forms of communication with others.

I watched Kim and Brian parent with calmness and compassion, and a sense of responsibility for their children. I watched Kim take my younger (adopted) sister, Omanii, out of public school in order to homeschool her, feeling she needed that one on one time to feel loved, enforce principles, and make sure her identity is rooted in God. I could see consistency in her actions when she spoke positivity, posted quotes around the house and played with the kids every day, even when she didn't feel like it. She reminded me "I'm not raising kids. I'm raising adults, husbands, wives, business owners, friends, and siblings. Our example will be what our kids learn from, for good or bad."

It amazed me that Kim and Brian consistently asked their children what they wanted—to eat, to drink, to wear, and asked them what their opinions were on a variety of subjects, granting them autonomy. I never felt like I really had a choice until I moved in and Kim asked me what I wanted. Before Kim, my life had been defined by other people's decisions; my aunt and social workers moved me according to their thought processes and judgment.

When the kids do something wrong, Kim says to them "Do you want to try that again?" allowing the kids a second chance to fix what they did. She also told me that she notices when they start acting out, it's because they want attention. For Omanii, the worst thing she can do is to isolate her and send her to her room because that only further justifies her trauma-induced thoughts of being alone, neglected, and unloved.

Recently, my six-year-old brother got in trouble for locking himself out of our RV that's parked next to our house. He ran to the couch hiding under the covers, scream crying until Brian got home because he feared that he would get spanked or yelled at. When Brian got home and was told about what Isaiah did, Brian said sternly, "Where's Isaiah?" I had never heard or seen Kim and Brian really scream at or spank their kids, but that tone made me think it was coming. I went to my room and came back to see Brian lying on the couch next to Isaiah, who was still hiding under the cover. Brian was rubbing his back, letting him know that what he did was wrong, but that he still loved him and wasn't going to hurt him. I stood watching in awe. What a beautiful way to communicate with your child and let them know that they are still loved and protected. I learned the importance of forgiveness and grace just by watching their behavior.

Of all the things I had to unlearn, the most profound was the idea that I didn't need anyone else to help me. In my childhood, I had no one mature and responsible enough to turn to, even during excruciating trauma, and so I learned that you could not expect help from anyone. I did not know that people existed in an entirely different way, in supportive, caring ways, living interdependently and being mutually responsible. I didn't know what community and companionship looked or felt like. Over time, Kim and Brian taught me to accept support. They taught me to let go of the survival mode I'd needed as a child and teen and to understand that my childhood circumstances were deeply abnormal.

TURNING POINT

"God doesn't call the qualified. He qualifies the called"
(1 Corinthians 1:27-29).

JUSTIN

THE FOUR MARRIED couples that built the group home brought a variety of mentors from various careers to interact with the four young men transitioning into adulthood. Meeting with numerous successful Black businessmen, lawyers, doctors, pastors, and engineers inspired me. Each person I interacted with told me that I was a bright young man who could go to any college or university I wanted. It was like rain on parched soil. I had begun to give up on the idea of higher education. Now I had the support I needed to build confidence. I even revived my childhood dream of working to rebuild communities in Detroit one day. It took leaving my family environment to understand and accept new concepts of healthy behavior and of life's possibilities. Unfortunately, my siblings didn't have the same luxury. The culture of our neighborhood remained deeply embedded in them, preventing them from imagining other ways of life.

In my junior year of high school, I worked twice as hard as I'd ever worked in my life. As my confidence rose, so did my performance in school. I boosted my GPA from a 2.3 to a 2.6 almost instantly. Years earlier, when I'd lived with the Bennett family, I brought home a 2.3 GPA report card. One D, a couple of C's, and a lone A to balance things out. The dad in the house said, "Wow, this is better than I thought you'd do." Hardly a message to inspire confidence.

It came time to take the ACT; I couldn't afford to have a bad score if I wanted to go to college, but a combination of anxiety and inertia prevented me from preparing properly. Maybe it was hard to envision success, and ensuring failure was oddly easier.

I got a score of 13. Embarrassed and depressed, I kept my score from my house parents. I couldn't face them. I was disgusted with myself. I had blown my opportunity with my lack of preparation.

Do you not realize that a majority of your family is living in poverty with little or no opportunity to go to college? And this is what you did with your chance? I decided to take the test again. Mrs. Cora refused to drive me to the ACT prep building this time. She said she wanted to see how badly I wanted to succeed. So after school, three days a week, I walked six miles to and from the ACT prep building to prove to myself.

The second test felt completely different. I dressed as if I were going to a job interview. I woke up early to pray and release my fears unto God. That morning, I felt at peace. After taking the test, I felt happy. I'd given it my all. This moment taught me to be happy with the journey before I knew the outcome.

I scored a 19 the second time. I felt invincible. Now it was time to choose where to go. I had decided to stop playing football in order to pursue a career in journalism, although football would always be my first love. When I was a child I wasn't always sure how to verbally express how I felt about the things going on around me. In an uncontrollable and chaotic environment, I became more fluent through writing and journalism. Writing became my way to understand my feelings and decipher my thoughts; it allowed me to process the things going on around me.

Eventually, I developed a passion for giving the reader a vivid image through descriptive wordplay. Though I never acted on my love of journalism, I had a burning desire to do so and I had finally been presented the opportunity. In my senior year of high school, my English teacher suggested that I join the school newspaper. Excited about the opportunity, I soon became the sports editor, covering all school sports at my high school. I wanted my readers to feel those Friday night pregame butterflies and smell the fresh turf under their feet.

College recruiters regularly visited my high school, and I attended every single presentation and filled out applications for each school. I needed to prove to myself that I could be accepted to any university I desired, going from a dwindling dream of college to having a variety of options gave me a surge of confidence.

Mentors told me about the Seita Scholars Program at Western Michigan University. The program offered a support system similar to the one I'd had in the group home. The Seita Program also offered a campus coach to help students navigate academic life, assist with budgeting, and offer general support. Plus, Seita offered a scholarship that covered most of the tuition.

Although it seemed perfect, I was torn. One of my mentors advised me to attend an HBCU (Historically Black College University). I was inspired by the number of successful graduates from those schools and fearful of the statistics that showed how few opportunities Black people were afforded after graduation. But ultimately, those schools were too costly; I hadn't received any scholarships that would allow me to attend an out-of-state school. Above all, I was determined not to graduate from college with a mountain of debt.

I heard that a college recruiter from WMU was coming to visit my high school. I was the first in the class to visit the recruiter, and I bombarded him with questions. I immediately submitted my application. The following Tuesday, I received a piece of mail from WMU. I opened it with shaking hands. There it was. I was accepted into Western Michigan University *and* the Seita Scholars Program. Despite all those years of suffering, now look where I was! I called my mom and Khalil to tell them the news. *Momma, we made it!*

PART 4:
REDEFINING NORMAL: BREAKING CYCLES

What the Statistics Say:

7 out of 10 girls who age out of the foster care system
will become pregnant before the age of 21.

One out of every three Black boys born today can expect to
go to prison in his lifetime, as can one of every six Latino
boys—compared to one of every 17 white boys.

What Does God Say:

"For I know the plans I have for you," declares the Lord,
"plans to prosper you and not to harm you,
plans to give you hope and a future"
(Jeremiah 29:11 NIV).

PART 4: INTRO

Breaking generational cycles can be a lonely, wrenching process. Children generally accept the practices of their family without question; looking back and questioning them later requires a determination stronger than the pain of separating from the only values they have ever known. For many people, choosing to leave their environment to do better comes with being shunned or shamed by one's family. Children are sponges; they soak up messages from the moment they are born. Ways of thinking and communication (and ways of behaving in general) become deeply ingrained in our formative years. The social world we grow up in defines for us what's normal, acceptable, and praiseworthy.

One thing is clear—we all want to be loved, but how we give and receive love is largely dictated by those who taught us what love is in the first place. **For those of us who have been traumatized in our youth, we have to redefine ourselves and redefine what is normal.** In our communities, sustaining and surviving abuse was a badge of honor, a proof of strength and character. Parents who protected their children from toxic situations were resented and ostracized, their children made to feel embarrassed to have received such "privilege." We would laugh about being beaten with shoes, extension cords, hangers and anything else our parents could hit us with. Again, how much trauma you'd endured was a perverse measure of your strength.

It's easy to think this way as a child until you learn about Adverse Childhood Experiences (ACEs). These have a tremendous impact on future violence, victimization and perpetration, and lifelong health and opportunity. An ACE score (0 to 10) is a tally of different types of abuse, neglect, and other hallmarks of a rough childhood. According to the Adverse Childhood Experiences Study, the rougher your childhood, the higher your score is likely to be and the higher your risk for later health problems such as alcoholism, obesity, drug use, depression, suicide attempts, cancer, heart disease, and more.

Alexis and I are careful about what we consume. With our high ACE scores and addiction running in both our families, we have to be.

As hard as those years were, we were lucky to end up in foster care and lucky that we got out of our violent and destructive homes. How many abused kids never make it to the relative refuge of foster care because they were afraid to tell anyone what was happening, or because the adults around them failed to notice the signs? We alone know dozens of people.

Trauma rewires the brain and can even change our DNA.

Too many parents think that just because they provide food and shelter that they are good parents. Or because they do slightly better than their parents did for them, that makes them successful parents. I didn't learn about Maslow's Hierarchy of Needs until my freshman year of college.

We need our parents to care for us on several levels.

Self-actualization
desire to become the most that one can be

Esteem
respect, self-esteem, status, recognition, strength, freedom

Love and belonging
friendship, intimacy, family, sense of connection

Safety needs
personal security, employment, resources, health, property

Physiological needs
air, water, food, shelter, sleep, clothing, reproduction

If they don't, then our needs seep over into our intimate relationships. Oftentimes, this takes a lifelong journey of unlearning and relearning what our definition of love, family, and parenting looks like.

Additionally, that there is significant evidence to prove that a child's success can be determined by drawing a 0.6 mile radius around where they grow up. Based on factors such as their environment, socio-economic status, neighborhood and parental influence, education, etc. This shows, even more, the importance of community, families, healthy relationships, and healing.

Our lives were on a certain trajectory of abuse, neglect, and brokenness but we had to fight through the millions of hurdles and societal expectations to become who we are today.

We believe that in many circumstances, our own actions determine the rewards we obtain (internal locus of control), but our parents and so many other people in our lives believe that their own behavior doesn't matter much and that what happens to them is generally outside of their control (external locus of control).

With the help of this book, we want individuals to redefine what is normal in their own lives.

REVEALING THE TRUTH
IN MY TRAUMA

*"Never get so comfortable in pain that you
forget happiness is an option."*
—Anonymous

ALEXIS

OW CAN WE do better in life if we've never seen what "better" looks like? It's hard to change the way you think and improve your mental and spiritual capacity with no examples. For this reason, victims of abuse often turn back to their destructive environment.

Outside of my godparents, Uncle Giles and Aunt Beverly, I had no role models on which to base an understanding of what healthy love looked like. Uncle Giles was the first man that I looked up to. Then I met Kim and Brian. Still, I believed that they must've done something right to receive love and mercy from God, things that I must not have deserved. I was always the girl who was abandoned, neglected, and abused. Children extrapolate their worth from how they've been treated and cared for. One Christmas, I pulled Brian aside to ask him if he had ever called Kim a "bitch." "No, why would I? I love her." **This shook up my understanding of "normal," and it began to dawn on me that just because I had experienced something all my life, that didn't make it normal.** In fact, my own experiences had been deeply pathological, not to mention criminal.

I remember going to an MYOI (Michigan Youth Opportunity Initiative) workshop session in Flint on healthy relationships. (MYOI is a program centered on improving outcomes for youths transitioning from foster care to adulthood.) There was a panel of five couples who were engaged, newly married, or married for years. I listened to the way they talked to and about each other. I watched their body language. I grew envious—and definitely more aware that my relationship with Shawn wasn't normal.

When I first moved to Kalamazoo, I wanted to go back to counseling. I hadn't gone since high school and usually someone else picked my counselor, so I had no idea how to even find one. I searched with Google and started making calls. The person that I thought I really wanted was on maternity leave and introduced me to her co-worker. On my first appointment, I saw a leaflet on the table that stated her specialties: Trauma, PTSD, anxiety, depression, domestic violence, family conflict, and several others. I thought to myself, "I found my person!" It helped that she was incredibly easy to talk to and was completely honest with me when I asked her questions about her integrity, character and faith. I needed to make sure that if she were giving me advice, I could trust her judgement.

I thought that I was entirely to blame for the destructiveness of my relationship. There had to be something wrong with me to be broken up with and called names daily. This was the backwards logic of an abused child at work: *I am being treated badly, therefore I am bad.* Rather than: *A parent who treats his child badly is a bad parent. My parent is a bad parent.* Most abused children apply this mirrored logic, perhaps because there is an illusion of control in it. *If I am at fault, I can fix it. If my parents are at fault, I have no power to change the dynamic.* A journal entry from that time reads:

If this is my fantasy and my dream (of running off and getting married and getting pregnant), how do I always manage to find ways to fuck it up? God, please don't give me such a wonderful loving man—just to take him away. What's the lesson in that? Is it to make me hate myself and live in regret forever?

My counselor asked me to fill out a chart (available at re-definingnormal. com), checking all the boxes of what I thought was healthy vs. unhealthy in my relationship. I checked almost every box on the unhealthy side and only one in healthy— and that one was a stretch. But I needed to cling to something. I would email my counselor constantly asking how to better handle situations, and asking her why I couldn't be the woman Shawn needed me to be. I always felt inadequate. Years later, I took the ACES assessment and got the highest score: 10. I was the most susceptible to dangerous relationships due to the severity of my childhood trauma. I also learned that I was diagnosed with PTSD—twice. Once when I left my biological dad and another time due to my relationship.

I've been told several times that I must've liked what Shawn did to me or I would have left sooner. However, I learned from my counselor that abusers are good at gaslighting: in other words, making you feel crazy and second guess yourself and your values. Also, when you're in an abusive relationship, you can't really see outside of it or even have the ability to listen to other people when they tell you that the relationship is toxic and that you need to leave. I think the reason why my relationship with Shawn had more of an impact on me than my relationship with my dad did was because my brain allowed me to dissociate with my dad as a coping mechanism. Whereas, in this relationship, I was vulnerable, I was with him during my formative years trying to figure out who I was and what place I have in this world. I was also introduced to the term "Escalation of Commitment," basically meaning that we have the tendency to continue to invest in something even though it's been years and we have seen no progress, even if it's getting worse. We tend to focus on how much time has been invested in a relationship, as if it were proportional to how much hope we should have for its success, and we overlook the actual quality of the relationship itself.

In my relationship with Shawn, I repeatedly did penance, as if over time I could purge my guilt or badness from my soul by continually offering more and accepting mistreatment. **Maybe proving my "worth" to Shawn was about trying to prove to myself that I was no longer the worthless person I felt I was with my dad.** Shawn had become a direct outgrowth of my father's abuse. He treated me as an object, not as a human being.

After taking that assessment from my counselor, I became obsessed with learning more about healthy relationships and the signs of an unhealthy one (manipulation, red flags, etc.). I asked couples all the time about their relationships, how they handled conflict, communicated, about their life after marriage and kids, etc. I could only go to people who were in a position to offer guidance—I couldn't go to people who were always indifferent, unstable, or in unhealthy relationships, or those who were never in a relationship to begin with—about what it takes to build a healthy, stable, and lasting relationship. You can't go to someone who's always broke or bankrupt for investment advice.

Then I had a realization:

> *This was not love.*
> *This was a need. I expected love to hurt. That's the only form*
> *of love I've ever known.*

I had to learn the difference between safety and predictable unpredictability. I knew what to expect: Chaos. Predictable chaos with predictable violence stemming from my childhood with rewards thrown at me in order to mollify me. I stayed because it was comfortable, and I didn't know what to expect after he left. I saw my entire world crash down around me so many times when he left that I couldn't even imagine life without him.

Shawn's torment was a form of domestic abuse. Many people assume that they are not being abused if they are not being hit or injured physically, and this belief is in itself dangerous. Controlling and manipulating with constant insults and threats of abandonment is a form of battering and abuse and it must be recognized as such. I have been both physically and psychologically abused, and I am here to tell you that the toll of the latter is just as high if not higher than the former.

At the end of the day: *hurt people, hurt people. Healed people, heal people.*

From gathering information on other couples, reading blogs, and observing Kim and Brian, I learned that love shouldn't hurt. That saying "What we allow will continue" seemed to fit. After witnessing Shawn's disrespect and abuse towards others during my study abroad and from others confronting me about his behavior, I knew deep down that I deserved better. When I returned from South Africa, I was ready to learn who Alexis was and what she stood for. This relationship was sucking away my happiness, peace, energy, and sanity. I had stayed so long due to a fear of losing him, and a fear that I couldn't tolerate that pain. I would not let fear hold me back any longer.

Once I broke up with him for good, a weight had been lifted. I could finally breathe. I could think rationally. **I had to love myself enough to walk away and accept better.** It was similar to the early healing people describe after drug withdrawal and recovery.

Almost exactly three months before meeting Justin, I wrote: "*Somewhere out there, God is preparing the man for me. I just haven't found him yet. If he's there, God will bring him to me.*"

I officially left Shawn on July 3, 2016. One week later I met Justin.

REVEALING THE TRUTH
IN MY TRAUMA

JUSTIN

HOW DO YOU identify what is healthy and unhealthy in your life? Have you ever reflected on the culture of your family and wondered if their influences have set you on a path to success or failure? It is not an easy question to face, nor is it always a pleasure to answer, but it's vital to growth and maturation.

In my high school, you were either the lady's man who messed with all the girls, or the relationship guy who messed with one girl. I decided I wanted to pursue the relationship route. The couples in school were corny but cool at the same time. They seemed close and loving; I also knew that they were having a lot of sex.

By the time I was in the 9th grade, I had only one sexual encounter. I was nine years old at the time when it happened. There was a girl named Chyna in our neighborhood who was about three years older. Chyna was one of those "fast" girls who was extremely flirtatious. Looking back, knowing what I know now, I wouldn't be surprised if she was being sexually abused in her household. Her parents allowed numerous men in their home without parental supervision, allowing them to stay the night.

Both of my brothers were having sex at the time, and I felt pressure to catch up. Chyna and I would often flirt and touch each other's private areas. A few of her brothers knew about it and decided not to do anything. It was only her oldest brother that would kill me if he found out. One summer evening, she invited me to the park. It was normal for me to stay out late after dark. I had freedoms you wouldn't believe at nine years old. At first, my mom had enforced the "streetlight" rule: I had to be in the house before the streetlights came on. But this turned into the "11 pm rule" that turned into the "Come Home Eventually rule."

Chyna and I went to the park with her brother and his girlfriend around 10:30 pm. None of us were above 13 years old. We played and joked around a little bit until she decided to pull me off to the side. The park was empty, and we were the only ones there. We went under the slide and started to have sex. I officially lost my virginity. She knew exactly what to do. I was prepared to try something I had seen in porn but ended up lying there frozen. Shortly after we started, her oldest brother discovered us. I ran as fast as I could with my pants around my knees.

A day or two later when I came to visit, I stood outside her window listening to her being beaten by her mother. I could hear the whipping from a belt hitting her skin. Chyna cried loud enough for people around the corner to hear. I was terrified to approach her from that point on. After my mom found out, she wasn't nearly as mad as I thought she would be. I knew for sure that if Chyna's mom beat her then I had something coming that was ten times worse. But all my mom said was, "Boy, do yo ass wanna catch AIDs or something? And I ain't taking care of no babies either. You better stop." That was my one and only sex talk.

I learned about sex from watching porn at about five or six years old. My brother Andre, who was 12 at the time, found a few tapes in my parents' stash and showed them to Khalil and me. Shortly after, I found a duffel bag filled with movies, and at least 30% of it was porn.

When I was ten and living with my oldest brother Dylan, my brother Khalil and I found hundreds of pornographic videos on Dylan's computer. My sister Tiffany and her boyfriend would eventually move into Dylan's apartment too. All five of us lived in a small one-bedroom apartment. My brother Dylan had the bedroom to himself, and my sister, her boyfriend, Khalil, and I slept in the living room, sharing two twin mattresses. We'd lean the mattresses on the wall during the day, to make space, and lay them down on the floor in the evenings to sleep.

I regularly found my sister and her boyfriend watching porn on his computer. It wasn't secretive—they watched midday, laughing and commentating as they did. When I poked my head in to see, they'd tell me to turn around and watch TV. I stepped back so they wouldn't see me and continued to watch. They downloaded the famous R. Kelly sex tape in which he urinated on a 14-year-old girl. I joined in the laughter this prompted, but underneath I felt shame for doing so. Something in me knew it was wrong, even then.

The school environment in which I grew up was highly sexualized. Once I got to middle school, a lot of girls were having sex, most of them with older guys. Sex had become a normal part of school and I felt lame because I hadn't had any sexual experiences since I was nine. Getting into a relationship seemed like the only logical way to do so. Girls would ask me to pull out my penis in class when the teacher wasn't looking. I was always too nervous because of what my auntie would do to me if she found out.

But before I entered into a relationship, regardless of the reason, I wanted to make sure I never treated the women I interacted with the way my father treated my mother. I had seen plenty of unhealthy relationships, but I had no idea what a healthy one looked like. I knew what *not* to do in a relationship, but I didn't know exactly what I *should* do. All I knew for sure was that I didn't want to put anyone through the pain I had seen my mother endure.

My parents' arguments were intense and ugly. Rarely did they seem to enjoy each other's company. I knew I wanted to be with someone I would enjoy conversation and genuine emotional connection.

In hindsight, I don't think I was looking for a girlfriend, but a mother figure. I was looking for someone to love me like my mother should have. Not long after meeting them, I would tell women about my experiences in foster care, about my lack of parental figures, about the chaos of my youth. The high school girls I interacted with were not interested or were understandably overwhelmed by the amount of difficult information I shared.

My goal was to do better than my parents had; but they had set an extremely low bar. This made me vulnerable to all sorts of manipulation by the girls I got involved with. I was both the abuser and the abused in some relationships.

My siblings also began to play out the pattern of domestic violence they had witnessed between my mother and father growing up. I would watch my nieces and nephews as they watched their mother being beaten up by their father. I knew very well what they were feeling as they watched it happen. It is unspeakably traumatic. But watching abuse repeatedly normalizes it and numbs you to its horrors. And the cycle continues down through generations. I realized that I needed to look beyond my siblings to find examples of healthy relationships.

After leaving my Auntie Cheryl's before moving to the group home at 16, my brother and I lived with the Bennett family. Living with the Bennett family was my first time having a hands-on interaction with a married couple. The parents in the house never seemed to agree on anything.

I wondered if Khalil and I caused the friction in their marriage. Ever since we entered foster care together, Khalil and I have depended on each other. When we bought food, it was only for us. When we bought clothes, we shared the clothes we bought. Our bond was close because we were all we had ever had. We weren't interested in adapting to someone else's household rules, especially after leaving my Auntie's house. How could this not cause conflict in a household with a more traditional family dynamic? We were two kids in survival mode that functioned as a separate unit.

The Bennetts called us "selfish." When in reality, we had never been socialized. I would eat whatever food I found in the fridge and it never occurred to me to save some for other people. I did only the chores that were convenient. I had never been taught the rules of regular, functioning households. Instead, I had grown up in an almost lawless environment, where survival was the only concern.

The bond between my brother and me made the Bennetts' life hard. They argued constantly, and although we might not have been the cause, our behavior certainly aggravated the tension.

After coming home from school, my brother would warn me to avoid stressing anyone out because they weren't in a good mood. Their way of communicating consisted of making jabs at one another and pretending it was all in fun. I never saw them handle a conflict in a peaceful manner. There was always one person unable to see the other person's point of view.

I understand that married couples aren't happy 24/7 but it seemed as if the Bennetts rarely enjoyed time with each other. When my biological parents were on good terms and not physically fighting each other, they seemed happier with each other than the Bennetts' parents were. Both the Bennetts and my parents stayed together for decades and **that was the only thing that was celebrated—the longevity of their relationship and not the quality of it.**

Year after year, both the Bennetts and my parents celebrated an anniversary. All everyone ever cared about was the fact that they *stuck it out*. That's what my siblings say today about my parents' relationship. "They stuck it out through thick and thin. That's loyalty. That's real love." I view it differently. First, my parents never got married; they never wanted to truly commit to each other. I remember being in class and telling my teacher about the cookout we were having for my parents' anniversary. The girls next to me asked how long they had been married as they fantasized about the romance they hoped to find one day.

"Oh no, they're not married, they've just been together for 30 years," I said.

I felt extremely embarrassed as they laughed and began to clown me.

"Boy, y'all celebrating a long-ass friendship."

No one in my immediate family had gotten married. My mom would always ask my brother Dylan and me "When do y'all plan on giving me grandbabies?" Not, "When do you plan on getting married? What type of person are you looking for? What type of family do you want to build?" It would never have occurred to my mother to ask these questions. The family structure was about having children, with no commitment to a partner or a cohesive family unit.

I don't know why my parents stayed together other than for the financial convenience. My mom stayed with my dad after being pistol-whipped. She stayed after having her jaw broken. She stayed after breaking her leg trying to run away from him by jumping off a porch.

Why was this normal and acceptable in our family? At what point do we discuss these issues and resolve them for a healthy and prosperous future? The mother of Andre's first child got into a custody battle with him over the kids. She brought up the fact that she was physically abused by Andre throughout their entire relationship. My mom went to court to defend Andre, saying that none of his girlfriend's stories were true, even though she had actually witnessed many of their fights and even had to break them up a few times. My mom protected the abuser, despite having been abused for decades herself.

My parents don't talk to anyone about my father's history of domestic abuse. They still argue, verbally assault each other, and threaten one another. Is this what we call "through thick and thin?" All my siblings have accepted the years of drug addiction and domestic abuse as normal. They don't ever talk about the desire to break the cycle for the sake of their children.

After the girls made fun of my parents, I began to reevaluate the normality of my family. I never felt comfortable celebrating my parents' anniversary again, mainly because I knew the unhealthy habits that have been practiced in our family for the 30 plus years. I wanted something different for myself and the next generation. I then started the journey of learning what was healthy.

VULNERABLE THROUGH THE PAIN

"She is clothed in strength and dignity and she
laughs without fear of the future"
(Proverbs 31:25).

ALEXIS

VULNERABILITY IS SOMETHING many broken youth grow to despise. Because foster youth are consistently neglected and disappointed, most build a wall to hide their feelings and protect themselves from the world. Even if you haven't been in the system, of course, you may find yourself building a similar wall after mistreatment, abuse, or neglect. Opening up to Justin on the grass that day was scary, but if he was going to bail, I wanted to get it over with.

So, I told him everything.

And then Justin took my hand, looked me in my eyes and said, "Alexis, I appreciate you sharing that with me. I am honored to hear your story. I want to let you know that you are amazing and I'd like to still get to know you more."

It wasn't just his words, it was the way he said them. Justin made me feel secure. I found myself beginning to relax into our friendship and open up to the possibility of more.

Of course, we were still two college kids. Not long after our chat, Justin flirted openly with our student leader at the closing luncheon, asking if she had a boyfriend. Naturally, I was jealous and confused. Had my revelations closed him off to the idea of being more than friends? It hadn't seemed that way at the time.

There was a break between the end of the program and the official start of school, so I took the opportunity to drive back home and spend time with Kim, Brian, and their children.

"Who's Justin?" Kim asked jokingly.

How on earth had she heard about him?

"He added me on Facebook," she explained.

I blushed. "Wow, he moves fast!" I replied. But secretly, I felt pleased. Usually I was the one who had to show initiative in relationships, but this boy had beat me to it!

"He must know what he wants."

"We slept in the same bed, but nothing happened, I *promise*. We talked for most of the night."

Since I had made a promise to Kim and Brian that I wouldn't date anyone for a year, I told Justin that we could only be friends. We saw each other again at a foster youth event in Lansing and we acted as though we had just met. Justin shook my hand and introduced himself. We tried to keep our distance because we didn't want people to think we were dating even though we were talking for six or more hours a night. I knew I was falling for him when we would eat cereal together—my favorite food. It also helped that he made me harder than I ever had with someone. It felt good and organic.

After about a month, I came to Kim crying and asking her, "How do you know if you're in love?" Although I had been in an eight-year relationship, I didn't know what love actually felt like. That was loving out of need—not want. I told myself that I would never love out of need again and only be with someone because I wanted to. I didn't want my identity to be defined by another person. All I knew was that this felt GOOD. We talked about things that I had never talked about with my ex—our faith and our journey with God. I always joked that I wanted to snatch Justin up before someone else discovered him and how incredible he was.

Out of the blue, I got an email from Shawn. He instructed me to pass it along to my new boyfriend. His pernicious driving jealousy led him to assume that I was already involved with someone new.

"Bro, don't make the same mistakes I did and waste eight years of your life on someone who isn't worth it. Alexis is selfish, evil, heartless and will only tear you down as a man. Listen to my advice and get out now while you can. Don't listen to anything she says, she's a liar and will only hurt you. She has too much baggage and trauma for anyone to deal with. She even has PTSD from her dad. It's not worth it, bro."

Despite Shawn's dire predictions, Justin seemed to find my company enjoyable, and our relationship flourished—no violent arguments or festering paranoia. I almost felt "normal"—like someone who had not suffered extreme trauma. A couple of months passed, and we saw each other again at another foster youth event at a local amusement park. Within only a couple hours together, I felt the happiest that I had felt in years—or ever, really.

The only actual "date" we went on in that time was to a restaurant called "Coney Island." I ordered pancakes, and Justin ordered the typical "girl" first date meal: a salad. I laughed. Naturally, when the waiter came out with our food, he put the salad in front of me. "Um, no. I ordered the pancakes," I said. After lunch, we went to a nearby park to walk around, swing on swings, and play on the monkey bars. As the day wound down, we went back to the car and sat for a while, listening to music. We deeply enjoyed our conversations; our time together was harmonious and gentle. I noticed that we didn't need much activity, simple conversation was enough.

Vulnerability is about more than revealing intimate experiences and feelings. It is an ongoing, daily practice, and a commitment between two people to stay present and connected. We must be able to forgive each other's transgressions, which we can do as long as we know our partner has fundamentally healthy intentions.

Mistakes happen. Learning from my past experiences, I now give grace and accept that we will disappoint each other sometimes. Partners will make mistakes, of course, and we have to apply a measure of grace when they do. I never had unrealistic expectations of Justin, and he never held me to unreasonable standards, either. After just a short time, my intuition told me that Justin was kind and gentle, and most importantly, trustworthy. I saw him as a kind and gentle man who was patient and intentional with his words and held him to that standard.

A few weeks before Justin started his freshman year, he texted me and said, "I think we should be friends because I want to go into college single and have fun."

Of course, I'd been the one to set a boundary from the start, based on my promise to Kim and Brian. Still, I was crushed. There was obviously more between us than friendship, and I had been sure he'd also felt the electricity between us. I'd shared so much with him. I felt betrayed. "Fine!" I texted back, feeling the old walls go back up. I didn't need Justin to save me. I didn't need anyone to save me anymore. I refused to beg another man to be with me. Maybe I had him all wrong. Maybe he was hiding something. Maybe he was sexually impatient and didn't feel I was worth the wait. Or maybe, given my past, I just wasn't worth it at all. These dark thoughts began to plague me.

VULNERABLE THROUGH THE PAIN

JUSTIN

WHEN YOU MEET someone for the first time, they know nothing of your past and don't immediately assume that you have unresolved issues. But what happens when they meet you in the midst of an emotional roller coaster? And what happens if you've met your life partner, but you still have unprocessed and unresolved trauma from your past? Your wounds, still open, might bleed onto your new relationship, staining and destroying a once-in-a-lifetime opportunity.

When I was 13 years old, I experienced one of the worst days of my life. The events of March 15th, 2011 would haunt me for many years to come. I was in the seventh grade, living with my Auntie Cheryl. My friends and I often hung out by Old Redford Academy's exit after dismissal. Before I headed to my bus stop, I saw a few high school kids smacking one of my classmates around. Two of the kids were hitting him and the third was recording it on his phone. The older kids noticed me watching. "What you lookin at?" They said. I knew I shouldn't have said anything, but I did. "I'm lookin at you," I replied. They immediately let the other kid go. Now they had a new target.

Parents and teachers got involved to de-escalate the situation, thinking it ended there on school grounds. But I knew that my walk to the bus would be isolated and scary. Sure enough, the bullies began to follow me. I scurried as fast as I could, but I knew they would catch up eventually. I assumed I'd have to fight my way out of this.

The bus stop was on Six Mile and Greenfield, in Detroit right next to the McDonald's that most of the students visited after school. I made it to the McDonald's parking lot and took off my bookbag, desperately hoping someone would intervene. Then, I saw one of the boys pick up a brick and walk toward me. The second boy was also closing in. But this time, there was no one recording what was about to happen. As I turned my head toward the first boy, he threw the brick straight at my face. Adrenaline rushing through me, I initially felt no pain. I knew that it was serious though, because the kids who'd just assaulted me stared in shock and laughed, possibly out of anxiety. Maybe they hadn't meant to go so far. I ran into the McDonald's, asking anyone who would listen to call my Auntie Cheryl. People stared, covering their mouths in shock. I tried to remain calm. Gasping, I dragged myself to the counter. All eyes were on me, but no one was offering to help. People seemed paralyzed by shock, which only made me more frightened of what had happened to me.

I kept begging for someone to call my aunt. I vaguely noticed that blood was pouring out of my mouth, and that this made it hard to speak. Then I saw one of my classmates. Her face was frozen in horror. Finally, the cashier came from behind the counter and handed me a warm wet rag. Once I looked down to grab it, I noticed the blood all over my coat, my hands, and even the cashier. From that point on, everything else was a blur, until my Auntie Cheryl arrived.

I was sitting on the ground outside the McDonald's when my aunt pulled into the parking lot. When she saw me, she jumped out of the car, petrified. She ran over to me and asked a police officer what had happened. Moments later, she and I were rushed to Sinai Grace Hospital. One of the guys in the ambulance asked me to open my mouth as he examined the damage.

He confirmed that I had lost six teeth, four of them partially gone and the front two completely knocked out. Later on, I found out that a part of the bone structure underneath my nose was damaged and partially gone as well. My heart sank and I began to sob...My Auntie held me, filled with anger that someone had done this to her nephew. I sat in the back of the ambulance, weak and ashamed. *How could I have let this happen to me? What could I have done differently?* These questions would weigh on me for years, causing me to spiral into a serious depression.

By the time we got home, my adrenaline had slowed and I was feeling the pain. My lip was so swollen, it reached the top of my nose. My gums were completely black and I could barely talk. I couldn't eat solid food for a couple of weeks, and it became difficult to eat or drink anything at all. Khalil hugged me as his eyes filled with tears. With my parents not around, he saw himself as my protector and he felt that he'd let me down. We were all wrung out emotionally that night.

I tried to sleep but I couldn't lie down—it put too much pressure on my head. I kept flashing back to the moment it happened. I sat on my bed with my back against the wall, asking *"why me?"* I reflected on all my sins and asked God what I had done wrong. I begged for forgiveness and apologized for all I had done. The pain was a constant reminder that life would never be the same. I shared a room with Khalil and didn't want him to hear me cry. Crying was seen as a weakness. I sat on the couch that night, praying and crying myself to sleep.

That Friday night, my aunt had told me that I was not to go to school the following Monday. But I did, maybe hoping that I could pretend my way back to normal. This was easily the worst decision I'd ever made. The entire school had heard what had happened, and every kid looked at me as I walked down the hall. I wasn't exactly popular, so I wasn't expecting anyone to care. But on this day, every single kid had an opinion or a joke. Rumors had spread around the school and the story had completely changed.

Because I wasn't that well known, some kids didn't know that I was the kid who'd been attacked and attempted to cover my mouth the entire day. Students right behind me in class talked about the incident, having no idea that I was the one they were discussing.

"I heard dude got stomped out so bad his teeth came out," one student said.

"Nah, I heard they whooped his ass, hit him with a brick and robbed him," another said.

Halfway through the day, almost every student was making jokes. Once everyone realized I was the one who'd lost his teeth, kids walked up to me, asking me to crack a smile, just for a good laugh. It wasn't until a kid in my third period class asked me to smile that I snapped. I knew only one way to deal with this type of pressure. I hadn't fought since fourth grade but the pressure was too much to bear. I stood over the kid, threatening to beat the crap out of him as our teacher removed me from the classroom. He knew what had happened and was very understanding, sitting next to me with his hand on my shoulder as I called Auntie Cheryl to take me home. I was overwhelmed by my new reality and didn't go to school for the next three weeks.

For the next couple of weeks, I suffered alone in depression. Meanwhile, my aunt and the rest of my family were bent on revenge. The police had gotten involved, but they weren't doing much. In a city like Detroit, my assault was forgettable compared to the huge amount of serious crime the police had to deal with. Frustrated with their inaction, my family decided to take matters into their own hands.

My auntie and I drove around my middle school, looking for the guys who assaulted me. I can't imagine what would've happened if we had found them. My aunt would have landed in jail for assault. I'd seen her in action before; she wasn't afraid to hop out of her car in the middle of traffic to cause a ruckus. We began to follow a few high school kids home. The situation became ridiculous. We were literally stalking kids who fit the description.

I tried very hard to forget their faces. Remembering who they were would only haunt me, pushing my anger and hatred even further. I certainly didn't want to make a mistake and point out the wrong boys, because my aunt was ready to pounce in seconds. Her rage didn't feel like love. It only made me feel more stressed and miserable.

I also quickly realized that **getting revenge would neither restore my teeth nor my mental health.** It was better to let the memory of that day fade. My family may have wanted an eye for an eye, but I wanted sanity. As it was, my world had been flipped upside down. I was now the kid with no teeth, an identity I hadn't chosen and certainly didn't want.

I didn't need my family to seek revenge or hurt anyone else. I needed them to pay attention to the badly damaged boy I had become, to offer some affection and guidance, some solace after surviving an act of fearsome brutality. Revenge was indeed soon forgotten, and the family moved on. I felt more alone than ever. No one was concerned with my mental, emotional or physical well-being, **it never seemed to occur to anyone that it was more than my face that needed to recover.**

Meanwhile, my parents hadn't seen me even once since I'd been attacked. I realized they must not have been too concerned with my mental or emotional health. Although my resentment grew, so did my desire to see them, or more accurately, for them to see me. It was hard to believe that they had so little interest that a grave injury didn't send them running to my side. When I got to their apartment, my mom told me how sorry she was that it had happened. My dad asked if I remembered their faces and told me he knew people that could take care of the situation. He was asking if I wanted them murdered. I was numb to my parents' words. **In their minds, if I didn't want revenge, I must be over it.** I wasn't, of course—and wouldn't be for many years—but I also wanted to move on and take care of myself. I needed to have my teeth repaired. I also worked toward letting go of my anger and forgiving the boys who had assaulted me. I needed that peace of mind.

For three months, I went to school without teeth until I received partials (also known as flippers) for my two front teeth. At night, I took them out and put them in a glass of water, as if I were a 70-year-old man. Khalil and

I would laugh about it. He was the only person who could make jokes about my teeth. He knew where the line was, and he also took care of me. Dental implants would cost nearly $20,000, and that option was not on the table. The partials would have to do. Meanwhile, there were still small pieces of my teeth left in my gums. I felt them as the doctor allowed me to eat more solid foods. I began the process of getting root canals for my other teeth. I went to a sketchy dentist who accepted Medicaid dental insurance. They gave me too little Novocain beforehand and I felt every needle ripping into my gums throughout the whole procedure. Over the years, it felt as though' I lived in that dentist's office.

The people who assaulted me didn't just steal my smile; they stole my happiness. I had a hard time making friends and enjoying life as a teenager. They knew that my teeth were fake. Kids would always watch me at lunch to see how I ate. Being a teenager is hard enough without that kind of attention. I began isolating myself from the world. I gave up on making friends because kids would eventually say "Aren't you the kid who got his teeth knocked out? Take your teeth out and show me."

In high school, I *needed* to take them out whenever I played football. Usually, if you're on the football team in middle school and high school, your teammates are your closest friends. **But because of my teeth, the jokes never ended.** I couldn't authentically be myself—I was always the kid with the missing teeth. I never made a true friend in high school. When I began focusing on college, and doing whatever it would take to fit in. The pain of my endless public humiliation in high school made fitting in my primary goal. I decided that I would do whatever it took—even if it meant abandoning my spiritual beliefs in the process.

On top of the merciless teasing, I had to continue to take the same route home from school. My auntie had gotten a job and had to work. I had no other way to get home besides catching the city bus I had used before the incident—the same route I rode the day I lost my teeth. Every day after school, I walked to the bus stop on Six Mile and Greenfield, next to the McDonald's where I lost my teeth. Every day after school I saw my blood and pieces of my broken teeth sitting in that parking lot. As I waited for the bus, I stared, reliving the incident, every single day.

One day, the McDonald's cashier who had helped me came out to the bus stop to check on me. I didn't remember her face, but she understood. She said, "I'm sure you don't remember me, but I wanted to make sure you were doing ok." We had a small conversation as I waited for the bus. It meant a lot. She asked how I was doing and how I was handling things. She seemed more concerned than my parents had been. Sometimes, the small things mean the most. She couldn't have had any idea what I was going through or dealing with. She didn't know that I felt alone and was deeply depressed. She didn't know that my parents weren't active in my life and I lacked support. **In only a few minutes, she had made my day and made me feel loved.**

Living with false teeth for the next eight years stirred up a number of different emotions. I felt unwanted by friends, family, and the world. Deciding to explore my career options outside of football once I entered college allowed me to keep my dental health a secret. I wanted to keep the damage to my teeth hidden to ensure that I could make friends in college. **I would rather have died than gone through the hell of revealing my injuries to another person. I just couldn't risk it.**

As I began to grow closer to Alexis, I felt like my secret was in danger of being exposed. The night we poured our hearts out to each other forged a powerful and irresistible bond. Yet I still hid my broken smile from Alexis. *No one could love or respect me as a man if they knew I had missing teeth and that I was the one who allowed it to happen.* This was what I believed—in high school, my "manhood" had been relentlessly questioned because of the assault.

"Damn, bro you let them knock your teeth out? I wouldn't let that shit happen to me." This ate away at whatever self-esteem I'd managed to build before. I was a fragile kid who'd been through so much and processed so little of it. As such, I couldn't imagine my dream girl respecting me after learning what had happened. It was simply beyond my experience with other people.

Meanwhile, we'd been talking all summer since we met at the scholarship program in July. At night, when we would talk on the phone, we always poured ourselves our favorite bowl of cereal. It became our tradition. Our friendship felt effortless and romance seemed inevitable.

But I began to panic. It would be my first adult relationship, which meant I'd have to come clean. I'd had numerous faulty root canals and was at risk of losing my teeth entirely. I was consumed with anxiety. Because of the cultural pressures of my high school, I associated my dental damage with weakness and a lack of masculine courage. I couldn't find the strength to tell Alexis. My teeth were at the very center of my tenderness, my most vulnerable spot, and I was desperate to prevent her from finding out.

With a heavy heart, I texted the woman that I probably already loved that I needed more time to "explore my options." I knew it looked bad, and Alexis was no dummy. She knew that meant that I wanted to sleep with other girls. She probably also suspected I was scared of commitment. I was, but not for the reason she had assumed. In so many ways, I felt very far from the perfect man she deserved.

The next day, I talked to my brother Khalil about what I should do. He was the only person that I felt would give me honest advice. He heard the pain in my voice. As I described Alexis to my brother, I thought *"Man… this is someone that I can't miss out on."* I told him about how often we'd talk and text., how she was so easy to talk to, and about how comforting she was despite her brutal honesty. But then I thought, *"If my parents didn't want me, who would?"* Khalil told me to relax. He said I already knew the answer." Give it your best shot," he said, "and if it doesn't work, it wasn't meant to be."

Alexis had been manipulated by so many men in her past. Having been abused or traumatized themselves, they projected their rage and pain onto her. I could not allow anything that had happened to me before I met her to poison our relationship or cause me to mistreat her. I had to stop flirting with other girls and take a step toward being an adult. After all the volatility I'd lived through, this felt like an enormous risk. I had no experience with stability. Were either of us equipped to be stable now, for ourselves and for each other?

When I talked to her later that day, I told her that I wanted to be the first in our relationship to be vulnerable and willing to show my vulnerability. If our relationship eventually failed, I would know that I had done everything that I could do to serve my partner.

Not long after, I told her about my teeth. I had always been convinced that no one would want me with the damage in my mouth. After telling her, she laughed at the fact that I thought she would leave me and began to further embrace me. I wasn't sure if she completely understood the gravity of the revelation. Most young people wouldn't know what a flipper or a partial was. Revealing my injuries lifted an enormous burden and made me feel safe with Alexis. I felt much of the shame dissipate for two reasons: one—I was no longer in hiding and two—the girl I loved was not the least bit phased by what I had assumed would be a deal-breaker. I had revealed the most sensitive details of my life and nothing bad had happened. She still loved me, despite the deficiencies of my upbringing and what I saw as a physical disfigurement. She loved me for who I was, damaged parts and all.

I didn't need Alexis to actively heal me from my childhood pain but support me along my journey. Knowing I had her by my side gave me a confidence I'd never before experienced.

MENTAL WARFARE

What the Statistics Say:
One in six U.S. adults live with a mental illness,
equating to almost 43.8 million adults.

90% of those who die by suicide have an underlying mental illness
with suicide being the 10th leading cause of death in the U.S.

1 out of every 2 kids who age out of the foster care
system will develop a substance dependence.

52% of youth in foster care are prescribed psychiatric
medication compared to 4% of youth overall.

What Does God Say:
""Come to Me, all who are weary and heavily burdened, and I
will give you rest. Take My yoke upon you and learn from Me, for
I am gentle and humble in heart, and you will find rest for your
souls. For My yoke is easy [to bear] and My burden is light""
(Matthew 11:28-30 AMP).

> *"Those that need help the most are the least likely to ask for it."*
> —Anonymous

ALEXIS

ENTAL WARFARE CAN often be more challenging than physical pain. I've internalized my struggles and expressed them in unhealthy and destructive ways. Growing up, I wasn't allowed to express my emotions and was constantly told that my feelings didn't matter. Money was used to cover up emotional pain. Eventually, I was lucky enough to be placed in a family that allowed me, and even encouraged me, to reveal my feelings while patiently guiding me in the right direction.

During childhood, my outlet was basketball. It gave me something to do for hours on end and would keep me out of my father's house. It also taught me resilience, as I was the only girl in my apartment complex to ever play with all teenage guys and adult men. I was always pushed and shoved to the ground. No one went easy on me because I was a girl and the shortest one on the court. But I didn't want their pity. I wouldn't go home until the blood from my knees soaked through to my socks. I perfected my 3-point shot while all the roughneck guys surrounded the basket for rebounds. I had no idea how to play on teams with positions. It was comical how ridiculous I looked playing organized basketball with my only experience consisting of playing street ball. I went to one basketball camp and dreaded it the entire time because I was forced to play different positions when I had never played before.

Planning my day down to the minute has also helped to stabilize my mental health. For as long as I can remember, I've been attached to my planner, scheduling almost every minute of my day. This provided a sense of stability and control. If I forgot my planner at home, I would have an anxiety attack. I struggled with anxiety throughout my first few jobs. It was the worst while I worked as a teller in Flint. When I found out that I wasn't going to graduate on time, I had panic attacks and cried uncontrollably at work. Thankfully, I had a phenomenal boss who was there to comfort me and allowed me to go home when it was so bad that I couldn't pull myself together.

The extreme stress not only had an effect on me mentally, but also physically. In 8th grade, I couldn't focus long enough to read and needed others to read my assignments to me. The extreme stress caused ocular pressure that required me to use trifocals to help my eyes focus. By 10th grade, I had been in counseling for a few years and was running track. My stress levels were lower, and I was able to stop wearing them altogether. Now, I don't need to wear glasses at all.

I used to cry in the bathroom in high school and eat in the counselor's office or with my teachers. Around 10th grade, I completely shut out the rest of the world. I would go straight from class to class without socializing. People thought that I had transferred schools or dropped out. **Later, I was told that people thought if anyone were to commit suicide in high school, it would have been me.**

I'm proud to tell people that I've been going to counseling since I was 13. I've been diagnosed with depression, anxiety, and PTSD twice. I've been hospitalized, placed on suicide watch, and attempted suicide more than three times. I've taken pills, drowned myself in tubs, wrapped a belt around my neck to the tightest hole I could latch the buckle into, and even made a goodbye video for friends and family on an old camera from my biological dad. Now it kind of reminds me of the book *Thirteen Reasons Why*. **I didn't know that suicide ran in my family, that both my mother and grandmother had died from it.**

I hated my mom for a long time. I was bitter and angry that she had abandoned me with my father. *How could she do that?* After she passed, I ended up getting rid of all of her jewelry and stuffed animals—anything that held memories of her. But I realized that those thoughts were selfish. I had no idea what she was going through or what pushed her to end her life—a decision that she can't take back. I have to believe that she thought she was doing what was best, or that she felt completely trapped and was driven to believe that she had no choice.

I didn't actually start to heal until four years after I graduated from high school because I didn't realize how bad everything had been with my ex and the severity of his impact on me until I left him. Every time I went to counseling before I graduated high school, I would just talk about my past relationship, how to cope with my home life, or just sit in silence. Sometimes, there were several weeks of silence. Group therapy was always my favorite. That was the first time that I felt less alone and like I wasn't the only one to experience what I had been through.

Healing is an ongoing journey. When I filed for adoption, I saw my mother's death certificate for the first time. "Death by suicide," it read. It stunned me. It looked so clinical and cold—so heartless. It took me a minute to pull myself together.

In counseling, I did an exercise in which I took a long piece of paper, like a banner, and drew a timeline. Then, I plotted out all of the major events in my life so far, such as being raped, molested, involved in an abusive relationship for eight years, my mother's suicide, switching from school to school, being diagnosed with PTSD twice, and more. **The exercise showed me that I've been through a lot, but also that I'd lived through 100% of it.** Afterward, I was supposed to rip it up, bury it, or burn it, but I decided to keep it to honor and reflect on my growth.

I always struggled with the idea that you can love a person you hate or hate a person you love. I had to learn to forgive my father, my mother, and ultimately myself. As my friend Aland calls it, "Maintained forgiveness." In counseling, I wanted to see if what happened to me was a generational occurrence. *Was my father abused as well? Was he not protected?* I wasn't making excuses for his behavior, but trying to understand the impact our environment has on us, and the damage it can cause in our lives if we don't deal with it head on. What happened to me isn't unique. I've met many women (and men) who've been in abusive relationships, have been sexually assaulted or raped. I consider myself one of the lucky ones. I had people to advocate for me. I had people who believed me. My abuser went to prison. How many people can say that? Not as many as you would hope.

Forgiving ourselves is also incredibly important. In order for me to be emotionally available, I first had to learn to love myself. I have my own toxic and damaging patterns and habits that will continue to plague my relationships if I don't deal with them and learn to be proud of myself for surviving my past. I do not want to be afraid to tell people that I was in foster care, no matter the stigma around it. It's my past and no one can take it away from me. I feel now that I was put through those things in order to become able to help others avoid the same type of misery. We all have powerful stories; it's how we use them to help others heal that has the ability to define our lives.

I've noticed (with myself and so many others) that when we talk about our trauma and the pain that our parents caused us, we tend to laugh and joke about it. I know that may be a coping mechanism, but we will never learn from it and improve if we don't take it more seriously. Sometimes, we laugh about how we were beaten as a kid and we laugh with each other as we discuss it, comparing how horrible our parents were or what we survived. This wasn't used as a means of coping, nor did it lead to any healing or growth. It was a reflection of the desensitization of children living in extremely abusive or trying circumstances. Eventually, you have been exposed to pathological and criminal behavior for so long that it ceases to seem abnormal. Oftentimes, when I try to challenge that mindset in others, I hear "Well, I lived through it," or "When I have kids, I'll beat them when they act up, too" or "I bet they won't do it again when I beat their ass."

I had to peel back the layers of hiding from the pain and the trauma so that I could be true to myself. So that I could know who I actually was underneath it. **My healing is up to me, not anyone else.** No one else can heal me or make me love myself. That's my job.

It's not fair for me to put my past and traumas on Justin. He didn't hurt me so why should it be his responsibility to save or heal me? Only Jesus and I can do that. It's not Justin's job to know all my triggers; I don't even know all my triggers. It could be a certain sound or smell that brings back memories. Sometimes, the sound of the front door opening triggers me. While I was in Peru by myself, I was in a bathtub and Justin was in Washington D.C. completing a summer program. He went to a club with his cousin and a few friends and I freaked out, crying, cussing him out, accusing him of cheating. Shawn had once cheated on me with a woman he had pretended was his cousin; now I was letting Shawn's bad behavior poison my trust in Justin.

It's up to me to communicate my triggers and it's his job to be empathetic. He knows not to touch my leg during the night in a sexual way or sneak into the shower, to always announce himself when he comes into the room, and to ask for consent every single time we have sex. Even today, I sleep with a nightlight on.

Although we have both gone through the foster care system, we've had vastly different experiences. I had never had the typical foster care experience of my belongings being thrown in a bag when moving. So when Justin and I were yet again rushing to pack up and move out of one of our dorms (which we've done often since we've moved over 14 times since high school), I put his clothes in trash bags after running out of suitcases and boxes. When Justin noticed, he was triggered. He bolted over to me and snatched the bag out of my hands. He dumped the clothes out quickly. "Why did you do that?" I snapped. "Don't ever put my clothes in trash bags again," he replied. He apologized for startling me and then explained that for him, trash bags symbolized how temporary and worthless he had been made to feel as a foster youth. His possessions had been thoughtlessly transported in trash bags time and again, stealing his dignity and making him feel like—well, like trash. He never wanted to feel like that again.

Each year, I would receive a letter the week of my birthday, notifying me that my dad was up for parole. I had to write a letter begging the parole board not to release him from prison enclosed with pictures of letters he wrote to prove my case. I didn't get the notification that he was going to be released because I was studying abroad in Senegal at the time. Brian called to tell me that he was released and living back in Flint. I called his parole officer but hung up before he could answer and then proceeded to ignore the officer's calls. I was scared of what he might tell me. The parole officer called me back several times a day until I answered, to reassure me that I was safe, that he had a tracker, and that he would *gladly* put him back in prison if he were to try to contact me.

Even graduating from college was a trigger. It represented foster care—instability, fears, the unknown, and so on. I didn't have a job lined up before graduating. I—the big planner—had nothing planned.

I made the decision to go back on anti-anxiety/anti-depressant medication to help me balance back out. When I told Justin, he said "If that's what you think is best. **I trust that you know more about your body than I do.** I trust your judgment and I support you in whatever decision you make." That was one of the most validating things my partner could ever say.

MENTAL WARFARE

Black children had the highest rate of suicide deaths within children ages 5–11. Suicide is ranked as the 3rd leading cause of death for Black men ages 15–24.

63% of African Americans believe that a mental health condition is a sign of personal weakness.

JUSTIN

MANY BLACK COMMUNITIES have been deprived of information on positive ways to maintain or improve mental health. The resources that other ethnic groups have access to compared to those available to Black communities puts youth like me at an immediate disadvantage. Society has put a dollar value on mental health and if you can't afford a counselor, then you're out of luck. Of course, mental health support and the stability it offers help pull impoverished communities away from the brink of destruction. Many impoverished Black communities have little if any access to information about mental health. Without these resources, Black youth are positioned for failure, stuck in patterns of unhealthy behavior, creating an imperishable cultural hierarchy among ethnic groups in the U.S.

Anxiety and depression are swept under the rug in Black communities, usually going unnamed and unaddressed. Black men make up more than half of the prison population in this country, meaning that huge numbers of Black children are growing up without their fathers. With the appropriate therapeutic resources, the number of Black men behind bars would drop drastically, which would contribute greatly to the stabilization of Black communities and households. Because I grew up in a household that lacked any knowledge of how to resolve conflict healthily, I was positioned to become another statistic. It wasn't until I took advantage of the resource (and privilege) of counseling that I learned how generational cycles could be reversed and how to disrupt the path of brokenness set for Black men in impoverished communities.

I remember going to counseling quite a few times during my early teenage years. My social worker thought it would be a good idea to seek therapy after losing my teeth. At the time, I wasn't sure how I felt about talking to a complete stranger, but I was at least a little open to the idea. Unfortunately, the therapist and I didn't talk much at all during our sessions. I didn't have the emotional capacity to express how I felt about losing my teeth and my counselor's seeming lack of interest enabled me to disengage. I just couldn't connect with him. Was it that he was an older white guy who didn't quite understand any of the trauma I'd experienced as a young Black man from Detroit?

I sat there with this stranger almost every day, and we often simply played cards together. Beating him in Uno grew tiresome, and eventually we sat in silence for the entire hour. I didn't know much about him and unfortunately, he didn't get a chance to know me either. Shortly after, he was moved to another facility and I had a new counselor. Most were short-lived and I started to see someone new almost every other week. I never built a rapport with any of my therapists and it became an annoyance to share my personal story with yet another stranger. I decided to give up on counseling and pursue mental stability on my own.

Years later, while in college, I decided to give counseling another shot. The pressures of college and my old family struggles were taking a toll on my mental health. Alexis suggested counseling but I wanted to share all my hardships with her, instead. She told me that asking her to bear all my pain would be unfair, and that I needed support from someone who was qualified. I realized that in most unhealthy relationships, it's common for someone to place all of their trauma and pain onto their partner without seeking professional help.

In counseling, I discovered that addiction is often the result of unresolved trauma and other mental health issues. Through conversations with Khalil, I learned that my mother had survived sexual abuse that mirrored some of the abuse Alexis had experienced in her childhood. Khalil told me that my mom was sexually assaulted almost daily by her stepmother. As a child, her father worked long hours and came home only at night to what he believed was a perfect family in which his children were loved and cared for. My mother never told him about the abuse—she didn't want to destroy his image of his family. She hangs a family portrait of her siblings, her father, and her stepmother above the couch in every home she lived in. She says that she smiles every time she sees it, because this was a time that made her father proud. Her dad is no longer alive, but she still keeps the portrait on the wall. Who am I to tell her she shouldn't? Maybe her response to her trauma is mysterious, but it belongs to her. Still, it hurts me to see it.

I am amazed that although the two most important women in my life have had such similar experiences, they chose such different paths. My mother never spoke about her abuse until a few years ago, at 54 years old, during a casual conversation with Khalil. She began abusing drugs at the age of 18, around the time she became pregnant with Dylan. That year, she also attempted suicide by shooting herself in the head. Somehow, she survived, but has suffered from seizures her entire life.

It was my responsibility to stop internalizing childhood trauma and to start seeing it as separate from my inherent value, not a reflection of it. I took my time and found the right therapist, trying several before finding the best fit. I asked friends for their input and to my surprise, found that many had been receiving counseling for some time through their health insurance. I learned how to search for resources and gain access to them.

During the fall semester of my junior year, Alexis started her internship in Washington D.C. Our physical separation allowed me to reconnect with my Christian faith on another level. I started attending Bible study meetings with the Collegiate Black Christians, along with a few of my friends. I began to understand the strength we have with God. Knowing that I'm made in the image of God gave me a new perspective: that **I'm in control of my destiny.** God gave us authority over the Earth, which means that He gave us authority over every earthly circumstance standing in our way. I just needed to exercise my authority over the barriers confronting me. My whole childhood had been about having my autonomy stripped from me; this journey was about finding and restoring it.

Additionally, my campus coach told me that the Seita Scholars Program offered counseling services for foster youth. These counselors specialize in helping trauma-surviving youth overcome the barriers of their past while teaching techniques to cope with anxiety and depression. At first, I wasn't sure if I should go or not. I felt that my life experiences were different from most foster youth because my biological parents were still in my life, to some degree. It seemed to me that so many youths, like Alexis, found a loving foster family and rode off into the sunset. Holding out for a miracle, I was still hoping my parents would transform into consistent, loving, and supportive parents.

I thought to myself, *"Why am I still feeling the way I did when I was a child? What triggered it?"* I asked Khalil if he still dealt with the pain of figuring out life without our parents. He told me that we were adults now and needed to get over it. He thought ignoring the pain of abuse and neglect would make it cease to exist. But doing so would actually internalize the damage and turn it into permanent shame and feelings of worthlessness. I refused to accept this for myself and I encouraged him to seek counseling as well. It wasn't our fault that we were put in this position, but we had to reject the habits of our only role models, whose behavior had been toxic.

My college classes pushed me to the limit and often forced me into a depression. I needed a parental figure to support me, but my parents couldn't understand my struggles as a university student, nor did they seem to care.

I did make a connection with one of the counselors and felt the improvement in my life immediately. We'd practice activities that would help me process my emotions and acknowledge them as real, but not all-defining. We walked through how to approach stressful situations in a healthy way, using a series of logical steps. I'd finally met a therapist invested in helping me heal and become the person I wanted to be. In the past, I'd barely engage in conversation with counselors. Today, I am able to laugh and cry freely and to express any emotion that comes up during our sessions. Counseling used to be torture, with barely a word exchanged the entire hour. Now my counselor and I regularly exceed the time limit and I am overcome with joy every time we schedule our next session.

God said, *"seek and you shall find."* I believe when I started counseling as a teenager, I was not in the right mental space to accept the love and support offered to me. I didn't understand how to love myself and I expected a counselor to swoop in and solve my issues. I don't know how many teenagers are good at receiving help, especially in a therapeutic environment or those with traumatic backgrounds. Maybe the counselors I saw weren't terribly effective, but until recently, I blamed myself for not getting much out of therapy as a teen. I realized that *I* get to choose when I'm happy by practicing healthy habits such as praying and exercising to combat anxiety or depression. I also accepted the responsibility of passing down this newfound information to other Black men and women. No longer should our race or economic status take away our God given right to mental stability.

The more I grew as an individual, the more my relationship with Alexis blossomed. I learned that I had to be secure and happy with myself before I could commit to another person. It was an intense period in which I focused solely on healing, mostly isolating myself in order to maintain stamina. It was the most intense work of my life and resulted in the most mental and spiritual growth I had ever experienced.

TRUE COLORS

"If God is for us, who can be against us?"
(Romans 8:31).

ALEXIS

EVERY SINGLE RELATIONSHIP with friends, family, and colleagues has boundaries, we just have to decide for ourselves what the parameters are in order to protect ourselves. Depending on the relationship, we can be taken advantage of, compromise beliefs, and be sucked dry financially, emotionally, mentally, and spiritually. For me, it took putting my foot down and setting rules or boundaries of behaviors that I was willing to accept and support. I had to cut off certain family members who would take advantage of me, even in high school, by guilt-tripping me into giving them money for an emergency, and there always seemed to be an emergency. It may seem harsh, but I told a family member to not ask me for money until he lost his apartment, sold everything he owns and is homeless because of how often I felt like I was being taken advantage of without saying no. I don't know if I meant that, but I was so tired of feeling manipulated, exploited and depleted by my family.

About four years after I graduated high school, and about five years since I had contact with my Aunt Karen, I studied abroad in South Africa. While there, I had a lot of time to think and reflect. Being thousands of miles away from home, dealing with culture shock, and not knowing anyone aside from one friend in my house, I'd never felt so alone. I used this time to get closer to God and try to make amends with people from my past. I reached out to my Aunt Karen and told her that I had forgiven her, and I apologized for anything that I could've done that made it difficult while I lived with them. It took a lot for me to get to this point, but I wanted to move forward in our relationships. After my apology, we stayed in contact over the phone and via email. I wanted to see them before they moved to North Carolina so that we all had a clean slate.

But the thing is, true colors always find their way of showing. It's not up to us to heal others, we can only heal ourselves and have to be okay with that. I had gotten accepted into a prestigious program at Georgetown University. Whenever I get into a program, I always have feelings of self-doubt as if I don't belong there. Since Georgetown is my dream school, this program added extra weight on my shoulders. My mentor Megan graciously allowed me to stay in her beautiful, quaint apartment just 10 minutes from campus. When I got there, she was on a call and texted me to come inside. When I opened the door, I noticed a cozy looking gray sofa. *Is that where I'm going to sleep?* On the ledge dividing the living room and the kitchen sat a pure white cat with bright blue eyes. Next to her was Megan with her enormous ginger curls. The moment I met her, I thought, "Wow, she's beautiful!" She was the first woman I had met who aligned exactly with my goals: she traveled the world, she lived in another country for several years, and she worked with orphans. I called her my twin, or my "DC wife."

As I was getting ready one morning, my aunt texted me. I didn't think anything of it because we were on good terms at that point. The conversation started off well and then went south. I started to feel defensive. She was saying things like "Honestly, very few people seem to follow your social media feeds. You're clearly wanting to make a difference, but it is so muddled and intertwined with everything about you that nobody can hear you. Your messages are not getting through. You need to get yourself out of the way so they can land. People don't care how smart and well-traveled you are. You do." I took a minute to walk away, breathe, and try to understand why she was coming at me like that.

I'm too old for this shit to keep happening.

I questioned her motives for texting me. She never asked me, "What are you doing in DC? When do you graduate?" or anything positive. When I asked her why she was being so hurtful, she immediately flipped the script. "You know what Alexis? You're trying really hard to make me mad and now I am...WE DIDNT FUCK YOU. Your dad did...You won't tell me what I did that was so bad. Oh, I figured it out...I didn't get you a new homecoming dress: I'm so sorry I traumatized you with that (kissy face)."

Then she blocked me so I couldn't get the last word—just like many others in my life had. This was gut-wrenching—and embarrassing, as this all had happened in front of my new mentor. But the worst of it was the stuff about my father. How could she use a word like "fuck?" How could she bring it up at all? It took awhile for me to understand that people who are truly grown up do not—ever—say such atrocious, violent things to anyone, much less to their children. The very word also implied some version of consent, as if I had been involved in some salacious sex act instead of having been raped repeatedly by my father. She was family, but family is not supposed to behave in this damaging, pathological way.

In the end, I realized that she was angry that I had publicly given credit to my foster mom, Kim, for helping me heal, and not to her. This proved to me even more that there's a reason we need to create boundaries, whether emotional or physical. I had to remind myself what my definition of family was, and what I was willing to sacrifice for the relationship. Blood means we're related; it doesn't mean I owe blind loyalty to anyone, especially those who have hurt me.

We have to know who is healthy in our lives and who isn't, and when it's better to love someone from a distance. This has been applicable for my brother Zach and for other family members. However, after going so long expecting negative outcomes from their proven track record it was hard for me to see the progress my brother was making with his son. Seeing my brother Zach, who used to terrorize me on his trampoline by throwing mini metal cars at my legs, leaving me with bruises and welts, now gently play wrestling with his son shows me that he is using this opportunity to shape him into a more compassionate adult so that he can better father his child. I can see how his son is softening his soul, changing him into a good, loving man that I am more than proud to call my brother. This reminds me of the power of my words and setting aside my personal feelings to let him know that.

Only five months after our breakup, Shawn had already moved in with a new girlfriend, who found me on Facebook and sent me a message while I was in Bible study. She asked me if he'd always been crazy. When I spoke to her over the phone, she told me that the night before, he had ripped the covers off of her and thrown water in her face. She thought she was doing something wrong because he was constantly punishing her and ignoring her. She said, "I started pulling back from God when I was with him and toward the end, I felt he was the devil."

Although I felt terrible for her, I was relieved to know that I hadn't imagined the cruelty of my old boyfriend, nor had it been my fault. Interestingly, she had also been in foster care and she had also had her share of childhood trauma. Shawn certainly had a type. He knew easy prey when he saw it. She had moved out and was staying with a friend; she was afraid of him.

I told her to get a restraining order but, knowing that I had been unable to get one, she told me that she didn't see the point, and it was hard to disagree.

Later that year, on New Year's Eve, she messaged me to tell me that she was pregnant. She felt that abortion was the only choice because "He will torture my child and my kid would hate me...I don't want to bring my baby into that world. I couldn't put my kid through that kind of mental abuse."

Then, in February of the following year, I received the following message:

"Alexis, Shawn isn't a bad guy like we made him seem at all...he didn't continue his bad habits after you, maybe he really did just fall out of love for you, but he wasn't a harmful person. I'm sending you this message because he didn't deserve what I did to make him spin out of control and for us to bring down his life more."

I was shocked. Either she had felt so hopeless that she began to identify with her abuser, or he had written the message himself. Or both. Whatever the case, I needed to draw a protective line. I could not save this girl from

Shawn or from her troubled life, I was just a kid starting over, myself. I had begun to see Justin and make progress in my academic life. I needed to cut any connection I had to her; being drawn into the drama maelstrom would be like going back to a toxic drug. I closed the door on that chapter of my life for good, even though I hoped the very best for her.

TRUE COLORS

JUSTIN

WHEN SITUATIONS BECOME stressful, we often run back to our old "normal." And I could only ignore my mother for so long before giving in and coming home.

Alexis was the type of student who could join five clubs, host ten events, take 16 credits, and still get a 4.0 GPA. Not to mention, she would rarely study and still ace her exams. I thought I could do the same, but things didn't turn out as well for me. I was failing my exams and I nearly failed a few classes my freshman year.

I had to balance a new relationship, university classes, and the pressure of being a first-generation college student and only the second in my immediate family to graduate high school. Most incoming students gain the infamous "freshman 15," I gained the "freshman 25." There were a few times where I thought I needed to go back to Detroit to live with my mom, not even knowing if it was an option or not. With how bad I was struggling, the idea didn't sound too bad. Deep down, I knew that was a cop-out. Everything came crashing down when I failed my second communications exam and found myself crying in Alexis' arms.

Alexis invited me over after and I tried to hide my emotional state but couldn't make it up the stairs to her apartment without bawling. I attempted to cover my face but when she looked me in the eyes and she noticed they were bloodshot, the tears started flooding down my face. I felt like a loser that was failing my entire family. In my mind, I saw it as a domino effect: if I failed my classes, I would lose my scholarship, drop out of college, and be forced to go back home to live with my biological parents.

That night, Alexis and I bought a planner and she helped me organize my life. We scheduled time to study, pray, workout, and spend time together. Our dates became study dates and we spent time together as students as well as partners.

In addition to the struggles of adjusting to university life, I dealt with a lack of parental figures through yet another life milestone. They always called to check on me, but this felt superficial and too casual. Did they miss me at all? Were they worried about their kid? If so, why didn't they visit me? If I had a child, I wouldn't let them suffer alone, as I did throughout my college experience. I would be there for them in a second if they needed me. I wondered if they didn't realize how much I needed them because they had never been through the college experience themselves. Or maybe because they lacked education, they assumed they had no advice or help to offer me. I wondered if I was being too hard on them. Now, I wonder how I held out hope that they'd become attentive and involved. Maybe children never quite give up on their parents.

When I became a Resident Assistant my sophomore year, I wanted to serve as an example for incoming freshmen on how to successfully make the transition to college. I watched with envy as parents eagerly helped their kids move in. Especially since it was just Alexis and me and sometimes my campus coach from the Seita Scholars Program every semester moving into my dorm. Some parents would take me off to the side to express their concerns for their child while they finished unpacking.

"We love our boy so much...," they would say, nearly through tears. "Please take good care of him and make sure he stays out of trouble."

The difference with my parents was so stark that it cut me to the bone. I had no real emotional connection to my parents at all. I would see parents embracing children up and down the hallway on move-in day and even though I knew better, I'd be suddenly inspired to go home to Detroit to see if maybe this time my parents would greet me with that kind of warmth and devotion.

I did express how much I would love for my parents to visit me while on the phone with them. I wanted to give them a chance while acting as if I didn't care if they disappointed me. Alexis noticed my disappointment every time I got off the phone with them. Just as in my childhood, I heard more false promises. My dad said he'd come and visit me as soon as he got his car fixed. My mom said she would come also but she didn't have the money. I told them that I would take them out to breakfast, lunch, and dinner, give them gas money—whatever they needed to come and visit me. Even as a broke college student, **I was more than willing to exceed my credit card limits to pay for my parents' love.** Never once did they come to visit me. **I felt worthless and still not good enough to be loved.**

Mrs. Cora and Mr. Melvin visited me once after I begged them to do so. While there, they would periodically call me "Son," which only confused me even more, mixed up as it was with their inconsistent behavior toward me.

With a focus on my mental health and more balance in my life, I decided to distance myself from my biological family and create a healthy boundary. Every time I returned home from college to visit my family; I always came back to school feeling depressed. I love my family and want the best for them but oftentimes it feels as if I wanted to help them more than they want to help themselves. I wanted to give my brothers Khalil and Andre small nuggets of advice I had learned in counseling, such as how to get out of debt, how to save money, or even how to get a driver's license. I always wanted to help, even if it was unwarranted. Looking back, I feel like I was out of line for giving unsolicited advice. This may have contributed to the friction between my family and me.

But the reason I wanted to create boundaries was much deeper. I cared most about their influence over the children in the family. I was never comfortable with my parents and siblings smoking weed, drinking alcohol, and playing explicit music, movies, and TV shows in front of my nieces and nephews. I didn't even notice this until I brought Alexis home, hoping to have a traditional visit between my girlfriend and my family. She was shocked to see the kids singing along to vulgar song lyrics. Overwhelmed by the chaos of everyone in the house screaming, cursing, and threatening to beat the kids at any given moment, Alexis and I left early. The car was silent as we drove home. In an uncertain tone, I asked, "Sooooooo.... What do you think?," knowing I didn't want to hear the answer, as Alexis could be brutally honest.

When I called my family out for this behavior, they would say "You think you too good to be a part of the family now." I'd talk about creating goals, personal and professional growth, and innovative ideas of how we could improve our circumstances and community. I was limited to what I could talk about and the ways in which I could express myself without offending anyone. When I brought news home about an exciting new opportunity I earned, it often fell on deaf ears and was soon forgotten. Conversations surrounding college, potential study abroad trips, and my career felt like speaking a foreign language and soon became frowned upon.

I told myself that I couldn't partake in ruining the kids' lives, so I eventually distanced myself from my family. As I distanced myself, I felt that I had given up on my nieces and nephews. Most of my nephews and nieces looked up to me and were always excited to see me when I came home from college. They always wanted to know what college was like and sometimes begged to come on a college visit with me.

On one of my last visits to my mom's house, I remember her desperately wanting to buy a pack of cigarettes. She needed to go to the store to get them but didn't have a ride. She asked me if I would take her to the store for cigarettes. I told her I didn't want to contribute to her smoking habit and giving her a ride would feel as if I were.

Once I said no, she asked any and everyone for a ride to the store to buy cigarettes. She begged at least five or six people and even offered a few dollars for gas money. It was crazy, she offered various business-like deals as if her life depended on it. It reminded me of when I was a child on 25th street, when she was completely consumed with drug addiction. Maybe this was silly of me, but I became slightly jealous. If she knew how much I needed her support, would she scrape up $30-40 for an Amtrak ticket to Kalamazoo to come and visit me even if I paid for the round-trip ticket myself? These may have been selfish thoughts of mine, but I seriously became jealous of how badly she wanted those cigarettes.

Later that year, I visited my family for Thanksgiving. Excited for the delicious holiday dinners my mother would make every year, I promised to help prepare dinner just so I could grab bits and pieces of food while cooking—an old habit of mine. I couldn't wait to taste her creamy mashed potatoes and enjoy her cherry pie for dessert.

As we began to cook, my mom noticed that she was missing quite a few essential ingredients for the meal. She looked at me and said, "Why don't you, just buy them with your credit card?" Puzzled that she knew I had one without my ever having mentioned it, I grew suspicious and declined. She asked that I give her a ride to the grocery store.

I was a broke college student and the youngest of the five, but somehow, I found myself getting ready to pay for part of Thanksgiving dinner. I dragged myself around the grocery store, my heart sinking. My mother has a talent for making others feel bad for her. She knows how to squeeze out a tear at just the right moment. By the time I made it to the register, I realized she'd grabbed many items she couldn't afford. She wept to the cashier, drawing the attention of everyone in the store. She begged for mercy, saying that she only wanted to feed her family for the holidays. I was humiliated watching my mother sob and carry on for the sake of "pity food." I grabbed the groceries and paid for them myself. I couldn't ruin Thanksgiving dinner for my family, even though I knew I had been played. I felt like I was eight years old again, like that little boy whose mother had just taken money from his cookie jar.

I was tired of my parents and my family controlling my emotions and making me feel depressed every time I visited. I wanted to be able to dictate my happiness for myself. **The burden of wanting their love was killing me.** I needed to emotionally separate from my family. I wanted to be happy with who I had become: a successful man of God and a soon to be a leader in my community. In order to overcome my resentment, I needed to draw even closer to God.

For those who have toxicity within their family, know that you are not required to feed into that relationship. Yes, you can love your family and friends while still acknowledging that their behavior is unacceptable. In fact, a part of loving your family is holding them accountable for their wrongdoing. Though I haven't yet mustered the strength to have these conversations with my family, I encourage you to create a healthy boundary that protects your mental and emotional wellbeing. **You must love others as you love yourself, but you cannot allow others to affect the love and respect you have for yourself.**

SELF-SABATOGE

*"Confront the dark parts of yourself, and work to
banish them with illumination and forgiveness. Your willingness
to wrestle with your demons will cause your angels to sing.
Use the pain as fuel, as a reminder of your strength."*
—August Wilson

ALEXIS

BECAUSE I WAS still holding onto the belief that I was too difficult to
love, I would revert to the tendencies I'd had in previous relationships.
Once I knew that I was falling for Justin, I tried to test his boundaries,
and his limits, to see if he'd stay. This is a common tactic used among foster
youth to see if they'll be kicked out of their foster homes. Subconsciously,
I was sabotaging our relationship. I would start arguments to see how far
I could push him. This tactic went hand-in-hand with continuing to have
an "escape plan."

In the beginning of our relationship, we would both passive aggressively
say we needed a "break" in order to end an argument. Then we wouldn't
speak for a day or two. This was our way of causing the other one a little
bit of pain, while protecting ourselves from being abandoned. I learned this
from years of "breaks," sometimes multiple times a day. Having that done
to me for years, especially the silent treatment—no calls, texts or anything
as a form of emotional "punishment," hurt like hell. *So why was I now doing
this to someone I loved?*

Justin and I had a petty argument that resulted in him walking back to his dorm to cool down. Upset that he refused to engage in the argument, I chased Justin around campus in my car yelling out the window, all because he didn't want to communicate when I was ready to on my terms. Looking back now, I am still embarrassed about this. I believe that every time you have sex with someone, you are becoming one with them spiritually, emotionally, and physically, creating a soul tie. Sex isn't just a physical act but one that carries into future relationships. Unless confronted and dealt with, it will affect any relationship in the future. Before moving forward in my relationship with Justin, I needed to address my past emotional and mental connections to my ex.

This explains why I started to pick up my ex's habits: a result of soul ties. Why was my past relationship weakening my ties with God? My ex still had a hold over my emotions whenever his name was brought up or I saw a picture of him. I knew that I separated emotionally when I was able to delete the emails, texts, and photos of him without feeling any pull for me to keep them...*just in case.*

I was trying to find reasons why Justin wasn't good for me or why we shouldn't be together. One of which was that Justin said that he didn't want to travel. Because I loved to travel the world, I couldn't imagine us together long-term.

I met with my mentor and pastor and told her how I was feeling. She said, "Honey, it's too late for that. You have to love like you've never been hurt before, as if this is your first relationship. Justin never hurt you, so why are you punishing him for something he never did?"

This made me realize that I needed to deal with my own crap. In order to be who we need to be for each other, we have to heal individually. We have to accept the fact that each of us potentially has toxic behaviors and mindsets that we bring to the relationship and that it's our individual responsibility to work through them. We have to be protective of each other's hearts. I don't think I realized how monumental a responsibility this was, but vulnerability provided a sense of authenticity in which we could hold each other accountable.

SELF-SABATOGE

JUSTIN

I T CAN BE the battle of one's life to simply feel worthy. Those that feel unworthy are often unaware of it, we unintentionally punish the people who appreciate and believe in us most. We slide into the comfort of old destructive habits and stymie any chance to grow.

The first few months of my relationship with Alexis were by far the hardest. Most married couples I know usually say that the first few years of marriage are the hardest, and that's how it felt. We were lovers that enjoyed spending time with one another, but we knew that our insecurities were getting in the way of our potential as a couple. As an adult, I needed to figure out what I wanted my relationship to look like. I wanted a relationship that was suitable for us. But how could I create a foundation for something I had never seen?

I was sensitive about several things. It was scary being with someone that had just gotten out of an abusive eight-year relationship, when I had no relationship experience at all. I always worried that I was just a rebound. Alexis would always enjoy the small things I did. The fact that I refused to call her "the B-word" or even play music where the word is used was something, she always loved about me. Honestly, that was the least I could do. I worried that being a gentleman and simply respecting my partner would lose its charm. She was used to being aggressively humiliated by her partner. After she had been with me for years, enjoying love and affection routinely, would she take it for granted? Being polite to Alexis was like giving a starving kid a cracker. But once she was accustomed to decency, would I grow bored? Did I have more to offer than that?

Alexis was so accomplished and ahead of her class. When we first started our relationship, I was still a freshman. Why didn't she choose the star athlete who had a more secure future ahead of him? Why wasn't she dating a soon to be doctor or someone seeking a PhD? I had nothing to offer other than being a nice guy. I barely had a savings account, and I didn't have the money I was spending on our dates. It got to a point where I sat down with Alexis and told her the truth.

"Look, I don't really have the money to cover all of our dates or even go out much. I'm pretty broke. I can support you mentally and emotionally, but financially I have nothing to offer right now."

But Alexis never had any financial expectations of me. She completely understood and was perfectly happy to go for walks, participate in free activities on campus, and share meals when we did go out to eat—something we still do today. But I was still plagued by the worry that I wasn't enough. What if I were simply filling a void for her? When we saw her friends, did they assume I was a rebound? My thoughts were, at times, paranoid. Sometimes the degree of trauma she had experienced felt like my burden too, and that there was no way I could support such a heavy load. If we had a fight or if things felt at all shaky, I would quickly remove photos of us together from social media, as if I were getting ahead of some inevitable breakup. It may have been immature, but it was my way of trying to spread a safety net. Between my persistent sense of inadequacy and the mounting pressure of schoolwork, I started to panic.

I had grown up with constant instability and it was impossible to imagine that this relationship would somehow be different. As a child, I'd had no power to stabilize or control my living situation and would sense a power imbalance between whomever was my guardian and me. They could pull the rug out from under me any given moment. And so with Alexis, I felt like I had to prepare for her to leave me. I had done the same whenever I entered a new foster home, preventing myself from becoming attached or emotionally invested in my foster family, which continuously resulted in them giving up on me and not wanting me to live there anymore. I felt, though, that it would be better to assume defeat from the start rather than experience the pain of being let down.

Also, I was extremely unsure of what my family's long-term influence on me would be. *What if I became my dad and physically abused my partner? What if I placed the pain of not having parents onto my partner?* There were so many questions that I needed to answer before committing to Alexis. I was certain I needed to end the relationship.

IMAGO

ALEXIS

MANY PEOPLE CHOOSE romantic partners with traits similar to those of a parent who denied the love they wanted and needed as children, choosing a partner similar to the one who raised us. Certainly, I have made that mistake in my own life. This tendency is called "imago" (pronounced like embargo) and it's built into our subconscious and contains all the positive and negative qualities of the caregiver(s) who raised us. This becomes our north star when we begin to look for a romantic partner.

In the Bible, it says "He who finds a wife," not a girlfriend. I had to walk in that mindset of being a wife with expectations. I'm not meant to date casually or be a serial girlfriend. I've always needed a goal and I have always known that I am a marriage sort of person, so I had to be very conscious of what partner I chose. That partner could very well become my husband, the person with whom I would spend the most time, seek advice from, make decisions with, and turn to for emotional support. And if I had children with him, those children would learn his habits and follow his example as well as mine.

After a few months of talking, Justin and I both felt it, though we hadn't yet said the words. We may have mouthed "I love you" over FaceTime or said corny things like, "I really wish I could say these three words to you right now." We told each other that we would wait to kiss until we started dating and hold off on sex because we didn't want to allow lust to cloud our judgment. I've seen too many people start having sex before they even start dating, even having kids with each other before being friends first, often ending up separated and with broken families.

I've seen friends and other women choose men based on the physical traits they might pass down—good looks, nice hair, height. But in my community, growing up, people never asked, "Does this person have integrity? Is he a good person? Would you want more people like him in the world?" **Without thoughtful parents to guide them, they turned to superficial images, other media, and celebrities whose Instagram accounts were more concerned with matching shoes and outfits than finding worthy soulmates with matching values.**

Kim suggested that I make a T-chart of what I need and want from a partner. Here's what I needed in a partner: kindness, compassion, vulnerability, and emotional availability. I also needed someone who had the capacity for forgiveness, someone who could provide stimulating conversation. Someone with whom I could build a legacy. Someone who could be both emotionally and intellectually my equal and who would encourage my growth. As for the wants: I desired someone tall and handsome who didn't smoke or drink. I knew that it was unfair to expect my partner to fulfill all of my needs—that's where my relationship with God comes in.

All the guys that I'd dated before Justin had things in common—they all had absent fathers, no ability to lead by example, and most importantly, they inspired in me a need to *fix* them. I tried to fix all of them. It's not my job to heal broken men or to parent them. Justin had similar heartbreaking experiences, but he was on a journey toward fixing himself. I deeply admired his self-awareness.

I never experienced or witnessed trust as a child. Justin was taken aback one day when I asked him if he'd get a paternity test if I got pregnant. "Why would I do that if I trust and love you?" he replied. Believe it or not, no other boy I'd dated had replied that way. All had said they would never trust that a child was theirs without a test.

So many men I've dated have assumed that buying me a meal or a movie ticket entitled them to my body. I've been called a tease, a bitch, ugly, and a "waste of time" when men realized this. But I am not obligated to offer my body to any man, my husband included. Justin fundamentally agrees with this. It's hardly a radical idea, but it's amazing how many men struggle with the concept of female self-determination.

My friend jokes that Justin and I "Are the same person." We always joke and say, "Give me, *me* back" because of how perfectly aligned we are. I found a partner when I wasn't looking. If I was looking, then I would have probably jumped into another relationship out of need instead of want.

To most people, I would say: take time to find yourself without a partner because I know what it's like to become obsessed and attached to the first man that gives you attention. Dating and learning what you like and you don't like is important. I've seen friends go through healthy breakups and remain with their ex-partner. Mostly, I've seen large, dramatic fall outs when people don't want to be with each other anymore.

Now, I'm blessed with a partner that has enough courage and strength where we both can heal and grow together. Since the beginning, we've set clear expectations that we are dating for an intentional purpose. One month with Justin replaced all eight years with my ex.

Our partners can't fix us, just as we cannot fix them. We can't fully love someone without loving ourselves first. I wanted a partner that would challenge me to reach my goals and allow me to support him as he supported me. I needed someone who shared my value system, because that is the foundation and scaffolding of every marriage. I was reminded by my good friend, Tere, **the importance of being equally yoked, of having similar morals and values. If not, we would spend the rest of our lives compromising them.** Our partners are a reflection of ourselves, meaning that if I'm broken, with low self-esteem and hurting, then that's probably what I'll attract.

We all crave consistency in our lives. When you don't have that consistency as a child in the form of your parents showing up, giving unconditional support, establishing positive daily habits, or exemplifying follow-through, then we won't know how to have consistency in our intimate relationships or professional lives. Once we became more comfortable with who we were individually, I learned to love the consistency of Justin's words and actions. It's different being with a man who does not run to other women when he feels that I fall short but instead, looks to God for guidance.

He is concerned when I feel stressed and reminds me to seek answers with God. He prays for me and with every day. When I'm truly overwhelmed and feel myself breaking down, I'll crawl into his lap and cry on his shoulder.

He gives me affection freely. His hugs and kisses come with no conditions. I call his hugs the "Justin Hugs," as if they were trademarked. He's the only person who can make me feel so loved, calm, and welcome with a single kiss on my forehead. **His arms are, for me, the safest place in the world.**

Even when I feel like a hot mess, he thinks I am beautiful and tells me so. He even blows me kisses in public, letting me know that his love for me is not a secret. This is something new for me. When I tell him that I'm not used to that, he says, "You deserve it!" We both are huge corn balls together, wearing onesies to a movie viewing on campus or matching "I Love my boyfriend/girlfriend" hoodies. Justin even sang "My Girl" by the Temptations on karaoke to me in Germany. He is the most selfless, patient, kind, loving human being that I've ever met. **If I had settled, I would have continued to block my blessings of meeting someone like him.**

I wanted to date someone that I could honor and respect. If not, then it's easier to disrespect them, hurt them, and be left unfulfilled and unhappy. From observing him around his nephews and my siblings, I know that he'll be a good father and a great example for our future children. I'd love for my kids to pick up his habits and behaviors. I wish we had a million Justins in the world. It's crazy that I used to call Kim crying late at night because of something that happened; now I've called her crying several times to report on how wonderful Justin is. She often has me pause to reflect on that fact.

To better understand one another's form of affection, we took the Love Languages quiz. I sent him my results and told him to send me his. I asked why he sent mine back to me. He didn't, we had the EXACT same results.

I think a reason why we work well together is that we both have similar backgrounds and yearn for love, acceptance, healing, and prosperity. We understand each other and our needs in that regard. It's almost like loving ourselves.

Right after we started dating, Justin wanted to meet Kim and Brian so that they could get to know him and, in his mind, "*do it the right way.*" While at dinner, Brian said to Justin, "I don't care about *you*, I care about Alexis and if she gets hurt." I knew he was trying to scare Justin a bit, to make sure that he was really intending to stay, but I remember thinking *I wish I'd had a dad like this my whole life. One who thinks there is almost no one good enough for his child, who makes my happiness and security his primary concerns.*

Now, Brian jokes that if we ever break up, he's keeping Justin! Even animals and babies love him. They always want to be around him, and often feel so comfortable with him that they fall asleep right on top of him. I know exactly how they feel.

Aunt Bev would say to me, "Alexis, I hope one day you'll have your own Uncle Giles." After she met Justin, I said, "I think I found my Uncle Giles."

IMAGO

"Likewise, every good tree bears good fruit,
but a bad tree bears bad fruit. A good tree cannot bear
bad fruit, and a bad tree cannot bear good fruit"
(Matthew 7:17-18 NIV).

JUSTIN

N A RELATIONSHIP with someone who's gone through extremely traumatic experiences, I needed to support her individual growth. Not for the relationship, but for her betterment as a woman of God. I believe my selfish ideas of who she should be in our relationship began to hurt the relationship. When she needed space to deal with her individual battles, I'd support her from a distance. If she needed me to just listen and acknowledge her, I would do so. We became aware of the things we needed to take to God and what we needed from our partner. Many people put Godly expectations on their partner and assume that they can fulfill them. Once our roles in the relationship became clear, we gelled together perfectly.

When choosing a partner and developing a relationship, I always want to be emotionally available for my partner. Maybe it was because I left my parents' home at nine years old that their influence over me wasn't as strong. My other siblings lived with them for the majority of their adolescence, learning that being emotionally closed off was normal, acceptable, and almost needed to survive the hardships they endured.

I knew if we disconnected emotionally, then our relationship would be headed for a disaster. Combined with being emotionally available, I wanted to ensure that we were equally yoked in our relationship. I wanted my relationship to be a partnership where we could hold each other accountable, support one another through our struggles, and work to serve each other. I wanted a partner who would be just as vulnerable as I was, and as well-intentioned.

My idea of leadership in a marriage consisted of protecting my wife from stress and loneliness as well as being open to her. **Men commonly accept the role of a leader without developing the necessary qualities.** One definition of "leader" is as a *servant* of his people. Leadership, for me, is not about establishing dominance over my partner. Within the context of marriage, leadership means serving my partner in a manner she sees fit.

Your parental figures can either save you from a life of difficulties or provoke a reckoning with the pain and trauma they've caused in your life. Parents are the tree of the family. **When choosing your partner, you are deciding what type of fruit you would like to produce.** Are you going to produce good fruit that your children can consume for a lifetime or toxic fruit from which your children will be poisoned? If that trauma is unaddressed, the poison can seep down into many generations. The fruit in this analogy represents culture, identity, and ideology. Some parents create a family culture in which kids thrive while others are unable or unwilling to do so, and many children suffer greatly as a result.

I'd noticed that people who have seen lots of divorce within their family often view it as a viable option when marriages hit rocky times. They have internalized the idea that marriage is temporary or conditional. I knew when I chose a partner that I wanted to avoid those who had absorbed that lesson.

Mr. Melvin told me about a woman he dated in his younger days and almost married before Mrs. Cora. He told me that one of the things that made him weary was the fact that his potential partner had parents who slept in separate beds. This prompted him to ask more questions about their relationship. His girlfriend at the time told him that it was normal for them to sleep separately but Mr. Melvin noticed that they lived almost completely separate lives. They were basically divorced but decided to live together in the same house. Being emotionally closed off to their partner was considered normal in their household.

The phrase *"play your role"* is typically used in a derogatory manner that demeans women and elevates men. Society uses this term as a way to force women into stereotypical roles. We all have a role and responsibilities in a relationship. The problem being that many people are forced to play a role that they don't exactly fit. In my relationship with Alexis, neither one of us knew our role until we discovered who we were individually and what we brought to the table. We had to make ourselves aware of our weaknesses and strengths and ways in which our partner could compliment.

Because one's partner is a reflection of oneself, I made sure to show Alexis the utmost respect. "Love is patient, love is kind…It holds no record of wrong and sees the best in one another." Along with this, Eve was described as being Adam's companion. A companion is defined as "One of a pair of things intended to complement or match each other." I didn't need another human to improve me but someone with God-given ability to build, with whom I could collaborate. I wanted someone who had the characteristics I wanted to see in my children—someone that was a leader, genuine, honest, and had the best intentions for everyone around them.

It's amazing how we meet the right person at the perfect time, even if we're not looking for them. My pastor described it as "God filling our partner with gifts that we need in our life, at the exact moment we need it."

Alexis was more than I ever could have asked for. She is my best friend. She is my sweetheart. She is my inspiration.

One thing that particularly touches me about Alexis is her gentleness with animals, especially her pet cats. I have memories of my family and me abusing our pets in scary and violent ways, memories so dark that it is hard, even now, for me to access the emotions they stir. Being around Alexis while she nurtures her animals has brought out a tender, gentle side of me I never would have realized was there, especially in the brutal days of my childhood.

Alexis is adamant about passing down every single piece of knowledge and information she feels could help the next generation. I hadn't felt as passionate about serving others until I met Alexis. She pushed me to advocate for those who have experienced bullying, neglect, and other forms of abuse that I had endured in the past. I was timid and fearful to share my life with the world. As though I were back in my high school days, I didn't believe anyone would care about what I had gone through. No one in my family bothered to pay attention to my struggles, so why would anyone else?

It wasn't until Alexis and I went to foster care advocacy panels and I watched her interaction with other youth that I began to see how important it was to share. She openly discussed the abuse she experienced with her father, as if doing so restored her power. Most women I know who have experienced sexual trauma would not have the strength to share their deepest moments of pain. Alexis seemed to do so with ease. She talked about resilience and regaining autonomy.

"Never again would I allow my voice to go unheard!" Alexis's voice was indeed heard; it echoed through the audience majestically. She gave everyone chills, such was her authority. Cheers rose from the excited crowd. Exhilarated by her ability to inspire, I sat in the front row gazing up. I knew the time had come to join my partner in advocacy, specifically for young Black men suffering through unfortunate circumstances.

The opportunity presented itself when I was a sophomore in college. I was inspired by the work of a professor in my communications class, Dr. Perry. An energetic lecturer who accepted no "B.S.", Dr. Perry had an ability to engage every student in a crowded lecture hall. After class, he stayed behind to talk with each and every student. This alone showed his investment into our future. I decided to attend his office hours to discuss my semester goals and create a lasting relationship. I told him some of my personal history, something Alexis had advised me to do. Curious about my involvement in the Seita Scholars program, Dr. Perry invited me to speak to a few students from the local elementary school. He introduced me to a child named Tevin who was experiencing the child welfare system. Tevin was a nine-year-old kid with worn down clothes and nappy hair, dry as the desert. I felt as if I were looking at my nine-year-old self when *I* entered the system.

This was intended to be a one-time visit to help with schoolwork and introduce myself, but Tevin and I formed a friendship and I ended up visiting him every week. The opportunity to nurture the potential this child possessed made me want to contribute more. I wanted to be the mentor I had needed as a child in foster care. A sense of excitement brewed in me every time I came to visit. I began to learn about his time in care, that he'd been through four placements before his tenth birthday. I would eventually come to his school play, as the only person there to support him. It was heartbreaking to witness his foster family abandon him for such a crucial milestone, and I felt compelled to make sure Tevin beat the odds and succeeded.

Every time I visited, I would discover that the teacher had placed Tevin in the back of the class on a computer because he had refused to do his schoolwork. I'd place my hand on his shoulder as we walked down the hallway, asking about his troubles at school. I knew he was internalizing his home troubles like I was once had but he refused to talk about it in much detail.

Before leaving and driving back to campus, the teacher chased me down, stopping the exit door before it closed.

"Mr. Black! Mr. Black! Do you have a second?" He said, nearly out of breath.

"I wanted to let you know we appreciate you mentoring Tevin. However, in our classroom, 75% of the kids are without a father at home and could use a male figure to support them." He looked terribly sad.

"This may be a lot to ask, but would you mind mentoring a few of the other boys?" I was shocked by the number of fatherless homes and overwhelmed with the workload of such a crucial task. Uncertain if I had the time to commit, I nonetheless accepted.

I was given the task of mentoring more than five children. My grades began to suffer and I was exhausted. Dreading the decision, I needed to make, I told Tevin and the other students that I could only visit once more before final exams. I wouldn't see any of them during the summer as I began my internship. I arrived at the elementary school with a heavy heart, depressed that this would be our last time together until September. I bought a few books for Tevin to read during the summer, hoping he would remember the bond we had developed. I returned to my car disheartened, sitting in silence and staring out of the window.

Once September came around, I was ecstatic to visit Tevin and hear about how his summer had gone until Tevin's teacher informed me that he had moved to another foster home and transferred schools. I was shattered. Tevin had been on a path of hope and self-discovery and the foster system derailed him once more.

Alexis assured me that Tevin would find his place in the world and eventually find happiness like we did. As I began to mentor foster care youth and other Black boys, I realized that the coping strategies and techniques that I used to help them build character were lessons I'd learned from Alexis.

A leader of her own but also my love, it would be the little things that would make our relationship flourish, and it will be those same things that keep our relationship strong. During a long car ride, it's easy for couples to become consumed with social media, staring at their phones for hours. But Alexis and I have our deepest, most satisfying conversations on the road. Whether we're discussing politics or how we want to raise our children, we simply enjoy one another's company.

There are times when I still feel that I don't deserve her, which makes me cherish our bond even more. I would love to have children who are like Alexis, and being around her makes me want to be more like her, too. But before we could consider marriage, our relationship had to survive some very challenging times and circumstances. There is one thing you can count on in life: there will always be times that test you.

SACRIFICE & SUBMISSION

"Whoever wants to be a leader among
you must be your servant"
(Matthew 20:26).

"Sacrifice" and "submission" are highly loaded words in our culture because they are often used in derogatory and elicit ways. A healthy partnership is based on sacrifice and compromise. We would like to redefine these words that we often hear in church and better explain how we can apply them as a mirror of our collaboration as romantic and loving partners.

ALEXIS

WHEN SHAWN AND other men in my life told me that I needed to be submissive, they meant that I should allow them to abuse their physical and emotional power over me—that I should accept their authority unquestioningly because of their gender. The dynamic was always about asserting dominance. I've been told that if I loved a man, I needed to bow down and kiss his feet to demonstrate this submission.

Because of this, it is even more difficult for me to be submissive to a man, even if he's deserving of it. Whether I like it or not, part of marriage is being submissive. **That, however, does not mean compromising your morals and values, nor does it mean mindlessly following or obeying someone.** Oftentimes, this turns into false narratives about what being submissive means and men twist it into a source of power and control over their partners. Too many men don't know how to lead by example with trustworthy, consistent character and aren't worthy of having a partner. With so many men abusing this power, it's causing more damage in marriages and families.

Submission doesn't mean bowing down to your partner but more of being on one accord. We can break down the term submission even further. According to Merriam Webster, *Sub* means "underneath" while the term *mission* is defined as "a self-imposed objective or purpose." Combining the two simply means that you and your partner are looking to satisfy the same goals and accomplishments as defined by God, exemplified when a couple operates as a unit, forming a family to serve the betterment of others.

This isn't something talked about in our culture today. Our culture promotes and encourages selfishness and greed with things like "Relationships should be 50/50" or "You do your part and I'll do mine," which means that acceptance, love and affection are based upon performance or merit (i.e., if you deserve it). Relationships are more "100/100" where both parties put full effort into making the relationship prosper.

I've had to learn to acknowledge the fact that I can be very controlling and hard-headed. I wouldn't change this about myself—it has benefited me academically and professionally. I go after what I want, and I don't take no for an answer. But this same quality often leads to conflict between Justin and me. I have had to learn to give up some control and to trust the man that I chose to lead me and someday, our children. If not, then it will minimize Justin as both a man and as my partner. Because of this, it is incredibly important for me to be with a man that I trust.

I am constantly learning how to sacrifice by witnessing Justin's love for other people and how he carries himself. Our first time in church together, he tithed over $300. I thought he was crazy and tried to talk him out of it because I couldn't understand why he would give so much when I knew we didn't have much more in our bank account. This was another way that he showed me how *he* is submissive and sacrificial to God. He reminded me that "Whoever sows sparingly will also reap sparingly, and whoever sows generously will also reap generously" (2 Corinthians 9:6-7).

We share our fears, desires, and passions with each other. A fear of mine is that, because I have polycystic ovarian syndrome, I won't be able to have kids—especially knowing how wonderful Justin is with kids and how much he wants to have his own. I'm scared that I can't give my husband what he needs as his partner and wife. This is just one of the many fears and insecurities we share because **we take comfort in being vulnerable together.** There is no plan B anymore, no escape plan.

When I was a kid, I was pushed down the stairs by a babysitter's kid, fracturing my sacrum. I didn't go to see a doctor even though it was black and blue for months. I was told that I had a bruised tailbone and I'd be fine. This resulted in a lot of back pain that has caused me to go to the hospital several times. In Flint, I was subscribed to pain medication that I refused to take because I knew that it would only mask the real problem and since addiction ran in my family, I needed to be careful. It wasn't until I moved to Kalamazoo and went to the hospital that I was finally referred to a spinal doctor. I've received spinal injections, went to physical therapy, and visited the chiropractor several times a week for seven years now. On several study abroad programs, I've had to go to the hospital because of back pain.

Sometimes, I wake up nearly paralyzed in pain and can't move. There have been a few times that Justin has had to help me get out of bed, help me get undressed, get in and out of the shower, and dress me again while crying uncontrollably because of the pain. We joke that I'm his "ol' lady."

When Justin got his very first car in 2018, mine happened to stop working the following week. Justin, being who he is, immediately said the car was "ours" now and I could drive it whenever I needed it. It quickly became more of my car than his.

When Justin was getting his temporary teeth, I was there every step of the way to make sure Justin's smile was perfect. The dentist looked to me for guidance and sometimes forgot to ask Justin if he liked how they looked. Justin would laugh and say that he trusted my judgment more than he trusted his own. The dentist taught me how to glue and screw in his teeth, just in case we needed to do so while we were abroad. On our second day in Senegal, Justin's teeth broke off after eating a baguette.

Justin's teeth, to me, have come to represent much about who he is. Justin was so young and already in a vulnerable place when he was brutally attacked and lost his teeth. His family believed revenge—violence—was the answer. But even at 13, at such a tender age and in such an already precarious circumstance mentally, physically, and emotionally, while undergoing the torment of being ostracized, Justin's spirit did not darken. I am still in awe that he did not become bitter, nor did he follow a path of vengeance. Instead, he bloomed into the most loving, gentle, and welcoming person I've ever met, whose strength lies not in displays of force, but in quiet displays of courage.

SACRIFICE & SUBMISSION

JUSTIN

THE CHRISTIAN COMMUNITY often discusses how women must submit to their partners but, as a society, we often overlook a man's responsibility in a marriage.

The Bible tells us to sacrifice for our wives as Jesus did for the church. That's a tall order. Jesus sacrificed his life. If He could do that, certainly I could give up privileges to focus on myself and improve Alexis and me for the sake of our mutual happiness. **God trusted me to take care of His daughter, and I needed to make myself into the kind of man capable of deserving that trust.**

When it came to discussing relationships with family, my brother Andre told me about his relationship with the mother of his children or his "baby mama" as he calls her. The power dynamic was a serious issue. He gave me advice on how to deal with women and how they needed to show men respect saying,

"She don't really love you until she kiss yo feet. I had my bitch kiss my feet. That's how a man is supposed to be treated. Do Alexis kiss yo feet?"

"No." I said, completely disturbed by his remarks.

"Then that ain't real love bro. She don't really love you until she kissing yo feet."

I was disgusted by his advice. It reminded me of my dad. It seemed manipulative and, by belittling his partner showed the insecurity of men in our family.

I was fifteen years old when I created my Instagram account. I followed every attractive woman I saw. Half-naked women flooded my feed. I became consumed with the images. The photos started to shape my understanding of beauty and sexuality. But the images were distortions, not just of reality but of beauty itself. Eventually, I entered relationships that were based entirely on sex. Apps like Instagram and Snapchat made sex seem like something inherently cheap and casual, a depressing circumstance for both parties involved. At only 12, I had become addicted to masturbation. These encounters, and looking at the Instagram images, were unfulfilling to say the least. Addictions always are. Most addicted people are trying to fill a void with a toxic substance or activity. I had confused my desire for sex with my need for love.

At some point, I realized I was trying to fulfill an emotional need with pornographic images, and with sex itself. I suffered alone and in silence. As Alexis and I deepened our relationship, I knew that I needed to cut ties with many of my Instagram followers.

When Alexis took another semester-long internship in Washington D.C., I seized the opportunity to deal with my demons. Isolating myself had always helped me find my way through spiritual challenges and, after these periods, I could feel my mental health improve. When Alexis left town, I took my problem to God. I began to sort out how pornography had sunk such deep hooks into me. I had first seen it when I was five, as though it had been downloaded into my brain at a very vulnerable and formative time of life. Perhaps I had conflated affection and sex from the moment I'd been unfairly exposed to these videos. Realizing this, I was able to understand the addiction's connection to my early loneliness and neglect, and forgive myself for it. It was at last time to **fight a battle I had postponed for nearly two decades.**

My sacrifice came when I decided to separate myself from all my friends and other social activities in order to focus solely on my healing. The majority of the semester consisted of going to class, bible study, and returning home. Intentional about every thought that came to my head, I began to develop an inner peace and comfort that I had never felt before. Though I made daily progress, I lay down at night knowing I was a click away from backsliding and negating all my growth. Calling Alexis at night to hold me accountable helped me through the temptations associated with being alone at night.

Similar to the emotional connection to my parents, it was once again time to cut an emotional tie that had been preventing me from moving forward. God confirms His truth to us through His word. "If you remain in me and my word remains in you, ask whatever you wish, and it will be done for you." I had asked God to help me strive in a career, to help me improve my relationship with Alexis, to establish boundaries with my biological family. But I had avoided asking God to help me end my relationship with lust. *What was I so afraid of?* I was consumed with guilt every time porn led me to have unrealistic expectations of Alexis even though ironically, my intimacy with Alexis was infinitely more fulfilling than any other emotional or sexual encounter I had had before her.

I deleted my Snapchat and unfollowed the women who posted provocative images. In general, I restricted my time on social media in order to focus on my schoolwork and my intellectual and spiritual life. In the end, the "sacrifice" of social media and porn, specifically, was not much of a sacrifice at all. It was like giving up empty calories and replacing them with nutritious food. But at the time, I called it my "Jesus in the desert moment." He was isolated and fasting, preparing for a fascinating journey. I think most people need these periods of solitude, divorced from the worldly expectations that are placed upon us daily. When I emerged from this time, I had strengthened my ability to reflect on whether the thoughts in my mind were useful and good or destructive and damaging.

I see a relationship as two individual journeys happening side by side, in which both parties share love and happiness along with grief and sorrow. I had been deeply ashamed of my addiction to pornographic images and this shame created a barrier to intimacy. Sharing my struggle made me vulnerable to Alexis, and when she supported me through it, we forged an even closer bond.

The masculine culture I and many other young men were born into has measured manhood according to our sexual prowess and the number of women we have slept with. **I had to unlearn the idea that sex represents manhood.** Some families see young boys having sex as an entry way into manhood, encouraging them to have sex even before their teenage years. Women having multiple sex partners is frowned upon but men doing the same is praiseworthy. Being with Alexis helped me realize that both scenarios may stem from trauma.

In relationships, sacrifice means to become selfless in mind and heart. It requires us to pay attention to the needs of our partner and put forth the effort of requiring us to support them. This process taught me self-control. As humans we are self-seeking in nature; looking to be dominant in every aspect of life. Men often want to seek empowerment by destroying and controlling others. I wanted to display a healthy idea of manhood for myself, one that entails building others up and validating their strengths. This example began in my relationship with Alexis. Sacrifice does not mean that we are "above" our partner, but rather in a relationship where both parties are equally validated and important. I feel that sacrifice creates an opportunity for men to be honest with themselves and their partner, no longer internalizing their trauma and displaying it in a destructive way.

I had to sacrifice my ego and my outward confidence to accept that I had issues that needed to be dealt with. The reason that so many men suffer in silence with sex addiction, drug abuse, and mental health issues is because society tells us that we need to "man up and deal with it," forcing us to see these problems as weaknesses that must be hidden. **I decided to**

use my acceptance and recognition of mental illness and addiction as a source of power that no one could hold against me while I overcome the obstacles that were set before me. I am a proud overcomer that will use my stories as an example of how other men can do the same.

TALK IT OUT

ALEXIS

E VERY ARGUMENT I had growing up consisted of screaming, yelling, hitting, and saying the meanest things that could possibly be said. To say my biological dad had an anger problem is an understatement. If he didn't take his anger out on me during his drunken rampages, he would take it out on our poor dog, Jake. He would tape together two foot-long pieces of wood and write "Butt Buster" on it, beating Jake until his blood splattered onto the bathroom tub, dripping slowly onto the floor. Jake would urinate and defecate as the hard wood slammed against his body, begging with his eyes for me to rescue him, squealing for my help. Jake became my father's punching bag, he kicked him whenever he got upset.

On days that I forgot to take Jake for a walk, he urinated on the living room carpet. My dad, filled with anger, would search for Butt Buster. I cried, screaming for him not to do it, feeling the shame of being the cause of Jake's misery. After my dad finished with Jake, I was told to clean the blood and feces that had scattered across the bathroom wall. I was mentally and emotionally detached from the abuse that I personally endured, but hearing Jake's innocent cries for help rocked me internally, causing me terrible distress.

I knew very well that this was part of the fun for my dad—demonstrating how helpless I truly was in his house, hurting me where I could not shut out the pain. Later, after much therapy, this terrible experience galvanized my determination to advocate for others. When I was a little girl, I could not help Jake but now, a grown woman, I can and will help others to safety.

Ever since I was in National Honors Society in high school, I've been committed to serving my community, both local and global, in any capacity that I can. Our environments—our families, schools, neighborhoods, and communities—will not change unless we invest in them. I never want others to endure what I have and I am going to continue paving the way for others in any way that I can. I am not sure if there is anything more personally healing than receiving a text from a person I have mentored, sharing their subsequent successes. I received this one not too long ago from a fellow foster youth:

> I won the presidential leadership award 😊

> I-

> Like you don't understand how much you set this table for me and how you pushed me even when I didn't believe I could even make it in this program

> Thank you Alexis, I know I don't say it enough but truly, your leadership and mentor ship continue to show me what is possible not only for me but for all foster kids and those who barely made it here

> OMGG!!!!!!!! IM SO PROUD OF YOU!!!!!!!!

When it came to filling in the gaps of my past, I searched for answers about who my biological father was and if he had suffered abuse in his life. I did this to fully understand how deep the trauma went in our family. I gathered the courage to contact his ex-wife, Lynn through Facebook to better understand who he was. She confirmed that my dad did cocaine regularly, even in the church on their wedding day. He was also an alcoholic. He trashed her home and ripped the phone from her hands when she tried to call the police. After she filed for divorce, he would follow her, sitting outside her job, showing up at her home and driving behind her to see where she was going, even after she had a restraining order and the police were called. All this was just two years before I was born.

Just after I was born, Lynn told me she had met my mother. My mom came into her place of work to find out where my dad was. She remembered that my mom had said, "I just want him to acknowledge that this is his daughter and help me support her." With that she had replied, "I doubt it because he can never take responsibility." This was apparent in the ugly custody battle. When I told her that my mom committed suicide, Lynn said, "Maybe she finally wanted him to be responsible."

Living with my dad every month when the phone bill came, I was terrified. He would go through my call record line by line to see if I was on the phone after my curfew. I would come up with anything to distract him such as acting like I got something in my eye, dropping a dish, or crying. If he saw that I had indeed made a call post-curfew, he would slap me across the face.

I was seven when I "slipped up" and said something about how my dad was hitting me to Aunt Bev and Uncle Giles and when we went outside to leave, he threw me down on the ground and started kicking me before throwing his motorcycle helmet at me to put on. The police were called by the neighbor, but nothing happened. I'm sure he told them that I slipped or something. At least once a month, I would hear him on the phone trying to manipulate my family into giving him money for the light bill or food to "support" me.

It's not surprising that at school I was getting into fights. I slapped a guy's glasses off his face and jumped over a table to pounce on someone in middle school. Thankfully, I had teachers and counselors pull me into their offices so that they didn't have to report me to the principal. Outside of that, I had a few out-of-school suspensions and in-school suspensions.

People express sympathy when they learn how my biological mom died but, unfortunately, I don't have any good memories of her. I do remember her getting into a few physical fights with neighbors on our lawn or theirs. She would ride a lawnmower down the street to fight, with us sitting on the back of it. When we reached her enemy of the day, she would immediately start throwing punches while Zach and I cheered her on to pull hair and aim for the face. All during the middle of the day, Zach and I would join in and fight their kids in the process.

Another memory of my mom is when she threw plates at our feet when Zach and I wouldn't stop arguing. Other memories included her getting upset with me and throwing all of my ceramic China in a trash bag before tossing it outside on the sidewalk. I ran outside, desperately trying to catch it before it hit the ground, but I was too late, and everything was smashed to pieces.

About two months into our relationship, Justin and I had our first big argument. Almost naturally, I raised my voice and yelled at him as I was used to doing. Only concerned with expressing my own feelings I said whatever came to mind.

Without saying anything, Justin walked out of my apartment. I was left confused and short of words.

I didn't know what to do. He didn't engage, yell back, or call me names. I just stood there staring at the waves in the carpet before running to my bed, terrified that meant that we were broken up. I cried for thirty minutes until he walked back into my room.

I will never forget what he said.

"I would never speak to you that way because I respect you. I grew up with everyone yelling and hitting each other and I promised myself that I would never do that, so I expect you not to do that, either. If that's not something you can do, then we shouldn't be together." I admired his willingness to set boundaries and expectations for our relationship

Ninety percent of communication is through body language. In the beginning of our relationship, we were pretty rocky when it came to handling disagreements. I'm the person that wants to figure everything out right at the moment of conflict. I needed him to stop being mad at me right away so we could move on. The idea of lingering bad feelings makes me feel powerless and out of control. But Justin is the type to think carefully about how he feels and what he wants to say before he says it, which takes a lot longer than what I'm comfortable with.

Holidays can be difficult for a lot of people, especially foster youth. Holidays always seemed to be filled with pain and loneliness. This didn't stop when I was in a relationship or when I moved out on my own—it actually got worse. It turned into a living hell with my ex—with my begging for him to be with me and spend time with me on holidays so I wouldn't have to be alone. Justin's reticence about joining my family at Christmas reminded me—whether that was fair or not—of those wrenching times and made me resent his reluctance even more.

When Justin and I started dating, the holidays were great. Maybe it was because it was a brand-new relationship and he was excited to meet Kim, Brian, and my siblings and for us to spend extra time together. Then, after about a year or two, something changed. Holidays were yet again a time of loneliness and arguments. It became a pattern, predictable. We didn't argue much in general until it came to holidays.

I wasn't sure if it was something my family was doing; I assumed they did all they could to make him feel loved and welcomed. I couldn't figure out why he would put up such a fight every time there was a family gathering. My friends often tell me that I can be too blunt, which makes me sound harsh and lack compassion. I wanted to try to understand his experiences and why they were so difficult so I could help him minimize his struggles while still getting to spend time with my family, something which had become increasingly important to me over the years.

I realized that it may not have been my family causing sadness and pain for Justin but rather that our closeness reminded him of what his family lacked. He longed for affection from his family. Holidays opened his oldest wounds. It didn't make it any easier that I refused to go visit his family. I escaped from that kind of life and I don't ever want to go back, not even for a visit. Spending time with Justin's family is like entering a war zone. I leave physically and emotionally exhausted.

I've had people tell me that when you marry, you marry your partner's family, too. Thankfully, when we marry, we create a new family, and new habits, traditions, and joyful memories. But this doesn't mean that it eliminates or alleviates family pressures.

Our last Thanksgiving and Christmas as an engaged couple in 2019 were the most difficult in our relationship. Over the break, Justin was doing what he usually did when we were together as a family: he kept to himself, usually on his computer or reading in a corner. I felt worn out from worrying and constantly checking on him.

I decided that I didn't want him to come for Christmas. It was a lose-lose decision. Seeing him unhappy made me unhappy, and not having him there hurt me as well. So, when it was time to start planning for Christmas, I knew an argument was coming. "Do I have to come? Does it have to be for a whole week?" These were the questions I was preparing to hear. As a way of getting ahead of it this time, I told him that I didn't think he should come, but that he needed to decide what was best for him not just that year but for all the years to come. I then told him I wanted him there the coming years, and that I expected him to figure out a way to be there happily. After all, Justin is my family just as much as my adoptive family is. I need them both and want them to be joined as family, too.

"What do you want to do for Christmas?"

"To stay behind."

I held back tears as he said that but I refused to make him feel bad for it. He stayed on campus with the other foster youth. To me, it felt like a declaration that he had no family. This hurt, because I thought that no matter what, we would be there for each other, with each other. I wanted him to see my family as his own because he was now a part of mine.

I texted Kim to let her know that Justin wasn't coming and asked her to please let everyone know. I didn't want to come in the door and have everyone ask where Justin was. Christmas break apart, especially our last Christmas before marriage, was incredibly difficult. I finished packing my belongings from Justin's dorm, fighting back tears as I walked past him, almost as if he were invisible. As I rolled my suitcase out of the door and I grabbed my toothbrush from the bathroom counter, Justin jumped in front of me.

"Wait! Are you sure you don't want me to come? Sweetheart, I really don't mind coming."

If he came, he'd be miserable, and I'd worry about him the entire time. At least if he stayed behind, I could be sad without worrying about how he felt.

"No, you're fine…" I responded with the least bit of emotion in my face but deep disappointment in my soul.

Road trips were our bonding time. When he drove, I'd look across at him, admiring the peace and comfort he gave with his welcoming smile as I softly graced his neck. Our usual drive to northern Michigan turned into a sorrowful trip filled with tears as I drove alone. A part of me was missing. I felt like I was being forced to choose between my family and my partner.

I slept every night with my pillow soaked in tears. My thoughts were spiraling. *Was I going to be alone at every family gathering? Would our kids be able to celebrate holidays with their father?*

I took my ring off (briefly)

This wasn't an area in which I was willing to compromise. I wasn't going to put my kids through that. I didn't talk to Justin much the entire weekend because I knew it would hurt more. He texted me as the weekend was wrapping up. "I'll find a way to make it work and come next time. I'm sorry that I hurt you, sweetheart. We are one and about to be married so we have to figure it out."

It took us four days to make it home after being evacuated from South Africa. Because of COVID-19, we had to be quarantined in an RV right outside my parents' house. That was really difficult for both of us—leaving so abruptly, not knowing our next steps and feeling trapped in a vehicle. At first, there was a lot of anxiety and frantic jobs searching and apartment hunting. Kim did everything she could to make the situation easier by delivering home cooked meals on our doorstep, to eating dinner and playing games together over Facetime. Almost daily, Kim and Brian reminded us that they love us being here and that they don't have a timeline for us to leave.

After several months of living back home during the months leading up to our wedding, what had felt burdensome at first turned into a happy experience of spending so much time together as a family, of deepening our bonds and relationships—especially between Justin and my parents. Since she is very good at being objective and thinking rationally, when we don't know how to handle a situation, personally or professionally, we often say "Let's ask Kim what she thinks!" Since she is very good at being objective and thinking rationally. Now, Brian and Justin hug and joke together all the time, calling each other "Huggy Bear!"

During this time, Justin was tempted to hide some of his culture, and mannerisms, and idiosyncrasies in order to be accepted by my family. I had to remind him that if he isn't authentically himself, then he was robbing others of the opportunity to know and love the real Justin. **When someone says they love you, they can't mean it without knowing who the real *you* is.**

TALK IT OUT

JUSTIN

ONE OF THE most vital aspects of healthy relationships is a willingness to communicate. As a public relations major, I learned the many ways in which people communicate, but that didn't make it any less challenging with my own romantic partner. I grew up in a household where there was virtually no communication and I wanted to be careful about how I approached it in my relationship.

I would sit quietly with Alexis, hands together on my lap, with my arms by my side. In the midst of a heated discussion or conflict, I'd try to collect my thoughts before expressing myself. Before taking action, I wanted to have a full understanding of my feelings so that I didn't speak impulsively or word my feelings the wrong way. Meanwhile, Alexis' style was very different. She spoke her mind immediately, barely leaving a breath between her words. She never held back. My seeming lack of emotion and engagement would often aggravate our conflicts.

When my mom and dad argued, they said exactly how they felt, when they felt it, with no regard for how the other person might react. While on the football team in high school, if there were tension between two of the players, they'd head to the locker room to resolve their grievances with a fist fight. They'd be forced by the other players to shake hands and move forward, still filled with fueling rage gone unresolved. Entering into adulthood, I rarely witnessed any sort of peaceful conflict resolution.

I had never seen anything successful come from violence and anger, so I wanted to approach my relationships differently, whether with friends, family, or a potential life partner. It is common for men to be aggressive or domineering in order to exert control over women and gain the upper hand in relationships. This can include yelling, degrading, and insulting their partners, among other abuses. When my mother confronted my father, he would respond with physical abuse. No one wins in this toxic dynamic.

I wanted to be able to remain calm and engage with compassion. For both partners to be "equally yoked," they must engage in active listening, sitting next to their partner, and making sure that they're physically sitting on the same level when confronting an issue. Standing over your partner is a belittling power play. I saw it as my responsibility to be aware of when my partner was projecting anger onto me unintentionally and approach the situation with love and support.

Violence had been a common theme throughout my family's history and I wanted to break the cycle. It had to stop with me. Through counseling, I discovered that our initial emotional reactions in the midst of conflict are typically not the most sensible or logical. The initial feeling may be satisfying but it leaves plenty of shame and regret in its wake. For a time, I used avoidance as a method to peacefully resolve our conflicts. Unfortunately, this technique also caused problems. Alexis would demand to know how I felt in the moment, but I couldn't express myself that quickly.

I needed time to understand how I felt about certain things. Intense arguments would cause me to leave the room in order to avoid feeling uncomfortable. I couldn't handle the pressure of expressing my immediate thoughts and feelings. I didn't want to do something that could permanently affect our relationship. **My father's impulsive anger ran through my body but biblical principles such as patience and understanding tempered that response. I knew I needed a better method of solving our issues.**

What I learned in counseling was to be willing to ask questions. What could have done differently in this situation? Or how do I make things better? Creating an open and respectful dialogue solves issues more quickly than the avoidance method I had been practicing. Alexis' previous partners enforced a power dynamic with aggressive attacks and slander. I felt that the best way to equalize the power dynamic without becoming overbearing was to listen to my partner and embrace her needs. We knew if we both were intentional about our actions without pointing blame, then our disagreement could be resolved peacefully. We also learned from mentors that instead of distancing ourselves during arguments, we actually needed to come together. It's hard to argue if you're holding hands. This form of physical communication indicates that the two of you are not against one another but instead working together to solve the issue.

The toxicity in my family kept me from being around them in general, and made holidays especially hard. But out of sight was not out of mind, and in fact, being without them made me miss them more. Every holiday season, my family would come together to crack jokes, laugh nonstop, watch the Christmas day basketball game, and enjoy the delicious food that my mother spent the whole day cooking. She'd make her mouth-watering macaroni with multiple layers of cheese, and her famous cherry pie that I always loved. My mother was a Southern woman who knew how to whip up a feast you'd never forget. Though we struggled through the year, holidays always had a special place in my heart, both as a child in the foster care system and as an adult. Each year since entering the foster care system, I'd visit my family on holidays and filter out the toxic behavior so that I could pretend that I had an ideal family.

Spending the holidays with another family was in some ways harder than spending the day by myself. Even though Alexis' foster family was loving and supportive, for the first few years, I felt that I could never be myself. I would be the only Black person in the family, with no one I could relate to in the slightest. I couldn't make the kind of jokes I'd make with my brothers, nor share that familiar plate of Mom's macaroni. I enjoyed talking about college and my career path with Alexis' family, but I didn't feel like I could be completely my real self, certainly not the self I was around the people I had known since childhood, however complicated that dynamic was.

Alexis' adopted family was filled with highly educated engineers. The adults would sit quietly in the living room and read books. On Christmas, Alexis' grandparents, aunts, and uncles would gather at Kim and Brian's house to go into the backyard and cut down a Christmas tree. Every day before, the family would wait until each person had arrived at the dinner table before saying grace. They were the ideal American family who believed in tradition.

My family was pretty much the opposite. Every time I'd come back home to Detroit, my father would grab my biceps, complimenting me on my physical stature while attempting to catch up on time missed. After a short stint in jail when I was about four, he taught me the importance of doing push-ups between time to gain muscle.

"You doing your push-ups? How many can you do?" My brothers and I would laugh as he'd challenge me to see who could do the most.

On holidays, the guys would jump around screaming at the television as the Detroit Lions lost yet another Thanksgiving Day game while my mom prepared dinner.

"Aye! Get y'all ass out the kitchen!" My mom would say to all nine grandchildren as they chased one another around her small one-bedroom apartment. I had grown comfortable with the chaos and ignored most of it, filtering it to find joy at my family's house. As I'd talk to my brother Andre about college and career options, I couldn't help but be bothered by all the negative influences surrounding the children. He'd be rolling a blunt of weed next to his youngest child, indifferent to whether he'd seen him do it. I'd awkwardly end the conversation to continue watching the game.

One Christmas in particular finally revealed Andre's deep pain and resentment he had internalized towards my parents, as my mother tried to tell him to take it easy and on disrespecting his children, especially in front of the entire family. "Shut up, Bitch! It ain't like we had an example to look up to." Andre replied to my mom in front of everyone. Neither my dad nor my siblings moved a finger. I was paralyzed by his reckless attack on my mother.

I'd call my mother to tell her that I would have to miss a few Christmas and Thanksgiving celebrations in order to spend time with Alexis' family. I was hoping to slowly make a clean break from my family and transition into creating our own one day. My mother's manipulative tears over the phone caused resentment between Alexis and me. She asked, "So we not good enough to be yo family no more huh? You wanna be with them now?" I felt torn between two loyalties. Though I knew they weren't true, my mother's words would replay in my head once the holidays approached and Alexis and I packed our bags to visit her family.

"What did my family ever do to you to make it so that we can't visit them? Why do you think your family is better than mine?" I said, as I pointed out any and every flaw in her family.

But it had been my decision to avoid my family's holiday dinner, and I was blaming Alexis. Maybe it was my fault that my parents hadn't shown me the love I wanted. If I had visited them more, then maybe they could show me their love. Sometimes we try to find the reasons for our family's shortcomings within ourselves because it gives us the illusion of control and the hope that we can fix things. I felt desperate for a real and peaceful connection with my family, but it seemed beyond reach.

Unfortunately, this caused arguments between Alexis and me every year around the holidays. Whether it was about how many days we wanted to stay or me not engaging in family activities, the pressure was just too much for me. I couldn't be my real self around her family, and I couldn't talk about college or any of my successes with my own family—so I decided that I wanted to stay at school during the break.

My goal was to eventually start my own family, so that I wouldn't have to deal with either branch too frequently. If I couldn't receive love from the family I wanted, then I didn't want to be around family at all. I'd rather spend holidays alone than with anyone else. I was stuck in a bind made out of my own selfishness and inability to move past the imperfection of a situation. I felt out of place with Alexis's family and, to some extent, out of place with my own. I was unmoored, caught between two versions of family, and neither one felt right. I felt like an outsider and it made me resent the holidays. Would I ever belong anywhere? All of this anger and resentment made me feel ashamed, which made me figure that maybe I didn't deserve to be happy after all.

Family meant everything to Alexis, and I knew as soon as I decided to stay behind that I'd made a terrible mistake. I single-handedly ruined her holiday. I knew that I needed to be there for her from that point on.

The more time I spent with Alexis' family, the more they became my family. I needed to accept the people who wanted to love and support me. My stubbornness and resentment were denying me the pleasure of having a family. Kim had wonderful, gentle ways of letting me know that I was appreciated and loved—that I was at home in their home. She made it much easier to let go of my resentment and open myself up to love. It was scary to make myself vulnerable, but it was only when I did that I relaxed into a new definition of family that wasn't about blood or childhood memories. It was about acceptance, support, mutual affection, and respect. It was about love. Alexis was no more blood-related to Kim and Brian than I was, after all, and she had defined them as her family when they embraced her. I could—and would—do the same.

CITY KIDS TRAVEL THE GLOBE

*"Just when the caterpillar thought the world
was over, she became a butterfly."*
—Barbara Haines Howett

ALEXIS

OR ME, TRAVEL began as a way to escape what was happening at home with my ex, and soon served as a way to experience new things and meet new people. I thought it was incredible that one of my mentors had friends all over the world and I wanted that too. This was how I rationalized my first few study abroad programs.

I traveled first to the Dominican Republic and then to South Africa for five months, and it changed my life forever. I've never felt more alone. I was away from everyone and everything that I loved but I needed this clean break to begin to like spending time alone again. I started going to lunch, dinner and to the movies by myself. I learned to be comfortable alone and to become unapologetically Alexis. This helped me nurture my self-worth and clarify the things in which I believed and stood for. I refused to be silenced by anyone or anything, ever again. At that time, my friend Angela said something powerful that I'll never forget: "What you went through doesn't have to define you. It can be reframed as a journey from pain to power, from struggle to liberation."

I studied abroad eight times during my 6.5-year college career. Travel showed me a world beyond my own history and circumstances. Because people didn't know anything about me, I was able to reinvent myself every time, only sharing what I wanted them to know, leaving the trauma behind.

I knew that I wanted to travel with Justin. Initially, he couldn't envision it and was pretty opposed. But over time, I wore down his resistance and he even took comfort in the idea of going abroad together. When we first started to travel, I would plan every moment of our trip: where we would stay down to all the activities we would do, which was exhausting for both of us. I learned to let go of some of that control and figure out our trip once we arrive. This allowed us to be more present, figure things out together, lower our frustrations, and experience things that we didn't plan. Some of our best memories are of the most unexpected, spontaneous moments on our trips.

After studying abroad in back to back programs in 2017, while abroad my credit card was being charged over $3,000 and we couldn't figure out why. It wasn't until we returned to Michigan and visited our storage unit that we realized all of our belongings had been stolen. Now, all Justin owned was his Dell laptop, his Bible, and the clothes he'd brought with him on our trip. I had a week break before going to Washington, DC for a semester as one of two students selected for a full scholarship from the Reagan Foundation to participate in the Leadership and the American Presidency Program while interning at the Congressional Coalition on Adoption Institute. During this time, we were filing police reports and buying new luggage while packing for the next adventure.

Unfortunately, this is a common story. Because universities close over Christmas and other holidays, many foster youths are left stranded in these periods, essentially homeless. They are forced to find a place to store their belongings, the trauma of hauling one's things from one place to the next still fresh in their minds from childhood.

We went to South Africa together in January 2020 for Justin's fifth and final study abroad program. He attended the University of Cape Town while I volunteered and worked on my business, The Scholarship Expert, remotely. We were evacuated in March because, like the rest of the world, the COVID-19 pandemic dramatically altered life as we knew it. We were terribly disappointed; we both loved it there. There were beaches, deserts, safaris, mountains, penguins, the best food we'd ever eaten, and some of the nicest people we could ever hope to meet. On our last day in Cape Town, we hiked Table Mountain. Several hours later, I couldn't believe we'd actually done it. I knew I couldn't have done it without Justin physically pulling me up the side of the mountain saying, "You got this sweetheart. I see you!" I had traveled some of these same locations with my ex, and now Justin was here with me and, together, we were replacing the devastating memories with happy ones.

Traveling made us feel like we were taking on the world together. There was something powerful about getting on a plane and flying somewhere far away from the backdrop of what we'd grown up with, taking life into our own hands. This was the physical embodiment of the *emotional* journey we had taken together. **When I was little, I couldn't just walk out and escape but, as adults, we were giving ourselves the power not only to leave, but to choose where we went.**

Alexis & Justin overlooking Blyde River Canyon in South Africa

In 2018, Justin and I attended a Kirk Franklin concert. There I was, singing *Imagine Me* in a completely different season of my life. I remembered the little girl I was when I held onto those lyrics for survival and I knew that she was here now, praising God for His grace and mercy which carried her through so much hardship. I cried that night, as I had cried all those nights when I was a battered child. But that night, holding Justin's hand, the tears I cried were different—they were not tears of sorrow, but instead, tears of joy.

CITY KIDS TRAVEL THE GLOBE

*Only 5.6 percent of all Black students in
the United States study abroad.*

JUSTIN

THOUGH THE CHILD welfare system is obviously far from ideal, it did offer a grudging gift. Being in the system pushed me to develop a kind of mental flexibility, an ability to adapt to multiple environments in fairly rapid succession. Every physical transition I made provided an opportunity for emotional and mental maturation. I held my head high and embraced the experiences for what they were, looking to find joy in my future.

Throughout my youth, I barely left Detroit until the age of 17, when I moved into a group home in Southfield, Michigan. At 18, I went to college in Kalamazoo, two hours away from my family. Who knew that at 19 I would be traveling abroad for the first time? Developing resilience and durability in the foster care system provided me with the confidence to travel to over 25 countries by the age of 23.

When I first met Alexis, she had just come back from South Africa, a place I knew nothing about. Alexis would talk about her time in South Africa nonstop. From the sight of Table Mountain bursting through the clouds, to the sweet taste of soft Malva pudding melting in your mouth, to the world-famous safaris and amazing people, South Africa seemed too good to be true. When I watched the news about foreign countries as a child with my mom, she'd always say, "Don't y'all go out the country, they gone chop yo damn head off." She said it jokingly but, as a child, I internalized those fears. The idea was that if you left the country you would be killed or kidnapped. Meanwhile, we lived in *Detroit*, which was the murder capital of the U.S. at the time. Murder could happen right at my doorstep, and violence surrounded us but we didn't fear the risks that Detroit posed, for some reason. Familiar dangers felt less threatening, I guess.

My Auntie Cheryl instilled her own fears in me in the form of her prejudice against Muslims and Jews. She would warn us about Muslim people, telling us they had evil spirits and that we needed to stay as far away from them as possible. Her ignorance influenced me for a time, causing me to shy away from those outside the Christian community. I believed it was dangerous to set foot in a mosque or synagogue at any time or for any reason. But I began to question and break down these beliefs for myself when I started college.

During this process, I did two things. First, I began to make the transition from identifying myself as religious into practicing more spirituality. After a deep dive into biblical scripture, I noticed that religion is a traditional practice that we believe will sustain our relationship with God. For example, some believe that the more you attend church, the more connected you are with God. That's what my auntie believed. But unfortunately, she missed out on the spiritual part of Christianity. She believed that engaging with individuals from different religions will disconnect you from God. I beg to differ! Within spirituality, I believe God will empower me and stand alongside me no matter where I am physically—as long as I continuously call for His help. The church is not a building created by humans but the presence of God within man. So, it didn't matter if I walked into a mosque or any other religious temple. As long as I am secure with who I am then I'll be fine. Plus, I believe that true faith means respecting people from all walks of life no matter how your beliefs differ.

Alexis had already caught the travel bug and planned to travel even more. As a freshman, I was set on staying domestic and focusing on rebuilding Detroit. I came to college wanting to do sports journalism, no minors or clubs. I just wanted to graduate. I was the first in my family to attend college and afraid to push myself past my limits. Combined with my wariness of travel, instilled in me from a very young age, I couldn't see an upside.

Near the end of my freshman year, Alexis suggested we study abroad together in Seoul, South Korea the following summer. Immediately, I heard my mother's warnings echoing in my ears. How would a Black man cope abroad? **Then, I remembered how much courage it had taken to apply to college and how much additional courage it took to actually attend.** There was a momentum to my life now—a new pattern of taking on challenges, experiencing the rewards, and shedding fear. I realized this could be the next big step. Also, I did not want to be without Alexis all summer. I made up my mind: I was going!

I was incredibly excited for South Korea at this point. I was awarded the prestigious Benjamin Gilman scholarship, which helped pay for the cost of the program. As soon as I received the email notifying me that I was chosen from thousands of applicants to be awarded—I bolted through campus, thrilled, indifferent to the strange looks. Alexis was completing a summer long program in Italy, which meant that I would be alone on my first very flight. I'd meet her in Korea after I landed. Since I was so used to transitions, I didn't have a nervous bone in my body. My mom called me, crying, thinking I was flying to North Korea. I kept reassuring her that it was South Korea, and that she didn't have to worry. Each time I spoke to her was a reminder to consciously shed the fear that she had imposed on me for so long.

I realized moments before my flight that I had a 13-hour layover in Shanghai, China before my second flight to Korea. I panicked. I arrived in Shanghai near midnight, completely petrified. The airport felt deserted; it was closing for the night. I stood in the middle of the airport lobby squeezing the handle of my luggage, paranoid about being stranded in a foreign country. My mother's fear fueled my every thought. I needed to book a hotel and figure out how to catch a taxi. Multiple people came up to help me—walking in what seemed like circles, it was clear that I was a lost traveler.

One of the airport employees scheduled a shuttle to take me to a nearby hotel. I was relieved until I saw the driver, who looked sketchy to me. He had a huge scar on his face, similar to Tony Montana's, he was smoking a cigarette, and he couldn't smile if his life depended on it. *"Nope! Not getting in the car with this guy."* But I did. Google Translate really came in handy as I cracked a few jokes to lighten the mood, but I was still very frightened. I called Alexis to relay the name of the hotel and my location just in case. Luckily, I arrived at the hotel just fine. The next day, I made it to the right airport and soon enough, I was landing in Seoul.

That night taught me some important things. Sometimes, you have to let go and trust people, trust that they are not out to get you. Second, be prepared! Had I checked earlier, I would have known about the layover and made plans in advance, avoiding the last-minute scrambling. Figuring these things out on the fly—no pun intended—did give me confidence though—I was capable of navigating through trying and unfamiliar circumstances. So began my life as an international traveler.

South Korea was a complete surprise! I wanted to get the initial fear out of my system, so I began to walk the crowded streets of Seoul alone, a few blocks from the university. Though it was risky, I wanted to fully embrace this experience, along with the sensation of entering an entirely new world. Eyes wide open, I was mesmerized, the proverbial kid in a candy shop. The shining lights of downtown Seoul left me frozen in amazement. The skyscrapers were tall enough to peek through the clouds. The food was so wonderful, it made me never want to go home. The spicy soup and chicken combined with the sweet Korean BBQ had me stomping for more. Hilariously, on the first day we arrived, I struggled through my meal, fumbling with my chopsticks. The waitress softly tapped my shoulder, handing me a fork as if I were the silly American who knew little about Asian culture. But I wanted to learn. It gave me a sense of freedom and re-birth; I felt refreshed by the adventure.

Although I struggled, I had grown accustomed to thriving through discomfort. I had an entirely new perspective on life after leaving Korea. After studying community development there for six weeks, Alexis and I journeyed through eight cities in Japan before returning to the United States. It was official! I had caught the travel bug too.

Experiences such as these were groundbreaking. Being a Black man who was the first in my family to travel out of the country meant that I could inspire others to do the same. The feeling I had in Korea was too extraordinary to keep to myself; I needed to spread the word to other Black men and women and encourage them to take similar risks. I became addicted to being the first' in my family to achieve such inspiring accomplishments. I began to plan my next trip before even returning from the first!

To further influence Black students to study abroad and defy the stereotypes placed on us, I went on to become the first Black study abroad president and advocated for other students to travel abroad and while walking through the process. I really enjoyed the title of being the first Black president. I immediately signed up to attend the Dominican Republic study abroad trip, where I conducted ethnographic research. This was followed by studying in Dakar, Senegal, a 95% Muslim country. I even stayed with a Muslim host family during Ramadan, learning all about a different culture than what I had grown accustomed to during my youth, putting to rest any lingering prejudice I'd held onto.

Today, not only are some of my closest friends Muslim, but I have a new-found respect for people from other walks of life. Senegal practices all Christian and Islamic holidays, which is proof that the two can coexist. I concluded my college career by creating Western Michigan University's first multi-country African study abroad program to Rwanda and Uganda. Traveling became about embracing other people and enjoying different communities, two concepts that were entirely new to me.

Alexis was my travel buddy. We spent so much time studying abroad that people teased that we were abroad more than on campus. Travel had become part of our relationship and an outlet that freed us from societal expectations. We bonded more with each trip. I soon realized, that given our love for travel, I wanted to propose to her while abroad!

THE PROPOSAL

ALEXIS

IN 2018, AFTER about two years of dating, I decided to travel to Ecuador to study Spanish. Meanwhile, Justin went to D.C. for a different program. We would have to be apart for most of the summer. Before I went to Ecuador, we had conversations about what type of ring I would like, and I even got my finger sized. Justin asked what sort of proposal I would like, and I told him that I wanted it to be simple, a surprise, and maybe around my family.

Justin drove me to a hotel in Chicago, where I stayed the night before I flew to Ecuador the next morning. When he dropped me off and brought my bags to my room, I didn't know if I wanted to cry or throw up. It was painful to think about a whole summer apart.

We were saying our goodbyes and I began to cry. We took a selfie and then I walked to the entrance of the hotel. As I stood there, waiting for Justin to drive off, I could see the tears streaming down his face. A few minutes passed and he finally backed out of the spot and drove away slowly looking at me through the rearview mirror. It felt very much like a movie moment.

I missed Justin so much that I asked him to join me for the two weeks he had off in between programs. He agreed, and before he left, I coordinated a trip with my class to Mindo, Ecuador for the first weekend that he would be there. Over the next few weeks, Justin started asking me strange questions like:

"Is there a rock we can both stand on together?"
"Is there someone that can take our picture together?"
"Is there a waterfall in Mindo? Which one is the best and biggest?"

Something told me he was planning to propose.

I noticed that he was talking to me a lot less, which made me doubt my optimism. I asked him relentlessly if something was wrong. Now I know that he was quiet because he was afraid of letting something slip before the big moment arrived. He was so used to telling me everything that he had to work on withholding the details of his plan.

On May 17th, 2018 he flew to Ecuador, but his flight was delayed. *Would he make it in time for the trip?*

He finally arrived around midnight. We were set to leave for Mindo really early the next morning. Once we were all on the cable car to take us to the waterfalls, Justin asked again, "What's the best waterfall?" Luckily for him, it was the first one on the tour.

The hike to the waterfall was exhausting and I found myself thinking that if Justin were to propose, I'd be all sweaty for the big moment.

Even though I knew it was coming, he managed to take me by surprise. He grabbed my hand and led me to a rock with a waterfall scenically located behind us. Then, he dropped to one knee. Tears rolled down my face before he'd even said a word.

"Alexis, I love you more than anything. Will you be my wife and the mother of my children?"

I responded quickly, "Yes! Of course." I cried. My legs were trembling. I thought I was going to fall off the rock we were standing on!

My entire class was standing there taking pictures, and a few people were even crying themselves. I glanced down at the ring, which was so beautiful, and allowed my own waterfall of shock and euphoria to cascade through me. Afterward, we walked to a butterfly garden. I can't think of a better symbol of the freedom and renewal that our relationship had given us and hoped that our marriage would continue to fill out lives with this newfound gift.

That night, we blissfully announced the news of our engagement to social media before falling asleep.

The next morning, our phones were flooded with personal attacks and threats on my life.

THE PROPOSAL

JUSTIN

MANY MARRIAGES ARE ruined before they begin before they even leave the ground. Because each person is a product of two cultures and identities, the relationship could be heading for a crash course. Specifically with interracial couples, families could be completely opposite of one another and oftentimes try to dictate the direction of the relationship. In order to make the relationship work, we needed the two may need to pursue happiness outside of external influences that do not contribute to the prosperity of our union.

Over the course of two years, the relationship between Alexis and me blossomed tremendously. We had been evolving through every step of the way, focusing our attention on how we could improve ourselves both individually and together. I dreamed of building a family that wouldn't have to suffer from the traumatic experiences of my childhood. I also wanted the mother of my children to balance out our household. The example given by my mentors in their marriages set the standard for the marriage I wanted. They prayed, built businesses, and nurtured their children together. These became components that I wanted as crucial parts of my marriage with Alexis.

Before asking Alexis to be my wife, I needed to pray and ask God for direction. I also needed to fast and remove distractions from the equation. We had discussed marriage a few times during our relationship, but I needed to make sure this was what we both wanted. I asked her foster parents in a joking manner (with a hint of seriousness) how they felt about us getting married, sneaking in the question before bedtime on a holiday visit. Nervous for their response, I didn't want to make a big deal of it. I also wanted to make sure I was making the right decision and not forcing my way into a lifelong commitment. They had grown pretty familiar with me over the past two years and we had developed a pretty close relationship. Marriage is easily the toughest decision of anyone's life. As usual, Brian cracked a few jokes,

"You sure you wanna join this crazy family?"

Like I hadn't experienced a few crazy things with my *whole* family. They told me that I had already become a part of the family and that they'd love for me to officially join. After sitting with the decision for a few weeks, asking my mentors for advice, and asking God for direction, I had found my answer.

It was May of 2018 and Alexis was studying abroad in Ecuador. My first plan was to propose in a large field of grass where Alexis and I could enjoy nature. Then, at the right time, I would pop the question. The perfect place was in northern Michigan at her foster parent's home on our anniversary in August. When I told my mom, she felt disrespected with the idea that I was proposing in front of her family and not with them. Luckily, I had an amazing backup plan.

I decided to visit Alexis in Ecuador while she was studying abroad. Since plans changed, I needed to hurry and buy the ring (and book a ticket to Ecuador!). After booking my ticket, to visit it had it become a waiting game until the ring was to be delivered. Sweating through the night, I was cutting it extremely close; having the ring arrived the day before my flight. It arrived just on time. I opened the wooden ring box and my heart skipped a beat. The rose gold sparkle felt as if it lit up the room. The ring was finally here but my worries nearly peaked.

Anxiety filling my thoughts, I had so many concerns about proposing. What if the ring didn't fit her finger?, What if I lost the ring on the way to the airport?, What if I was robbed once I landed in Ecuador? I couldn't hold the secret any longer and needed to pop the question immediately. I asked Alexis to meet me at a popular waterfall in Mindo, Ecuador where I would propose the next day.

The day went as planned—and I asked Alexis to be my wife. She said yes and the rest is history.

LOVE IS NOT ALWAYS BLACK AND WHITE

*Interracial couples are 10% more likely to divorce
than couples who marry within their race.*

ALEXIS

ONE OF JUSTIN'S aunts, Patty, commented on several of our posts, including our engagement post. She called me "White trash," "nasty," "old," and messaged me, "I don't know you [you] are not right for my nephew. No no no," and "White bitch I'm fucking her up. If I ever find out she in Detroit that's her ass. Believe that."

We were devastated, hurt, and angry. I even felt resentful that Justin was hesitant to defend me in the public comments his relatives had left on my Facebook page.

I told him that if we had a bridal shower or a barbeque in Detroit, I would attend only through FaceTime. I knew that his family's threats weren't just threats. I had heard all the stories. Besides, there was no reason I should subject myself to their hatred and contempt.

After a while, we gathered our courage and decided that we would not let anything ruin our special moment. We had been through too much. **We had to remember that we were a team, even when it felt like the world was against us.** We learned that day that we must guard our oneness, because when we are bringing purpose into our marriage, there's nothing the enemy can do to break it.

Justin never wavered in wanting to marry me, but he did consider skipping a formal wedding, thinking that maybe a City Hall ceremony would suffice. I understood his pain—this was the holidays all over again, and once more, he was caught between his desire to have a connection with his family and the realities of what it cost him to maintain that connection. But it also caused tension—how could he ask me to give up my dream of having a traditional wedding day?

Especially because in our case, a wedding would celebrate more than just the start of a marriage, but our hard-earned victory over our demons, and the mutual support that made that victory possible. Additionally, so many people have poured into us to make this moment possible. I never want to minimize the pain of Justin's ongoing struggle to reconcile his present with his past, nor his longing to build a bridge with his family, still being so rooted in the problems that plagued his childhood. I have to be careful to advocate for the peaceful celebration we both wanted and deserved, while still being mindful of the undercurrent of grief that the day would hold for Justin.

Once we decided to throw a wedding, we wanted to do it right. We decided to use local vendors, startup entrepreneurs, and as many Black and brown-owned businesses as possible. We even planned to have a business table set aside so our vendors could network and gain connections and potential for future business opportunities. We wanted our special day to be of real value to others, as well as a joyful and happy day for us.

Racism is a deep-rooted issue in this country and my family is saturated in it. Living in Flint, I had all Black friends and my dad hated it. He was a racist and everyone knew it. He was never shy about saying the "n"-word.

One time, I was at the library to do "homework" when he came in to check on me. He found me on Myspace scrolling through a Black boy's page. He grabbed me by the back of my neck, dragged me outside, and threw me to the ground. "I drop you off to do homework and I catch you looking at "n****ers," he spat. When I visited family later that day, they picked on me for looking at "black boys" instead of ones I should be looking at instead. In a stack of old letters I found at Aunt Bev's, several read like this one:

"This whole mess started the summer between her sixth and seventh grades. As you know all of Alexis' friends started to become more and more black during that time. You also know that I was not pleased with that situation, but I was trying to make the best of it. I told her many times that she needed to find more white friends to hang around with. Well, in time, as you know all her friends were black. She started acting, talking and trying to dress black around me and her friends. By the time she started her new school, 7th grade, there were four black boys coming over, on the bus, from the north end of town. I told my dad [my grandpa] that it was all about not letting Alexis have a black boyfriend, and possibly half-black grandchildren later in my life. I will stick to my beliefs, that my daughter will not see a black boy. If I have to go to prison for it, then I guess I have to go. I will not back [down] from this."

In one letter, he added:

"I've been okay except the time I was beaten by 4 black men 1 year ago this month. My left side of my face was so swollen I couldn't see out of my left eye."

It is difficult to describe what I felt when I read those words. I did not feel any sympathy, that's for sure. In fact, I felt that some justice had been served.

But once I read these letters, I couldn't help but worry for Justin's safety. *Would my dad ever break his parole to hurt Justin?* Even though Justin and I were out of the country the day he was released, when I got the news, my heart stopped for a moment and my world felt threatened.

He was free.

On so many levels, this was a terrible thought. I had hoped that he'd die behind bars, that I'd never have to imagine him roaming free.

In 2018, my dad's sister (who is now retired from the Flint police department) was posting extremely racist and prejudiced things on Facebook. At first, I tried to talk to her about how her posts were hurtful to people of color, especially with her being a white woman. After a while, several other family members started commenting on posts and sharing so many other harmful things that I had to block most of my family on all social media platforms. This didn't stop their hurtful and hateful rhetoric. This also didn't stop her from messaging me, "Don't you know they're [black people] the problem?" and "I'd accept Justin because you love" him and "He's one of the good ones."

Our decision to marry one another has only reinforced the emotional and moral necessity of removing toxic people—even family members—from our lives.

Justin and I talk about race almost every day, since it is such a glaring part of our lives. My husband and my future children will be Black, and with that comes a long list of worries and specific social barriers. Race isn't something that Justin can just walk away from, although I could easily walk through my life never even considering race if I weren't in love with and marrying a Black man.

Seeing him break down crying, thinking that his life has no value that he could be killed on camera for the world to see (and that no one would care) tears me apart, but there's no true way for me to comfort or protect him. Justin's already been through so much and has to deal with these feelings on a daily basis simply because of the color of his skin.

I feel helpless knowing that I can't protect him. There are no words to describe the trauma of watching countless videos of Black men being murdered by police with impunity. Watching my soulmate witness it fills me with a whole new type of dread and despair. Knowing how much Justin has already been through and conquered adds to this despair, but it also tempers it. No one should have to gather the strength to fight systemic racism every day of his life, but if anyone has that strength, it's Justin. Whatever comfort I can offer, however I can help him with that struggle, he knows I will be beside him doing my utmost to support him in every way possible.

In order for us to work, I must strive to be actively anti-racist in our relationship and in the world around us.

Before we got married, I wanted to finalize my adoption. Over the course of many years, Kim and Brian had repeatedly reassured me that I was their daughter and that they didn't need paperwork to prove that. But it was of vital symbolic importance to me. The only thing that I wanted for my 26th birthday was to be adopted. I had known for years that I wanted to be adopted, but I had to wait until age 26 so that I wouldn't lose my Medicaid insurance.

On December 3, 2019, over Thanksgiving weekend, Kim, Brian, Justin, and all five of my little siblings (Anna, Eli, Isaiah, Obadiah, and Omanii) came to support me at the local courthouse. When we arrived, I sat in the car, looking in the mirror and trying to hold it together. I could feel the tears building up. Then, I looked up at the courthouse itself. Since my father's trial, courts have been a major trigger for me.

Before going inside, I recorded our reactions to document the day. We all sat down in the same aisle waiting for our turn to approach the stand. I was looking around the courtroom and saw one of Brian's brothers sitting in the back row for support. Next, I looked at the family I was about to permanently join. I had an overwhelming sense of joy and peace as each one smiled at me. Brian sat to my left with his arm around my shoulder, Obi on his lap. Smiling, the judge called out "Up next, the adoption of Alexis Lenderman." *This is it!*

The floodgates opened. I openly wept the most cathartic tears of my life. We approached the table and the judge asked us our names and if I was giving Kim and Brian the permission to adopt me. I managed to gasp the word "Yes!" and sat down between Kim and Brian. After answering a few more legal questions, the judge proclaimed, "Kim and Brian, you are now legally the parents of Alexis Lenderman." When I thought I couldn't cry anymore, it all came out. I now had parents that *I chose and that chose me back*.

The judge had each sibling go up to the wooden podium to say their name and whether they were excited to have a new sister. I stood there with such pride as I was claimed in court by my family! One by one, from my oldest sister Anna to my youngest brother Obadiah, all five of my siblings pushed themselves out of their comfort zone to speak up and say "Yes!"

For years, courthouses had always symbolized pain, heartache, and loss. But this time, it represented wholeness, joy, and love. The warm hug I received from my now father, Brian, reminded me that I was now loved and protected. Kim, gentle and kind as she is, shed tears as she welcomed me officially as her child.

The day before my adoption, they threw me a party with a cake that read "We love you, Alexis" and several gifts that filled my heart with joy. One was a book called "Wherever You Are" by Nancy Tillman. Inside, Kim wrote, "Our love will find you wherever you go and whatever you do. We love you no matter what." I also received a puzzle piece ornament with each of our names on it and a necklace saying, *"Always my daughter, forever my friend."*

My new family and me on my adoption day

Until that point, I had insisted on calling Kim and Brian my "foster parents," keeping that wall up for my emotional protection. Now, I could let it down. I realized this when I overheard Justin on a call, referring to them as "Alexis's *foster* parents." I felt hurt and defensive. After his call, I said "Babe, can you please stop calling them my foster parents and refer to them as my parents?"

Places, roles, and names that once had negative connotations have now been restored. I am able to reclaim those words and places.

That lost six-year-old girl, searching for a mother, has now found her place of belonging, a home, a family, a mother.

LOVE IS NOT ALWAYS
BLACK AND WHITE

JUSTIN

DATING OUTSIDE YOUR race has always been a tricky thing in my family. A majority of my dad's side of the family is from the South. Before moving to Detroit, my grandparents lived in Mississippi during the 30s, 40s and part of the 50s. Being a Black person from the segregated South alters your view of white people, to say the least. It burned a kind of fear and rage into the generations that survived that time and place.

Living with my Auntie Cheryl, Khalil and I would joke about what would happen if her son were to bring home a white girl. She didn't find it funny.

"His ass better not bring home a white girl." We knew for sure not to marry a white woman or there would be hell to pay.

About two or three years later, when I lived with Mrs. Cora and Mr. Melvin in the group home, I asked the same thing in a joking manner, not knowing that I would marry a white woman one day. They said they didn't care about her race as long as she treated me right. That was the first time I had heard something like that from a Black person. That's when I felt like I received "approval" to focus solely on compatibility in a relationship. Dating outside my race wasn't even considered as a teenager. I rarely had interactions with white people aside from my social workers and a handful of teachers—never with anyone close to my own age.

When I met Alexis, things happened so naturally that I didn't even think about her race. Another one of our first conversations during the Seita Scholars SET week occurred when I jokingly asked the white people in our cohort, "What are you doing to support the Black Lives Matter movement?" This was back in 2016 when a majority of White Americans still could easily ignore racial injustices. Most of my white counterparts stated that they hadn't heard of the movement. Alexis gave a real response, one that I hadn't expected. She stated how she was actively involved in social justice initiatives and reading books about how to be a supportive ally. With her being more involved than I was at the time, I felt weird about continuing the conversation.

Surprisingly, once Alexis and I started dating my biological family was supportive of us. I brought Alexis to see my Auntie Cheryl, who was very welcoming. A few years after leaving my aunt's house, we patched things up and had continued a relationship with healthy boundaries. At the time, I wanted everyone to like Alexis and was slightly worried about receiving my biological family's approval.

My Auntie Cheryl barely mentioned the fact that Alexis was white and actively supported our relationship. Maybe she had changed a lot since Khalil and I left her place. Regardless, I wasn't as nervous about Auntie Cheryl as I was about my other aunt, Auntie Patty. Auntie Patty was the one to stir up drama in the family and the main person who openly displayed her hatred for white people. Often aggressive and hostile, she was the auntie to be nervous about. I remember her and my Auntie Cheryl regularly getting into arguments. On one occasion, shortly after Alexis and I started dating, Auntie Patty got into an argument with my Auntie Cheryl and sucker-punched her. Things got so bad that the police needed to show up to deescalate the situation. Being in their 50s didn't change a thing about their behavior, for that reason, I refused to bring Alexis around much at all.

I didn't exactly want or need Auntie Patty's approval, but I knew she would bring up my interracial relationship the second we had an encounter. A few months later, we saw one another at a cookout. One of my cousins said, "Uh oh, Auntie Patty about to talk to you about messing with a white girl." I laughed it off but was ready to explain how nice of a person Alexis was and how much she would love her. Before getting a word out, she said,

"Does she treat you right?"

"Yea," I said, nervous about what to expect next.

"That's all I care about."

"Wow! That was easy." I thought to myself. I washed my hands of it, and moved on.

In May of 2018, after I asked my best friend to marry me, we woke up the next morning to over 100 Facebook notifications, assuming they would be filled with congratulations from our friends and family.

Instead, it was Auntie Patty. Auntie Patty began to attack Alexis in the comment section. She wrote that she wouldn't allow a white woman to come into our family. She called Alexis every name in the book, wished death on our children, and threatened to attack Alexis if she came to Detroit. I couldn't imagine welcoming Alexis into a family like this. Alexis turned away from me and started to cry. I felt responsible for her misery. I grabbed Alexis' hand and told her that no matter what, we were in this together.

A year later, I had distanced myself from my dad's side of the family completely. I was returning home to Detroit from yet another trip abroad in the summer of 2019, one of the most exciting summers of my life. I traveled to Senegal, Rwanda, Uganda, Thailand, Cambodia, and Hong Kong—all in one summer. I studied abroad, did some personal travel, and ultimately made memories and friendships that I would never forget.

When I returned home, my mom invited me to a cookout to celebrate my dad's birthday. She told me that they would also be making it a "Welcome Home" party for me. I had been ignoring her requests to visit for almost a year now, and I really missed my mom's famous macaroni. I yearned to be with my family, too.

My motivation for returning home was to deliver a three-day educational workshop I prepared for my oldest nephews. I wanted to discuss career planning, financial literacy, and manhood from a Christian perspective. I also wanted to let them know that no matter the situation, even if I were to completely separate from the family, that they could always contact me. I was excited, but also nervous. This would challenge the reality they see on a daily basis. Some of my nephews had begun to follow in the footsteps of their parents. Some had already smoked weed and had sex, none of them were 12 yet—there was no time to waste.

After every workshop, I dropped the kids off and left immediately after, deciding to no longer engage with the behavior of my family. On the last day of workshops, I took a chance and stayed to relax with my family with the cookout being the next day. One day wouldn't hurt right? When I arrived, I immediately recognized all of my family's old habits, like doing drugs and drinking alcohol around the kids. I couldn't speak my mind, nor could I discuss my amazing summer. It began to feel like torture all over again.

At some point, while discussing the people expected at the cookout, they mentioned that Aunt Patty would attend. I was stunned. Aunt Patty was known for resolving conflict with violence. "How could you put me in that situation?" I asked my mother. I reminded her of the things Aunt Patty had said about Alexis. "I don't want that swept under the rug," I insisted. My brother Andre interrupted. "You still worried about that? She ain't gon do nothing," he said. Tiffany agreed, failing to notice or understand how upset I was. The drama and violence in my family had become so normalized that no one thought twice about Aunt Patty's arrival; no one considered her abusive comments to be a problem at all. It felt as if they approved of Aunt Patty more than they did of Alexis.

I wanted no part of the cookout that was supposed to be held in my honor. I would have returned to school that night, but I had no room to return to yet; the semester hadn't started. I spent the night at a friend's instead, where I slept badly, seething with resentment.

That night, I drove to a bar to drown my sorrows. I drank an entire fishbowl of alcohol and smoked weed until I forgot the deep pain my family had caused with their indifference. The next day, I drove back to Kalamazoo with a hangover and a sense of deep shame. I had numbed my pain in the exact ways I had warned my nephews to avoid. I had told them to turn to God with their problems. Yet that night, I had instead done just what my parents did.

Skipping the cookout, my phone blew up with texts and calls from all my siblings and parents. I ignored all of them. Eventually, I answered my mom's call and my sister snatched the phone and began to curse at me. My voice quavered and I hung up quickly, pulling the car over and crying into the steering wheel.

I sat in my car for a long time, staring out of the window as the afternoon sun glared, wondering how long I could bear this dysfunction. Sitting in the parking lot of Biggby Coffee, I saw that Khalil had texted me, and it calmed me. I knew he would understand how upset I was, and why, and that he alone would be able to comfort me. Khalil and I had been through everything together.

Then I read his text.

"You acting like a hoe, I can't believe you turned yo back on the family bro. I see how it is…"

There was nothing left to say. I knew I had to close a door in my mind, to stop trying to get blood from a stone. This was who my family was, and the level at which they could communicate. I could not expect more of them, and it would only wound me further to hope for more.

It wasn't just the sense of loss and abandonment that Khalil's text filled me with, it was the dawning realization that deep within the culture of my family lay a need to pretend that pain did not exist, to refuse to validate anyone's feelings who dared to feel deeply, who dared to be truly hurt by someone else, who dared to expect sympathy and empathy from another living soul. I had challenged this need, this method of extinguishing other people's emotions and humanity as well as their own. I had challenged it by explaining how upset I was about Aunt Patty, and by saying her presence under the circumstances was unacceptable. I had violated our code. We did not show vulnerability or weakness, heartache or sorrow. I did not want to be a part of that kind of culture anymore. I had come too far, grown too much, lived a different kind of life for too long. I could not go back to that.

With a heavy heart, I suggested to Alexis that we elope. I dreaded the idea of family dictating the direction of our special day or, even worse, spoiling it. I wanted nothing more than to marry away from the cruel judgments of the world and ride off into the sunset, just Alexis and me.

I believe that self-discovery requires resilience and acceptance of one's past. Animosity toward Mrs. Cora, Auntie Cheryl, the Bennetts, or my parents would only deter me from mental and emotional growth. Forgiveness was the word placed on my heart as I entered into marriage with Alexis. Both our experiences and interactions with family, friends, and loved ones had prepared us to become who we are today. With this in mind, I hold no resentment towards anyone in my past and accept responsibility for the pain and suffering that I caused others. I recognize my wrongs within every single household I've been placed and would ask that they forgive me as well. The only option for Alexis and I to start our marriage with a renewed mind and spirit was to cleanse ourselves of our old ways of thinking and accept the lessons we gathered from each circumstance.

As the night dwindled on a windy October evening, Kim and I sparked deep conversation shortly after eating dinner and putting the kids to bed. With Alexis by my side, pushing me to be the vulnerable and confident partner I was with her, I knew I wanted to share details about my traumatizing childhood with Kim. Though I presented myself as the perfect gentleman, they knew life in foster care was no easy task. Kim's soft and warming tone of voice made me want to share more about my deepest pains, leading me to describing how I lost my teeth. Kim was distraught and immediately told me about an organization named Watermark. I smiled and thanked her, but I held out little hope. I couldn't imagine they'd donate more than a few dollars, and I needed a lot more than that for corrective surgery.

After contacting Watermark, Alexis and I drove to several dental offices from Detroit to Canada to see which office had the most affordable rates. She kept saying:

"Don't worry about the amount of money needed, things will work themselves out and we'll find the perfect fit!"

Given the amount of damage, no dental office gave an estimate below $25,000. Driving back from Canada, I sat with my head in my hands. Accepting misery was nothing unusual, though, and at least this time, I had Alexis there to comfort me.

Then, suddenly, my phone vibrated. Holding the wheel with one hand, I scrambled to find my phone with the other. It was the Watermark organization!

"Is this Justin Black?"

"Yeah," I replied nervously.

"We wanted to let you know that we were inspired by your story and your resilience."

People admire my story all the time with no follow through or support. I didn't expect this time to be any different.

"Justin, our team has discussed it and we've decided to cover the total cost of your dental surgery."

I nearly crashed the car. Could this really be happening?

Just when I was prepared to accept failure and misery, happiness walked in. Had I not trusted Kim and shared my story with her, it never would have happened, and that taught me a valuable lesson. In January of 2020, after my implants were installed, I felt my tongue touch the top of my mouth for the first time in almost a decade.

A week later, my gums healed just in time to attend the Nsoro Foundation's 2020 Starfish Ball in Atlanta, Georgia. I took the stage and spoke publicly about my experiences in the foster care system and about the moment that I lost my teeth. In fact, in front of an audience of over 1,000 people, including prominent politicians, celebrities like T.I and famous athletes like Steve

Smith and Jerome Bettis. I was the keynote speaker. With every word, the weight of years of suppression and anxiety lifted off my shoulders. Years of secretly crying in the bathroom had led to this bold public moment. The shame of being the kid with missing teeth was at last behind me, and I felt the peace and grace of God within me. That night, we raised over $1 million to support foster youth working toward degrees in higher education.

Alexis and I realized that we wanted to share our wedding day with the friends and foster relatives who had supplied their unwavering love and support for us. We also wanted a wedding that celebrated the fact that we had survived the trials life has handed us, beating the odds together.

Family supports you during your moments of sorrow, as well as joyfully celebrating your successes. Family is truthful and patient and sees the very best in you. Envy, bitterness, and resentment are not routine states in a healthy family. Peace, respect, and compromise are instead its organizing principles. I will no longer allow someone else's pain or damage to influence my identity. Alexis and I have defined for ourselves what family and love should look like, after experiencing both deeply dysfunctional families and families that know how to love.

If I could go back and talk to that nine-year-old kid living in abandoned housing and preparing to enter the foster care system, I'd tell him that in this world there will be battles that seem hopeless and circumstances that will test your durability and strength. Though you may stumble, you will not fall. Life is a marathon. Find joy in as many moments as you can; take comfort in the pain that some lessons necessarily offer. Sometimes, there is no other way to truly learn. Take a breath and respect the person you are becoming. Your hardship does not define you but can strengthen your character, your heart, and your soul. Your victory will be accepting true love and giving it fully, too.

PART 5:
AGREEMENT

What the Statistics Say:
40-50% of marriages end in divorce. The leading causes
are infidelity, finances, and family conflict.

Around 70 percent of child poverty occurs in single-parent
families. Children in single-parent homes are about five times
more likely to be poor than are children in married-couple
homes, showing that family structure is the most important
factor in predicting the upward social mobility of children.

The welfare system imposes substantial financial penalties on low-
income parents who marry, reducing the marriage rate among
the poor. A recent study found that an anti-marriage penalty of
$1,000 in the Earned Income Tax Credit (EITC) reduced the
probability that low-income women would marry by 10 percent.

What Does God Say:
"Such love has no fear, because perfect love expels all fear"
(1 John 4:18).

INTENTIONALITY

"Watch your thoughts, they become your words;
watch your words, they become your actions;
watch your actions, they become your habits;
watch your habits, they become your character;
watch your character, it becomes your destiny."
—Lao Tzu

STATISTICALLY, WE SHOULDN'T be where we are today, but with God's grace and love, we've been able to use our circumstances to help others. We all have a story that will help others. Sharing our story gives others the courage to share theirs. People look at us and what we've been able to accomplish, and they can't imagine—or would never guess—what we've been through along the way.

We have the power to speak life and death into our lives and our relationships. For the sake of our friendship, our marriage, and our children, we have to live a life of intentionality and be careful of what and who we allow around us—what we listen to and watch. Jim Rohn says that "We are the average of the five people we surround ourselves with." They are influences on the way we think, our confidence, self-esteem, and largely our life trajectory. If we surround ourselves with negative, unhappy, and bitter individuals that aren't ambitious or driven, then we probably will be the same. We've had to make the difficult decision to leave behind friends from high school because we've simply outgrown them.

Too often, we inherit that which our family or our community does and believes, rather than choosing our own thoughts and opinions and deciding for ourselves what it is that *we* believe in. We want to make sure that every thought, perspective, and opinion we have is because we arrived at those conclusions ourselves, rather than inheriting them from the generation before us.

To accomplish this, we had to define what our values *are*, how we want others to see us, and what *we* want to leave behind in this world. Personal growth consultant Richie Norton says, "*Intentional living means making choices for your life based on your greatest values, not the habit of others.*" We are not a product of our parent's choices—we are instead defined by our own decisions.

We didn't want to have children without first developing a healthy friendship and marriage. We wanted to make sure that when we decided to bring a child into this world, he or she would have a covenant and a covering. If we had children without agreement in place, then our children would unfairly face challenges by furthering generational patterns of brokenness.

We are breaking cycles of generational dysfunction. It stops with us, it ends here; It doesn't matter what kind of family we come from; we can be the start of a healthy generation.

We grew tired of merely surviving. We wanted to *live* a life with greater meaning—with greater purpose. We wanted to serve people, because we believe that we have a duty to others, especially future generations. We didn't want to be like so many people around us who had become complacent and comfortable with the status quo. Every day, we think of ways to test our boundaries, because real growth doesn't happen in our comfort zone. Most of the time, people do things because "my parents did it" or because "It's always been that way," but both of those ways of thinking can be harmful to families and relationships. We strive to question ourselves and others, and to find alternatives to damaging behavior.

Thankfully, through foster care, we've learned that we have the power to choose our own families. We've been through so much, which is why we are committed to keeping our relationship as drama-free as possible, building each other up, to keeping each other accountable. Our relationship is our haven. We want to feel safe, secure and vulnerable in that space that we've created together. We are each other's refuge.

From the beginning, we had a purpose for our relationship. We weren't just dating without a plan or some sort of direction for our relationship. We both knew that we wanted marriage, which was something to work towards. We didn't have a time limit, but around that two-year mark is generally when people decide if this is the person they want to spend the rest of their life with.

We thank each other constantly, even for just existing and being who we are. Positive words of affirmation are another form of speaking life into each other and letting the other person know that they are loved and appreciated. We are each other's biggest cheerleaders. We are protective of our space and the energy around us. We consider our time and hard-earned happiness to be precious and chose to reframe it as a privilege for others to take part in it.

In college, we even made a chart of our daily schedules so that we could be more intentional on spending time together. This included walking each other to class having lunch and dinners together on certain days because, if not, we both are so busy that we could go an entire week without seeing each other. We exercise together because our physical health has a direct impact on our mental health. Knowing each other's strengths and weaknesses makes it easier for us to hold each other accountable, too.

Marriage is a partnership and ultimately, your partner is a reflection of yourself. This means being present with each other, making each other feel loved and heard, and validating each other's feelings while being patient and kind. We do not believe in following gender norms. We are a partnership and our role is to serve each other.

Our pastor once said, "If you don't know the purpose of a thing, you'll abuse it."

People look at us, not realizing what we've gone through and how much work we've put in to be who we are today. **Imagine if we looked like what we've been through!**

Foster care saved us. Sadly, our stories aren't unique. There are thousands of individuals who experience the same trauma that we have: domestic violence, abandonment, neglect, abuse, and sexual assault. Less common is establishing a commitment to overcoming, unlearning pathological ways of behaving while choosing to live a life that isn't rooted in the past.

We have been committed to serving others individually and together, which is why we mentor youth, offering guidance from what we've learned and overcome. That is why we are federal National Youth in Transition

Database Reviewers (NYTD) who assess states' policies and practices to ensure that foster youth are equipped to transition out of care.

We had to go through individual journeys to define who we are, our values, and our own healing before we could come. We couldn't do any of those things for each other. Just as we couldn't rely on our partner to make us happy. We had to find ways to make ourselves happy.

Together, we push each other to be the best possible versions of ourselves. With this, comes the benefits of being recognized as a Presidential Scholar, a Phi Beta Kappa inductee, a Horatio Alger National Scholar, and Clinton Global Initiative alumni.

FOUNDATION

"Make it your goal to create a marriage that feels
like the safest place on earth."
—Greg Smalley

WE ARE DESIGNED to be interdependent, not independent. With that, we have to know how to serve our partner. Kim and Brian told us that every day, they are in a competition to see who loves each other more as a way of constantly courting each other and keeping the spark alive. This means enjoying the little things that we do with and for each other every day. We believe that God is love, and therefore, if you have God first in your marriage, you have love first, too.

But even in a healthy relationship, with agreement, communication, and vulnerability, sometimes one partner will fail the other. That's where unconditional love, faith, and grace come in. Again, much of our culture promotes and encourages selfishness, not selflessness and serving each other.

But if we want a long-lasting healthy marriage, then we believe selflessness and servant leadership should be the foundation of our marriage. Love is an action. The amount of time you spend with someone isn't as valuable as the daily commitment and love you give one another.

Marriage is not about the piece of paper that makes it legal. It's the promise and commitment before our community and God that is crucial. It's about the lifelong partnership that follows.

ONENESS

"Every marriage is either moving toward oneness or drifting towards isolation. Oneness in marriage involves complete unity with each other. It's more than a mere mingling of two humans— it's a tender merger of body, soul, and spirit."
—Dennis Rainey

THE DECISION TO get married is one of the biggest we ever make. Our relationship can set the tone for the next three to four generations. We will not take it lightly and we want to position ourselves for success in our marriage just as much if not more than we do with our academic and professional responsibilities. Kim suggested we attend a pre-marital conference called *Weekend to Remember* and it was absolutely worth it! This allowed us to be surrounded by hundreds of couples (everyone from newlyweds to people who have been married for over 60 years of marriage as a way to learn and grow from one another. Within the conference, we were shocked by how much people openly talked about sex. This was mainly because in our upbringing, sex had always been a dirty, taboo topic that people didn't speak freely of. But sex is meant to be beautiful, intimate, and vulnerable.

We also went to pre-marital counseling with our pastors, where we completed several exercises together. In one, we assessed which areas of generational curses we should be aware of so that we won't bring them into our marriage. These included dominance, addiction, selfishness, materialism, unfaithfulness, divorce, lack of ownership, a life of struggle, settling for less, domestic violence, brokenness, and more.

> Justin: During the premarital counseling, one of my physical expectations was for Alexis to put her 10 PM bowl of cereal in the sink after she was done. We always joked about how much we enjoyed our late-night snacks! The only issue was that by the end of the week, her bowls would be stacked up to the ceiling.

We learned to recognize red flags such as poor spending habits, frequent disagreements, poor ways of disciplining our children, taking each other for granted, breakdowns in communication, and one or both of us compromising our career goals.

We did another exercise that focused on our physical and spiritual expectations. We learned that the quickest way to end a relationship is to put God-level responsibility on your partner. We each came up with three to five spiritual and physical expectations we have for each other and then held hands while communicating them with our partner. Some of ours were to pray together before big decisions, motivate each other, support each other's dreams, be considerate of each other's thoughts, feelings, expectations, dreams, and desires, and put aside our egos—meaning learning how to forgive quickly and offer grace.

Additionally, we read a book called <u>131 Necessary Conversations Before Marriage</u> by Jed Jurchenko. We discovered that we'd already talked about everything except for one silly question: What make and model of car would your partner most likely be like?

We've seen couples get divorced because they hadn't had these conversations before marriage. They didn't discuss expectations regarding money, if they wanted children and how they'd plan to discipline them, how they were disciplined as a child (and if that's okay or not) for their children.

The two of us have created a game plan with regard to finances. We see finances as a representation of our relationship: open, transparent, one. Meaning—no secrets. For any purchase over fifty dollars, we discuss it in advance as well as having a no purchasing after midnight rule to avoid impulsive spending and promote accountability. We are both committed to being debt-free because we want to remain unburdened by the anxiety debt can bring on.

Searching for jobs can be a challenge in any committed relationship. We have to make choices, for example, about the cities where we are willing to apply for work; both of us need to be happy about the idea of living there. We also want the kinds of schedules and hours we can negotiate. All we know with certainty is that we don't want to be geographically separated. Wherever we go, we know that we will go together, finally settling down roots.

Given our traumatic childhoods, we've obviously talked about how we plan to raise our children—along with whether we even want to have biological kids. Ultimately, we want to be prepared—we certainly don't want our kids to have to heal from our parenting. Our friend Jameshia said something that struck a chord: "Our parent's voice becomes our inner voice." Think about how your parents spoke to you, were they loving and caring, or the opposite? Next, think about how you speak to yourself. Children internalize everything their parents tell them, especially how the parents choose to characterize them. If a parent tells you that you are bad or stupid, that is a hard thing to shake in later life. We tend to live by the myths our parents create, good or bad.

Early on, we decided together that we wouldn't hit our kids. We grew up around violence and know firsthand the dissonance of being told that your parents are hitting you out of love. As we said before, **love shouldn't hurt**. It also unquestionably leads to violent behavior down the road, or being more likely to become a victim of violence—or both.

This also applies to how you choose to raise your kids and to what and who you choose to expose them to. We refuse to allow our kids to be exposed to behaviors and habits that we worked so hard to get rid of and leave behind. It will be our duty to protect them. We hate when people say that they survived it, so their kids can too. This is foolish, ignorant, and toxic to kids because they do deserve better and for us to put in the effort to do so.

We've agreed that divorce isn't an option for us. If we go into marriage with a "Plan B," then we subconsciously seek a way out. If divorce isn't an option then, separation won't even be considered as we battle through our issues.

I'M NOT YOUR ENEMY

A GOOD MARRIAGE (AND any relationship) is built on communication, honesty, and trust. True intimacy is when you can 100% be your true, authentic self with someone 100% of the time without the fear of not being rejected or unloved. We don't keep secrets. We talk openly about our insecurities, pain and fear. We have never checked each other's phones or social media because we've never felt the need to. Instead, we make it a habit of trusting each other's judgment.

All relationships and marriages have conflict—it's actually healthy (so we've learned)! Conflicts are unavoidable, it's *how* conflicts are resolved and what comes from it that's important. On the flip side, there are lines that should never be crossed, and damage that can't be undone once inflicted. Both of us have had more than enough experience with our boundaries being ignored and are constantly aware that this is so. We are committed to not arguing via text; We've gone down many rabbit holes that way. Texts are also easily misinterpreted because there is no tone to go with it. In public, we back each other up even when we don't agree, then talk about it later, privately.

We've learned to not say things like "you always" or "you never" because those are unnecessarily weighted phrases. When one of us does something wrong, we try to remember to say things like "When you do this…it makes me feel…" This takes the blame off the other person and encourages dialogue. We also remind each other that we aren't each other's enemy. During a disagreement, with adrenaline and stress hormones flowing, it can be easily forgotten.

FRIENDS FIRST

"The Lord God said 'it is not good for the man to be alone.
I will make a helper suitable for him'"
(Gen 2:18).

BECAUSE OF THE trauma that we've been through, and our desperation for love, we take deep pleasure in spending time together. Although we are individuals with our own goals and dreams, our favorite parts of the day are those we spend with one another.

We love to be cozy, no makeup, sweatpants, just lounging around. Even when we go on dates, we usually wear what we're already wearing, because we are the happiest when we are both comfortable.

Alexis: I have so many outfits that I want to get dressed up and look cute and Justin will say, "No, just be cozy." If I try to wear heels, he'll say, "Wear those for you, not me because I'd rather you be comfortable." *How great is it for someone to love your authentic self?*

When we were in college, if we hadn't seen each other all day and spotted one another on campus, Justin would throw his arms out and start running towards me without caring who may see how silly (and adorable) he looked. Even today, if we catch each other's eye, my heart races—I can see his face light up as we smile at each other.

We even ask each other when or if these feelings are supposed to fade. Ultimately, we are best friends and bring each other joy. When we are together, we joke, laugh, play, wrestle, and play basketball almost every day. We can be in the same building and still text each other as if we're far apart. We can sit and watch cat videos for hours when we're having a bad day. We can be around each other and not have physical touch or sex. Our favorite times together are when we just lie in bed or sit and talk for hours. We don't have to go anywhere or do anything special. One weekend when we were in D.C. after not seeing each other for a month, we'd stay in the house all weekend.

BUILDING A LEGACY

"At the end of the day, it's not about what you have or even what you've accomplished… It's about who you've lifted up, who you've made better. It's about what you've given back."
—Denzel Washington

WHEN YOU GET married, you should focus on building and leaving a legacy behind. Before we could do this, we had to define what success meant for our lives—both individual success, and success in our marriage. As we started to get closer to each other, we talked about what we want to leave behind in this world, especially if we have children.

Our gifts (purpose/potential) need to be extracted by each other to transform others. As our pastor said, "When you leave this earth, you should die empty. Give everything you have to this world." Each January we develop goals together, then reassess those goals every few months to see our growth and what we need to change or improve.

Part of our legacy building has included working together to develop The Scholarship Expert, starting a publishing company called Global Perspectives Publishing, and founding The ROSE Empowerment Group. We wrote this book, and developed a full online course called The Scholarship Blueprint that walks students through how to find and apply for scholarships. We know we work well together and strive to create kingdoms for future generations.

THE TWO SHALL BECOME ONE

"Love binds us together in perfect unity"
(Colossians 3:14).

SINCE, WE DIDN'T want our marriage to affect Justin's financial aid (if you're married, you could lose scholarship funding), we decided to have a two-year engagement.

We were in full agreement that our wedding planning process would be a fun and enjoyable experience. We planned our whole wedding in the course of two weeks in January of 2019. We planned it so far in advance because we didn't know if we would be in the same state or country together until the wedding. Thank God we planned our wedding before COVID! Christmas night, we downloaded Pinterest and picked out our colors, theme and general location. It was super fun and we worked together every step of the way.

When we visited our venue, we teared up because we both knew this was the place where we wanted to get married. An organization called One Simple Wish that provides support for foster youth (no matter their age), funded part of our wedding! This was unexpected and greatly appreciated.

What a year to be married! Between COVID, the resulting economic crash, and being recent graduates, everything we want to do has been an uphill battle, but we were determined to make it work! Luckily, we are used to being adaptable.

> Alexis: Our bridal shower was in April and because Justin was graduating the next weekend, I used this opportunity to throw a surprise graduation party for him. I was incredibly disappointed that he wouldn't be able to have the experience of walking across the stage to officially receive his diploma in a formal ceremony that he so deserved. He was the very first in his family to graduate from college. But Michigan had opened up its COVID lockdown just in time to have a party with over 30 of our closest family and friends at a local park. We both were surprised, because two of our closest friends came and without expecting it. The day went perfectly thanks to family and friends showing up and showing out!

WHAT'S NEXT?

*"You are the fruit sent to the earth to develop as a tree
so the earth can earth from your fruit!"*
—Myles Munroe

W E ARE CONTINUING to build our relationship together and set the foundation for a healthy, long-lasting marriage. The odds have always been stacked against us—but we hope that this book is only the beginning of us creating a dialogue of teaching people strategies of identifying healthy and unhealthy habits. We are challenging the next generation to create communities and families filled with love, healing and growth.

We hope this book inspires people to become mentors, to foster, to adopt, but most importantly, to be intentional on how we behave and how we interact with one another.

Lastly,—and maybe most importantly—choosing to adopt or foster should not be seen as less fulfilling than having biological children. Ultimately, foster care saved us, which is why we feel so strongly about discussing it and also about giving back in some way. It's why we are passionate about sharing our story—we want others who are walking or have walked that path to know they are not alone and that they can achieve anything they want to. Now, we leave it to you. What will *you* do? How can you redefine normal in your life or in the community around you?

Justin as an infant and at his college graduation 2020

Alexis as an infant and at her college graduation 2019

08.08.2020 - Our wedding day

Baby, I'm dancing in the dark with you between my arms
Barefoot on the grass
Listening to our favorite song
When you said you looked a mess
I whispered underneath my breath
But you heard it, darling
You look perfect tonight
Well I found a woman
Stronger than anyone I know
She shares my dreams
I hope that someday I'll share her home
I found a love
To carry more than just my secrets
To carry love, to carry children of our own
We are still kids, but we're so in love
Fighting against all odds
I know we'll be alright this time
Darling, just hold my hand
Be my girl, I'll be your man
I see my future in your eyes
Perfect cover by Leroy Sanchez

More photos available on our website re-definingnormal.com/gallery.

EPILOGUE: WHEN THE UNIMAGINABLE HAPPENS

Justin dancing with his mom at our wedding

T'S FUNNY, NO matter how rough our road had been, I felt a need to have my mother by my side during the time leading up to our wedding. Excited for the big day, my mother FaceTimed me to show me the silk burgundy dress and black shoes she was going to wear. We joked about her two left feet, and how comical our mother-son dance would be. We laughed so hard that we cried, and I promised her that I would take good care of her on the dance floor.

My parents arrived the day before the wedding and Alexis and I heaved a sigh of relief when we saw them: our ceremony would be complete. My mother gazed at me with tears in her eyes and told me how proud she was. She hugged me in a way that allowed me to free the pain and tension of all that had come before this moment.

Khalil and I danced with my mom to *Losing You* by The Temptations. We pranced around her as though we were her back-up dancers, just the way we'd done as little boys. The sun shone down on her as though she were an angel. The whole world seemed to smile upon me, my family, and my new wife. Everything crystalized.

One week later during our honeymoon, Khalil called.

"Mommy is gone, bro," he said. It was a video call, and I could see white walls and an exit sign above him. A woman was screaming in the background. My heart stopped.

On Saturday, August 15th, my mother was murdered by her neighbor. My father and brother, Andre had gotten into a fight with him and my mother tried to diffuse the tension, as she always does. But the neighbor (who was inebriated and abusing drugs), got into his car and ran her into the wall outside her apartment building, fleeing the scene afterward.

She died serving as a peacemaker.

Who knows how or when I'll be able to make sense of the violence that took my mother's life? Meanwhile, she didn't get to travel the world, create businesses, own a home, or write the book she had asked for my help with. For now, I hold onto that afternoon of dancing, my mother in her burgundy dress, with all that sunshine and laughter lighting up her face.

CAN YOU HELP?

THANK YOU FOR reading our book. We poured our hearts into it and would greatly appreciate it if you could leave a review on Amazon, Barnes and Noble, or any platform that you purchased it from. We believe that sharing our story will help other people heal from theirs. By sharing your review, this is the best way for us to gain exposure and to get the word out there.

Please share this book with others whom you think will benefit from it as well as share any story or quote that impacted you on social media with the hashtag #redefiningnormalbook.

Join our email list to stay up to date on our journey and to learn more about all of the topics covered in this book at www.re-definingnormal.com.

ACKNOWLEDGEMENTS

(Be sure to at least read the last paragraph!)

T HE LAST STATISTIC of the book: Only 2% of people publish a book. Now we've done that twice. Thank you for allowing us to be a part of your life. We hope to continue inspiring others to question their definition of normal and to develop healthier habits throughout life. Our time at Western Michigan University has been challenging but incredibly rewarding as WMU has cultivated an environment filled with leaders and trailblazers. We've learned to utilize our resources on campus while nurturing a community filled with friendship and prosperity. Resources such as Starting Gate in the Haworth College of Business were critical in helping us develop an entrepreneurial mindset. Because of Western Michigan University, Kalamazoo, Michigan will always be our home.

During our time at WMU, we had the privilege of being a part of the Seita Scholars program for foster youth in higher education. The Seita Scholars program has helped us navigate the struggles of college as foster care youth and successfully transition into our careers. The campus coaches within the Seita program have personally impacted our lives in numerous ways. Whether the Seita Scholars program was providing assistance to students over winter break or giving us step-by-step instructions on how to successfully navigate life on top of graduating, Seita has been the support system we've all needed. The Seita Scholars program will forever have a special place in our hearts.

The importance of mentorship and support is heavily underrated both academically and professionally. With the multitude of mentors, we've had throughout our collegiate career, we've been able to obtain knowledge that many wouldn't have. Because of this, we've garnered year's worth of wisdom and knowledge that has positioned us to grow tremendously.

Thank you to all who have poured love, guidance, and positive examples into our lives. You've helped make this book possible and helped us heal. Special thanks to Kim and Brian for being phenomenal examples and to The Seita Scholars Program, The Nsoro Foundation, Hope Pkgs, and One Simple Wish for continuing your relentless work to support foster youth like us and for pushing us to have big, bold dreams.

Thank you to our pastors for planting the seeds of being business owners and authors. Because of your faith and words of encouragement, this is possible!

Thank you, Leslie Kendall Dye (www.lesliekendalldye.net) for helping to bring this book to life, and for being the greatest editor through this process, making it possible and even fun!

We wouldn't change anything that we've been through because it made us who we are today. Remember that there's power in your story. Own it! No one can take it away from you! Telling your story gives others the courage to share theirs. You are not alone.

Last, but certainly not least, thank you to all of the scholarships and fellowships that we've received. They've enabled us to pursue our academic studies and positioned us to prosper.

A portion of each sale will go to Hope Pkgs, The Nsoro Foundation, One Simple Wish, and The Seita Scholars Program.

ABOUT THE AUTHORS

AS YOU CAN see throughout this book, Alexis and Justin are beating the odds and showing others how they can beat the odds too! Fewer than 3% of foster youth graduate from college. They both did that! Fewer than 2% of people publish a book, they both did that—twice (and are planning to write more). Together, they studied abroad 13 times, earned three degrees, graduated with over $340,000 in scholarships, started two companies, and have written two books. Both are foster care advocates, business owners, authors, and speakers.

Alexis Lenderman-Black is a proud foster care alumna, as well as a graduate of Western Michigan University. She believes that she is not defined by her past, but rather by what she does with it. She is the founder of The Scholarship Expert, co-founder of ROSE Empowerment Group, and author of The Scholarship Blueprint.

During her undergraduate career, she completed eight study abroad programs in Africa, Asia, South America, and Europe, covering topics such as sustainability, business ethics, international humanitarianism, political economics, and global marketing. She utilized her passion for program development and relationship building to co-develop Western Michigan

University's first study abroad program with a foreign service component to volunteer in a refugee camp in Lesvos, Greece. With Justin,

Alexis has continued her advocacy work by participating in the International Relations Career Challenge at Johns Hopkins University and the Global Institute for Human Rights, hosted through Penn Law and the United Nations. Alexis has had the privilege of speaking at such events as the Reagan Presidential Library's Leadership Summit, The Nsoro Scholarship gala, The Bravo Scholarships of America Gala, and Western Michigan University's Night of Excellence. Because of her commitment to her college campus and community, she was the sole nominee from the former president of her university for the Newman Civic Fellowship.

Justin Black is the co-founder of Rising Over Societal Expectations (ROSE) Empowerment Group, and due to his experience as a Black male in the foster care system, has a strong vision for how to close the information gap for today's generation of Black and Brown youth. He has pioneered youth conferences and workshops that teach methods of economic sustainability, principles of healthy relationships, and collective impact.

Justin is committed to serving as an example for other youth who want to better themselves through character development, resiliency, and seeking support. He created the ROSE Model to show youth the effect they can have on their local and global communities. Justin is also the current Communications Director for The Scholarship Expert, which was founded to help scholars find the funding and opportunities needed to maximize their college experience.

Justin has presented at numerous conferences and served as the student keynote speaker at the Nsoro foundation's 2020 Starfish Ball, helping to raise over $1,000,000 in scholarship funding for foster youth around the United States. He received prestigious Benjamin Gilman Scholarship for his time in South Korea, as well as the Yvonne Unrau Innovation award from Western Michigan University's Seita Scholars program, for the development of WMU's first multi-country study abroad program in Africa.

Together, Justin and Alexis hope to inspire those who want to heal from traumatic childhoods and fulfill their potentials.

NEXT STEPS/WORK WITH US

Let's keep connecting on Facebook, Twitter, Instagram, and through our business, The Scholarship Expert and ROSE Empowerment Group.

To contact Alexis and Justin about media appearances, coaching or speaking at your event, email press@re-definingnormal.com

To subscribe to their email list to learn more about their journey, information on healthy relationships and stay tuned for their upcoming books, visit re-definingnormal.com or listen to our ROSE From Concrete podcast at www.rosefromconcrete.buzzsprout.com

To connect with Justin and Alexis on
Twitter @Roseegroup
Facebook @ redefiningnormalmemoir
Instagram @re.definingnormal
Justin's Blog: akidfromdetroit.com

ROSE Empowerment Group, a youth-serving organization on the importance of self, community and impact.

For more info, go to roseempowermentgroup.com
Contact: info@roseempowermentgroup.com

Follow us on social media:
Facebook @Roseempowermentgroup
LinkedIn @Roseempowermentgroup
Instagram @Roseempowermentgroup
Twitter @Roseeg

The Scholarship Expert, scholarship coaching business to help students graduate debt-free.

For more info, go to thescholarshipexpert.com
Contact: thescholarshipexpert@gmail.com

Follow us on social media:
Facebook @thescholarshpexpert
Instagram @thescholarshpexpert
LinkedIn @thescholarshpexpert
Twitter @ScholarshipXprt

If you're interested in supporting students, we have sponsorship packages available at thescholarshipexpert.com/sponsorships

SELF-PUBLISHING
SCHOOL

This book would not have been possible without the Self-Publishing School. We read the book *Published* by Chandler Bolt to help us write our outline and generate ideas, but it was the course that pushed us and helped bring this book to fruition.

You can get a FREE copy of the book Published via this link: https://self-publishingschool.com/friend/.

If you choose to join a Self-Publishing School program (listed below) you'll get $250 and we'll also receive $250 via PayPal as a big thank you from SPS.

Become a Bestseller
Fundamentals of Fiction
Sell More Books
Course Building for Authors

Be sure to include our names for who referred you!

RESOURCES MENTIONED

- All resources are available at re-definingnormal.com/resources
- Healthy vs Unhealthy Checklist
- The 5 Love Languages: The Secret to Love that Last by Gary Chapman
- Weekend to Remember Conference
- 131 Necessary Conversations Before Marriage
- ACEs Score

CPSIA information can be obtained
at www.ICGtesting.com
Printed in the USA
LVHW030921221120
672362LV00044B/1074